PRASHANT SHAH is one of India's leading practitioners of one dir
worked for a number of years with various financial firms, usin
noiseless charts in particular. His first book on point and figure cl
He appears on business channels and writes regular blogs and columns. He also comm
live market trading sessions on rule-based trading systems. His mission is to help others
become objective, noiseless and process oriented traders. Prashant is the architect of a
market analysis software called TradePoint, which is being used and appreciated by
professional traders and market analysts due to its advanced and unlimited capabilities.

Prashant is a founder member and CEO of Definedge Solutions (www.definedge.com),
a company which develops high quality financial products and research services. Prashant
has won a number of coveted and renowned professional designations in the financial
industry. He has been awarded Chartered Market Technician (CMT®) and a Certified
Financial Technician (CFTe) by CMT Association and International Federation of
Technical Analysts (IFTA), respectively. He is also a holder of the right to Master of
Financial Technical Analysis® certification designation by IFTA for the original research
conducted by him on line break swing trading techniques.

~

PROFITABLE TRADING with RENKO CHARTS

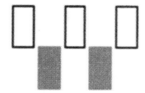

PRASHANT SHAH

www.visionbooksindia.com

Disclaimer

The author and the publisher disclaim all legal or other responsibilities for any losses which investors may suffer by investing or trading using the methods described in this book. Readers are advised to seek professional guidance before making any specific investments. This book is meant purely for the purpose of investor and trader education.

First Published 2019
Reprinted 2021, 2023, 2024

A Vision Books Original

ISBN 10: 93-86268-27-2
ISBN 13: 978-93-86268-27-3

Published by
Vision Books Pvt. Ltd.
(Incorporating Orient Paperbacks and CARING imprints)
24 Feroze Gandhi Road, Lajpat Nagar 3
New Delhi 110024, India.
Phone: (+91-11) 2984 0821 / 22
e-mail: visionbooks@gmail.com

Printed at
Ashim Print Line
38/2, 35 & 36, Sahibabad Industrial Area, Ghaziabad
Uttar Pradesh 201010, India.

Contents

Part 1

~

Technical Analysis of Renko Charts

Part 2

~

Trading with Renko Charts

Part 1

~

Technical Analysis of Renko Charts

Chapter 1

Introduction to Renko Charts

Technical analysis can broadly be defined as the study of historical price action of a financial instrument, commodity, currency, etc. that helps in arriving at a reasonable conclusion about its prevailing demand and supply equation.

The following are the basic tenets of technical analysis according to the classic work, *Technical Analysis of Stock Trends* by Robert D. Edwards and John Magee:[*]

1. Stock[**] prices move in trends, and a trend is deemed to continue until it gets reversed.

2. Stock prices are determined by the interaction of demand and supply, and the shifts in demand and supply cause reversals in trends.

3. The price discounts everything. Shifts in demand and supply can be detected in charts.

4. Price history and chart patterns tend to repeat themselves.

Popular Charting Methods

There are many ways to capture, or chart, the historical price movement of a financial instrument. The popular charting methods include line chart, bar chart and candlestick chart. Figure 1.1 explains their construction.

Line charts are drawn by connecting closing prices of the chosen time interval. In bar charts, a bar is bullish when its closing price is higher than the earlier period's bar; it is bearish when the closing price is lower than the earlier period's bar. In candlestick charts, a candle is bullish when the close of a period is higher than its open, else it is bearish.

---

[*] Published in India by Vision Books Pvt. Ltd. (www.visionbooksindia.com).

[**] Throughout the book, the words "stock" or "instrument" may be understood to mean any financial security, derivative, commodity, currency, etc.

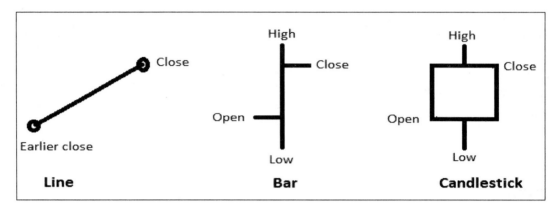

Figure 1.1: **Line, bar and candlestick charts**

~

Figure 1.2 shows a typical candlestick chart. As you would observe, there are two dimensions to the chart, namely price and time. In such charts, time is plotted on the X-axis and price on the Y-axis.

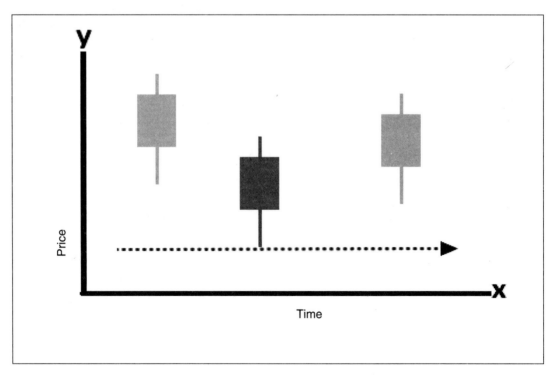

Figure 1.2: **A candlestick chart with time plotted along the X-axis and price along the Y-axis**

~

A line chart is plotted by connecting successive closing prices. Breakouts and patterns based on closing prices are relatively clear and noise free. This is perhaps the reason why eminent technical analysts such as Charles Dow, John Murphy and many others prefer line charts over bar charts. Charles Dow considered the daily close as the most significant price and relied exclusively on closing prices. The usual line chart that plots only closing prices is one of the oldest and most important methods of plotting prices. Also, as Murphy argues, "Many chartists believe that because the closing price is the most critical price of the trading day, a line chart is a more valid measure of price activity." [*]

Renko Charts

Renko is a charting method that belongs to the "noiseless" category, i.e. a chart which is free of relatively minor price moves. Apart from Renko, other noiseless charting methods include Point and Figure, Line-break and Kagi.

Renko charts have their origins in Japan where they were used during the 19th century. They were introduced to the rest of the world by Steven Nison who discussed this methodology in his book, *Beyond Candlesticks*.

In Japanese, Renko means brick; that is why Renko charts are also known as brick charts. A Renko chart is categorised as noiseless because it eliminates insignificant price action. Also, the Renko chart is a one dimensional chart because its plotting only takes price into account. On the other hand, popular charts, such as bar or candlestick, have two dimensions — price and time. In two dimensional charts, price is plotted on the Y-axis and time on the X-axis. A new price point gets plotted on the chart when the specified time passes by, irrespective of the extent of the price move. A Renko chart, on the other hand, filters out insignificant price movements and captures only significant price action. The elimination of noise is achieved by selecting a suitable brick value. We shall discuss more about the brick value a little later.

Simplicity and objectivity are the major advantages of Renko charts. Renko is a complete charting system that is objective in nature and applicable on all types of financial instruments and over all time frames. Recent advancement in technology has made it easier to plot and study patterns in a Renko chart. Besides, the technology today offers the facility to plot log scale Renko charts, but more about that later.

As you go with the flow and process of this book, you will understand all aspects of Renko charts and you will be able to trade any instrument on any time frame.

---

[*] Murphy, John J., *Technical Analysis of the Financial Markets: A Comprehensive Guide to Trading Methods and Applications*. New York: New York Institute of Finance, 1999, P.36.

Construction of Renko Charts

Let us begin by understanding how Renko charts are constructed. This is a most important and fundamental aspect. Readers are often more interested in immediately getting to the trade setups; they don't focus enough on the basics and struggle later in grasping the nuances of trading strategies. I urge you to spend enough time in understanding the basics before moving on to chart patterns and trading.

The method of plotting Renko charts is slightly different as compared to the plotting of traditional candle or bar charts. Renko charts are constructed, or plotted, by connecting two prices. The method is explained step-wise below.

Figure 1.3 is the image of a simple line chart that is drawn by connecting successive closing prices. In the chart in Figure 1.3, the closing prices at 100 and 105 are connected by a line.

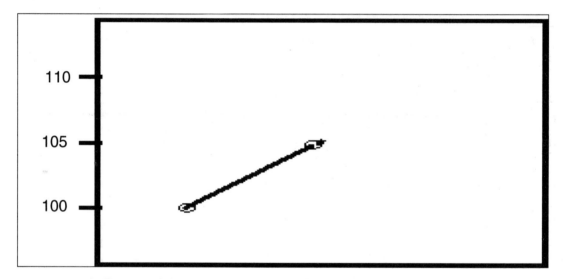

Figure 1.3: **A line chart connects successive closing prices with a line**

~

Instead of connecting the closing prices with a line, a Renko chart connects the two prices by drawing a box as shown in Figure 1.4.

The box drawn by connecting the two prices is called a brick. So, every brick would represent two prices, a high price and a low price. In the example in Figure 1.4, the brick's low price is 100 and its high price is 105.

The brick shown in Figure 1.4 is bullish because the price is rising. **Typically, bullish bricks are drawn hollow while bearish bricks are filled with colour.** The charting software may use customized colour coding for the bricks, which is fine so long as the difference between a bullish and a bearish brick is easily identifiable. In this book, hollow bricks represent bullish price action, and black, or filled, bricks represent bearish price action.

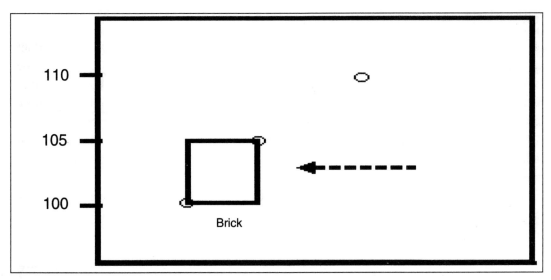

Figure 1.4: **A Renko chart is drawn by connecting closing prices of a minimum stipulated price difference as a box, called a brick.**

~

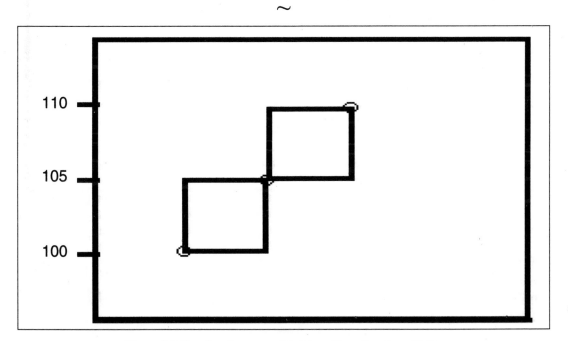

Figure 1.5: **Drawing the second brick as the price rises higher**

~

Continuing the example of Figure 1.4, if the price goes up to, say, 110, another brick would be drawn diagonal to the existing brick, starting from the existing brick's top right corner (*see* Figure 1.5).

The second brick plotted in Figure 1.5 is also a bullish brick as the new price has closed above the previous brick's price level. The low price of the new brick is 105 and the high price is 110. Note that 105 is also the high price of the previous brick, and we drew the current brick starting from that price.

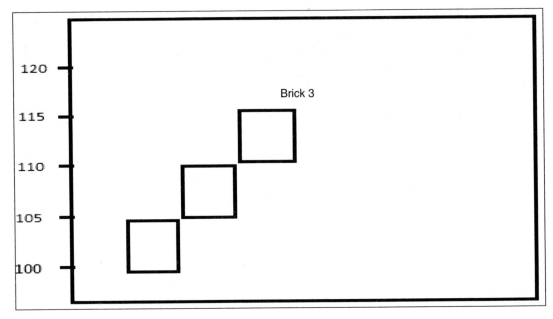

Figure 1.6: **Construction of the third brick**

~

Another bullish brick will get drawn in the same manner if the price advances further (*see* Figure 1.6).

The low price of the latest brick (Brick 3 in Figure 1.6) is 110 and its high price is 115. Further bricks will be formed in the same way if the price keeps moving higher. If the price starts moving down, however, and falls below the low price of the previous brick, we need to draw a bearish brick.

In the example in Figure 1.6, the current high price is 115 and the low price is 110. For a reversal, the price has to move down to 105, or below that, which is the low price of the previous brick.

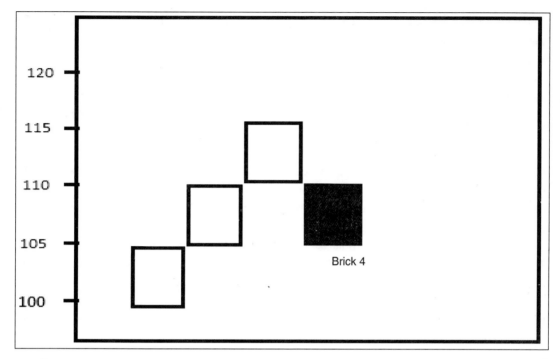

Figure 1.7: **A reversal brick, bearish in this case, would be formed were the price to fall to 105**

~

Figure 1.7 shows that a new bearish brick is drawn diagonal to the bottom right corner of the previous brick. In the example of Figure 1.7, if the price falls even further and goes below 100, then another bearish brick will get drawn, starting from the bottom right corner of the current bearish brick. On the other hand, if the price moves back up above 115, a bullish brick will get plotted from the top right corner of current brick.

Based on the above discussion on brick construction, you will readily appreciate that the level where a continuation, or a reversal, brick will get plotted is known in advance. For instance, in the case of the Renko chart in Figure 1.7, you know the price levels where bullish or bearish bricks will get printed. This is an important aspect from a trading perspective which we will discuss further in the coming chapters.

Brick Value

As mentioned earlier, Renko charts are categorized as noiseless and what makes them so is the appropriate selection of the brick value. In the example in Figure 1.7, the brick value used was 5 points, which is the difference between each brick.

The brick value selected defines the price action which the user considers is significant enough to be captured in the chart. In Figure 1.7, for example, a brick will be plotted only when the price has moved by at least 5 points, or multiples thereof.

So if price moves from 100 to 105, a bullish brick is formed. A brick will not be formed if the price is even one tick below 105. Accordingly, if the price is at 104, the Renko chart will not plot anything. Thus, the defined brick value also determines the frequency of bricks and the noise that we want to eliminate.

Renko charts can be drawn by using different brick values but the principle remains the same. Later, we will discuss how best to decide what the appropriate brick value should be. Before that, notice in the example of Figure 1.7 that because it is a 5 brick value chart, the next bearish brick will be plotted only if the price falls to at least 100, and a bullish brick will be plotted only if the price goes up to at least 115.

It is important to grasp that the next bullish brick will be plotted if the price closes either at, or above, 115. It is not necessary that the price must break out, or close, above 115. Similarly, for a bearish brick to be plotted at 105, the price has to close either at, or below, 105.

Thus, the rules for forming the bullish or bearish bricks are clear and objective. Objectivity and noiselessness are the two most important advantages of Renko charts, besides their visual appeal.

Exercise

Let's do an exercise in constructing a Renko chart to test our comfort with the basics.

Table 1.1 is a price table which we will use to plot a Renko chart with a brick value of 10. I recommend readers to try and make a Renko chart on their own using the price data in Table 1.1.

Table 1.1
Price Table for Plotting a 10-Brick Renko Chart

S. No.	Price	S. No.	Price
1	99.15	15	152.05
2	110.20	16	159.70
3	117.05	17	147.10
4	110.50	18	160.70
5	121.85	19	169.85
6	107.00	20	160.90
7	124.00	21	175.25
8	99.90	22	182.30
9	120.80	23	188.65
10	124.55	24	193.75
11	115.20	25	180.05
12	130.90	26	164.85
13	141.75	27	157.15
14	131.65		

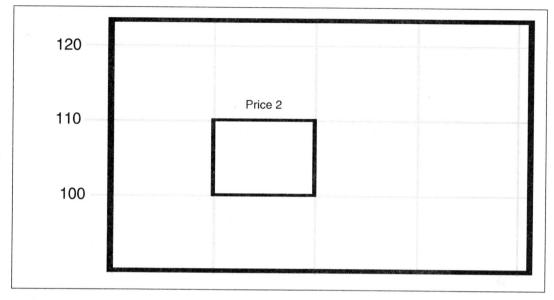

Figure 1.8: **The first brick, a bullish one. The number '2' written above the brick is a price series number for reference, indicating that this brick is formed after the second price.**

~

The method I adopt to plot a Renko chart is that I define the scale as per the brick value chosen to keep it a round number for better readability. If we choose the brick value as 10, the scale used will be 100, 110, 120, and so on.

Let's begin with the first price. We cannot plot the first price simply because we don't know whether we need to start with a bullish brick or a bearish brick. Because it is a 10 brick value chart, if the price goes up by 10 points we'll begin with a bullish brick and if it declines by 10 points, we'll start with a bearish brick. A Renko chart cannot be plotted with just one price; we'll have to wait for another.

As the second price is 110.20, which is higher than the first price, we begin with a bullish brick and draw it as shown in Figure 1.8.

Table 1.2

Price Table

S. No.	Price	Plotting
1	99.15	No plotting
2	110.20	Bullish brick

The next brick will be plotted if the price either goes to 120, or above, or falls to 90 or below, the low price of the previous brick. Any price that occurs in between these two is insignificant and is considered as noise for this chosen brick value.

The third and fourth prices, 117.05 and 110.50 respectively (*see* Table 1.3), fall between these two reference levels and thus don't warrant plotting. The fifth price in Table 1.3 has gone above 120, hence a bullish brick needs to be plotted. The sixth and the seventh prices are ignored as they do not warrant plotting either bullish or bearish bricks. The eighth price falls below the requirement of the bearish brick price level and hence a bearish brick is plotted (*see* Figure 1.9).

Table 1.3

Price Table *(contd.)*

S. No.	Price	Plotting
1	99.15	No plotting
2	110.20	Bullish brick
3	117.05	No plotting
4	110.50	No plotting
5	121.85	Bullish brick
6	107.00	No plotting
7	124.00	No plotting
8	99.90	Bearish Brick

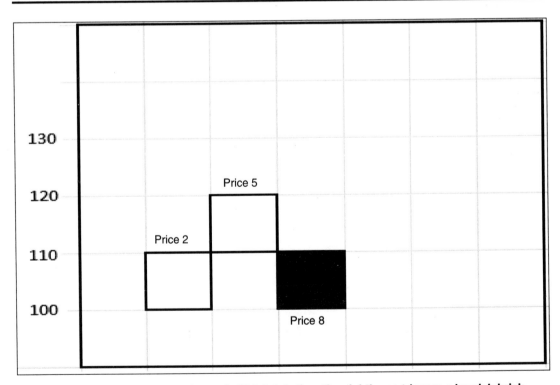

Figure 1.9: **The fifth price leads to a bullish brick, then the eighth one triggers a bearish brick** (*see* **Table 1.3**)

The ninth price (*see* Table 1.4) triggers a reversal from a bearish to a bullish brick as the price moves back above 120. The next bullish brick level is 130, and the subsequent bearish brick level is 100. The eleventh and twelfth prices remain between the bands, so no bricks. The thirteenth price warrants plotting a bullish brick as the price moved above 140. The fourteenth price doesn't allow plotting. Table 1.4 summarises the status of the plotting thus far, and Figure 1.10 is the resultant Renko chart.

Table 1.4
Price Table *(contd.)*

S. No.	Price	Plotting
1	99.15	No plotting
2	110.20	Bullish brick
3	117.05	No plotting
4	110.50	No plotting
5	121.85	Bullish brick
6	107.00	No plotting
7	124.00	No plotting
8	99.90	Bearish Brick
9	120.80	Bullish brick
10	124.55	No plotting
11	115.20	No plotting
12	130.90	Bullish brick
13	141.75	Bullish brick
14	131.65	No plotting

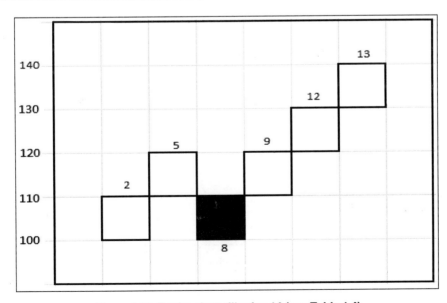

Figure 1.10: **Renko chart till price 14 (*see* Table 1.4)**

~

Table 1.5

Price Table *(contd.)*

S. No.	Price	Plotting	S. No.	Price	Plotting
1	99.15	No plotting	15	152.05	Bullish brick
2	110.20	Bullish brick	16	159.70	No plotting
3	117.05	No plotting	17	147.10	No plotting
4	110.50	No plotting	18	160.70	Bullish brick
5	121.85	Bullish brick	19	169.85	No plotting
6	107.00	No plotting	20	160.90	No plotting
7	124.00	No plotting	21	175.25	Bullish brick
8	99.90	Bearish Brick	22	182.30	Bullish brick
9	120.80	Bullish brick	23	188.65	No plotting
10	124.55	No plotting	24	193.75	Bullish brick
11	115.20	No plotting	25	180.05	No plotting
12	130.90	Bullish brick	26	164.85	Bearish Brick
13	141.75	Bullish brick	27	157.15	Bearish Brick
14	131.65	No plotting			

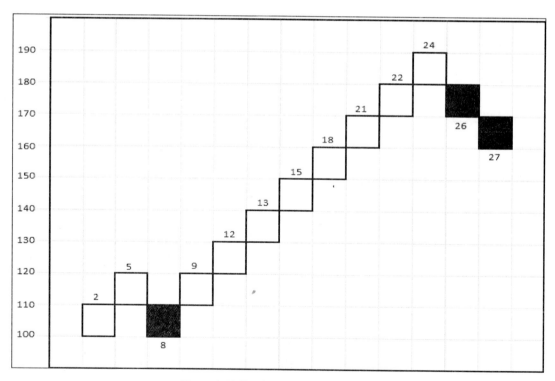

Figure 1.11: **Renko chart for Table 1.5**

~

If you have followed the logic behind the plotting so far, the rest of the sequence should be easy to comprehend. The remaining price action is illustrated in the chart in Figure 1.11.

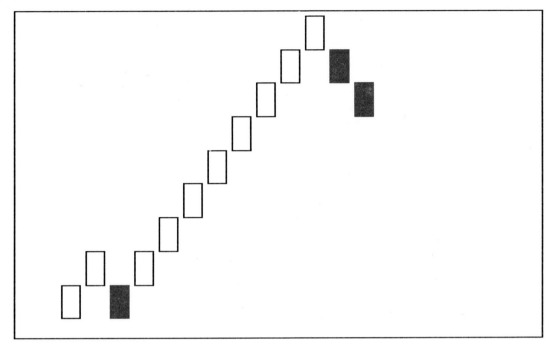

Figure 1.12: **A 10 brick value Renko chart of Hindalco (July 2013 to September 2014)**

~

The chart shown in Figure 1.11 is actually based on real time daily closing prices of Hindalco between 2013 and 2014. Figure 1.12 is the chart showing the same.

High-Low Brick Value

Thus far we have plotted Renko charts using closing prices. As observed earlier, Renko charts can't be plotted with only one price.

A. W. Cohen made a remarkable advance in the field of Point & Figure charts when he devised the high-low method of plotting such charts in his brilliant work in the late 1950s. The same method can be used for plotting Renko charts as well. Instead of the closing price, the high and low prices of a particular period can be utilised for plotting a Renko chart. To plot Renko charts with this method, either the high price or the low price of a period needs to be considered. The rules are as follows:

- If the price forms a new high and qualifies for the next bullish brick, the low price is to be ignored and a bullish brick is to be plotted connecting the high prices.

- If after forming a bullish brick, the price doesn't form a new high price that qualifies for a bullish brick, then check if the low price of that period fulfils the criteria for the formation of a bearish brick. If yes, plot a bearish brick. If no, move on.

- If the price forms a new low price which qualifies for a bearish brick, first consider the low price of the next period to check whether another bearish brick can be formed. If yes, plot a bearish brick. If not, check the high price of the period to ascertain whether the reversal criteria is fulfilled. If so, plot a bullish brick. If not, move on.

Hence, with this method we first consider the high price if the last brick was bullish — and the low price first if the last brick was bearish.

Table 1.6 and Figure 1.13 provide brick-wise explanation of the construction of a high-low Renko chart.

Table 1.6
Price Table for Figure 1.14

S. No.	Price	Plotting
1	98.75	No plotting
2	112.55	Bullish brick
3	89.40	Bearish Brick
4	110.40	Bullish brick
5	122.40	Bullish brick
6	99.80	Bearish Brick
7	121.20	Bullish brick
8	131.70	Bullish brick
9	142.95	Bullish brick
10	152.95	Bullish brick

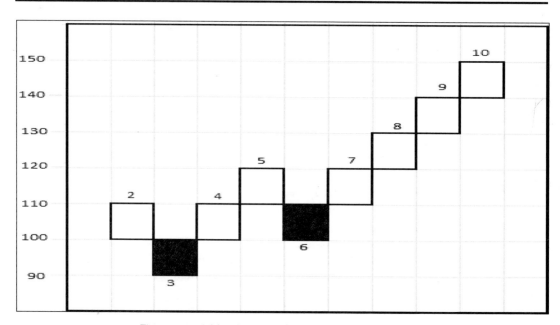

Figure 1.13: **A high-low Renko chart based on Table 1.6**

~

Those who are familiar with the point & figure (P&F) charts will realise that Renko charts are similar to P&F charts in more ways than one. The key difference between Renko and P&F charts is that we don't have to define the reversal method or value in a Renko chart. We only need to define a brick value to plot the Renko chart. It is possible to introduce reversals also to the Renko charts, but let's not complicate it just now.

Log Brick Value

In the earlier examples, we discussed the plotting of Renko charts using absolute brick values, such as 5 or 10. Actually, Renko charts can be plotted with any number. But often a chart moves in a wide range which makes defining the brick value difficult. Take, for instance, a stock like Aban Offshore that was trading at ₹5,000 in January 2008 and subsequently crashed to ₹300 in March 2009, and then traded below ₹200 in January 2016. A brick value of 50, when the stock was trading at ₹5,000, would have represented 1% of the prevailing price. But if the chart were plotted with the same brick value when the price had dropped to ₹200, the brick value of 50 would represent 25% of the prevailing price.

This example illustrates the problem associated with using absolute brick values for Renko charts, especially when studying a long term chart. There are many examples of stocks moving in a wide price range where it would be illogical to use a single brick value to sensibly capture the price action over time.

Technology came as a saviour in dealing with this issue. With the advent of computers, it's become easier to use log scale, or log brick values, to plot Renko charts. So, if we use a 1% log scale, a bullish brick will be plotted when the price moves higher by 1%, irrespective of its absolute value. Similarly, the next bullish brick will get plotted when the price again moves higher by 1%. On the other hand, a bearish brick will be plotted if the price drops below the low of the previous brick. For a reversal from a bearish to a bullish brick, the price must move past the high of the previous brick.

To summarise, while the manner of chart construction remains the same but a log brick value is used while instead of the absolute brick value. This makes the chart consistent in terms of brick value, and price patterns too become more relevant.

Remember, the X-axis in a Renko chart does not capture time. Therefore, a series of bullish or bearish bricks can represent the price action of many days. In all the charts in this book, the period covered is therefore specifically mentioned in the chart.

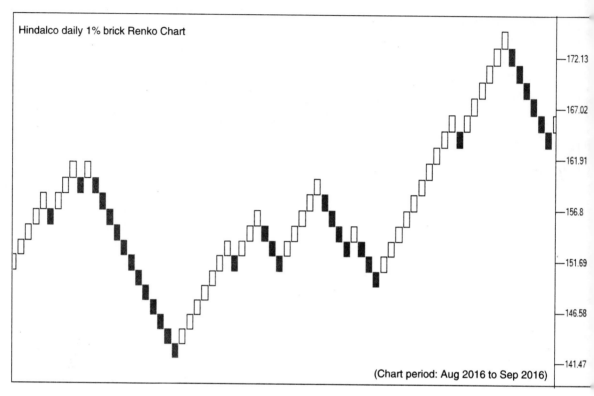

Figure 1.14: **Daily Renko chart of Hindalco with 1% brick value**

~

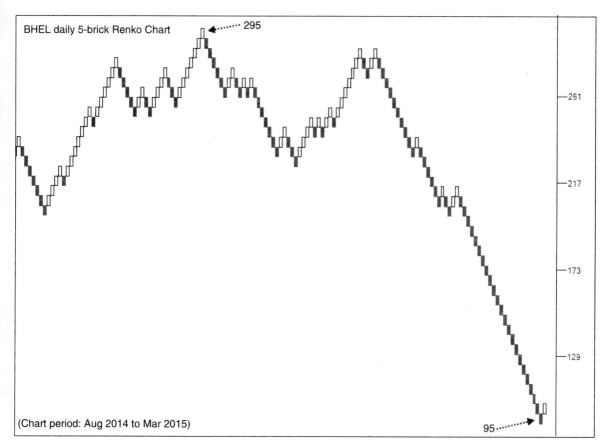

BHEL daily 5-brick Renko Chart 295

—261

—217

—173

—129

(Chart period: Aug 2014 to Mar 2015)   95 ········►

Figure 1.15: **The BHEL stock was trading around ₹300 in February 2015 and then fell below ₹100 in March 2016. This 5-brick value chart looks good but is difficult to trade in the later stages because of the brick value issue. In simple words, a brick value of ₹5 when the stock was trading at ₹300 is 1.66% of the price, but when it is trading at ₹100, it represents 5% of the price.**

∼

Figure 1.15 is the Renko chart of BHEL plotted with a brick value of 5. It aptly highlights why log bricks are of great advantage while studying longer term charts.

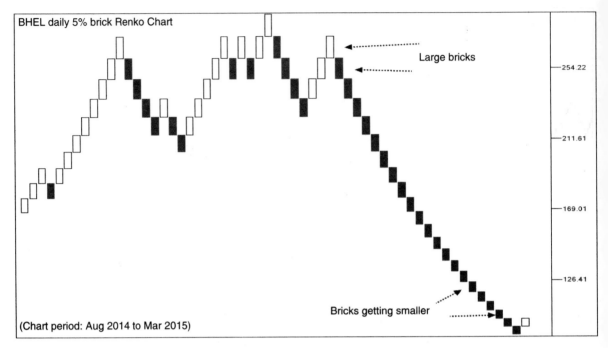

Figure 1.16: **Daily Renko chart of BHEL with 5% brick value**

~

Figure 1.16 is a Renko chart of BHEL plotted with a daily 5% brick value for the same period as in the case of Figure 1.15.

The brick value changes as per the price level due to the log scale, which is logical for analysing longer term trends. Notice that in the chart in Figure 1.16, the earlier bricks are larger because the price level was high and they later turn smaller as the price fell to lower levels.

Log scale allows the user to plot consistent charts and, more importantly, it makes the chart tradable in practice. Figure 1.17 is the BHEL chart plotted with 1.5% brick value for the same period. Compare it with the chart in Figure 1.15 and notice the difference in the latter part of the chart when the stock started falling.

A huge advantage of log brick charts is that they lend themselves to screening for opportunities across a universe, or a group, of stocks. A brick value of 5 point for a stock trading at ₹1,000 and for another one trading at ₹100 is incompatible and hence scanning is rendered meaningless with absolute brick values. But 1% across the charts remains 1% of prevailing prices, irrespective of the absolute price level a stock is trading at.

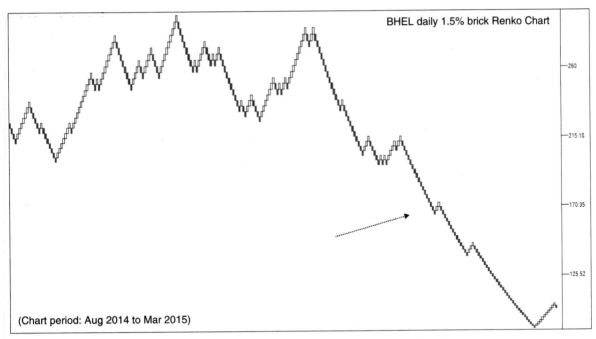

Figure 1.17: **Daily Renko chart of BHEL with 1.5% brick value**

~

We can therefore run a scanner for a given strategy or pattern across a group of stocks or instruments using a log brick value. The use of log brick value also facilitates the testing of a trading system.

You would have notice that the chart plotted with brick value of 5 has more bricks than a chart with a brick value of 20. The number of bricks plotted in a chart depends on the chosen brick value.

By now it must be clear that changing the brick value alters the amount of information captured in the chart. This possibility of changing brick values on the same time frame (data frequency) is a key feature of these charts. To look at the larger degree price setups, higher brick value can be used. To look at the short term price structure, lower brick values are useful.

ATR Brick Value

Apart from fixed or absolute brick values and log scale brick values, it is also not uncommon to see the 14-day average true range (ATR) being used as brick value in Renko charts. Thus, the 14-day ATR is first calculated and the Renko chart is then plotted using that value. For example, if the 14-day ATR of Nifty is 50, then the ATR based Renko chart of Nifty will be plotted with a 50-point absolute brick value. Since ATR is a volatility based indicator, an ATR based brick value chart is based on the current volatility of the instrument. However, it is better to plot percentage ATR when this method is followed. Thus, in the above example, if the Nifty is currently trading at, say, 5,000, then a 1% log brick value chart (ATR value of 50 divided by current price of 5,000) can be used for plotting instead of using the 50-point absolute brick value, so that past Renko patterns become relevant for the analysis.

All the methods and analyses discussed in the book are applicable to charts plotted using ATR based brick values as well. The logic is that ATR factors in an instrument's inherent volatility and plots the chart accordingly. The problem with this kind of method is that the brick value would keep changing as the value of ATR changes. So if you enter a trade based on an earlier ATR-based Renko chart, how do you deal with the changing ATR value? A change in the ATR will lead to a change in the brick value and the chart structure. Which is why log brick values are preferred over dynamic methods of determining brick values.

Keeping track of the price setups on higher brick values and lower brick values is not possible with ATR brick value charts. The ATR method could be useful when only a chart pattern is analysed on the Renko chart while the trade is executed using some other method. I would rate this as serious under-utilisation of Renko charts since Renko is a complete charting system in itself, which can be used for every type of trading.

From a trading perspective, there is a very important advantage in using log brick values. It is possible to design patterns that fit one's risk appetite. For example, if someone is comfortable with a 5% risk, a Renko formation can be traded with the stop loss of not more than 5 bricks on the 1% brick value chart. Scanners designed this way will produce outcomes where there is a price pattern which fits into the risk parameters.

Other Methods of Plotting Renko Charts

Renko charts are plotted using only a single price and we have discussed the methods of plotting charts both with closing price and high-low prices. A Renko chart can also be plotted with a typical price (high + low + close). It can also be plotted using a weighted average price, or such other calculations. While the latter is ideal from an analytical perspective but it is difficult to trade with it. A Renko chart of open instead of close can also be experimented with. There can be other methods as well, but all of them come with their own pros and cons, so one should understand a method well before using it. It is not that one method will generate higher profitability than the others; it is the understanding of their nature and how you trade them that will lead to success. The key is consistency.

Personally, I prefer log brick value charts plotted with closing prices on all time frames.

Repainting

There is a common complaint of a repainting issue with Renko charts. There can be only two reasons for a brick getting repainted. The first is when you are using ATR as brick value. In that case, the chart will change whenever the ATR changes. The second reason is that some bricks may disappear by the time the period is over. For instance, if you are using a 15-minute time frame for a Renko chart, some bricks might disappear after being printed within that 15-minute period simply because the time frame is yet to be completed. This is similar to bar or candlestick charts except that only the last candle changes in that format so it can be easily understood. With Renko charts, several bricks can appear and disappear, leading to possible confusion.

Time Frame

In a traditional candlestick or bar chart, we can plot higher time frame charts by using monthly, weekly or yearly prices. We can do that in Renko charts as well by simply adjusting the brick value, instead of switching between weekly, monthly or yearly prices. A weekly chart is locked at the end of the week, but a higher brick value daily chart gets locked every day but fulfils the same purpose.

Thus, instead of plotting charts using weekly or monthly price data, I recommend plotting higher brick value charts using the daily price data in order to analyse the bigger time frame picture, as follows:

- For short term analysis, one can use a 0.25% to 1% brick value based on daily price data.

- Use a 1% to 3% brick value daily chart to get a medium term picture; and

- Use a 3% to 5% brick value daily chart to get a much larger time frame picture.

Figure 1.18 is a Renko chart of TVS Motors plotted with 0.50% brick value.

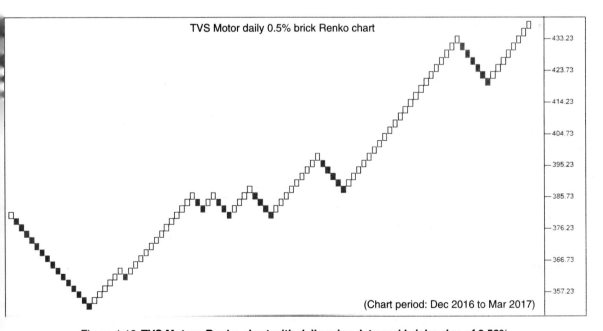

Figure 1.18: **TVS Motors Renko chart with daily price data and brick value of 0.50%**

~

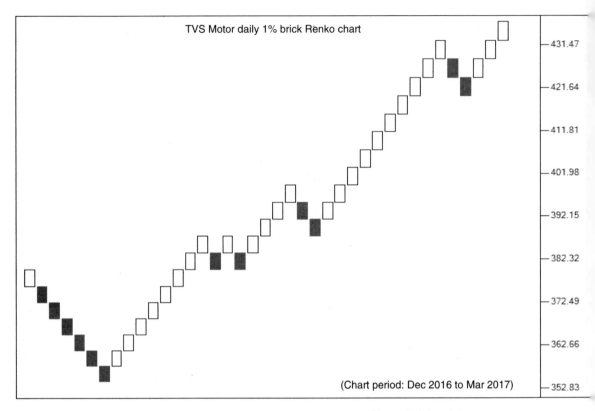

Figure 1.19: **TVS Motors daily Renko chart with 1% brick value**

~

Figure 1.19 is the corresponding chart plotted using a 1% brick value. You would notice that in this chart, brick values are more compressed and the noise is reduced.

Figure 1.20 is the corresponding daily chart of TVS Motors plotted with 5% brick value to get the larger picture.

You can see in Figure 1.20 that the size of the brick is increasing as the price goes up. This is the advantage of log charts. Trend lines and other analysis also become more logical on these charts.

For intraday time intervals, I recommend using one-minute price data for plotting the charts. One can use 0.25% brick value for stocks. I recommend using 10- and 25-point absolute brick values for Nifty and Bank Nifty charts on the one-minute time frame. With experience, one can adjust these brick values as per one's trading style and preferences.

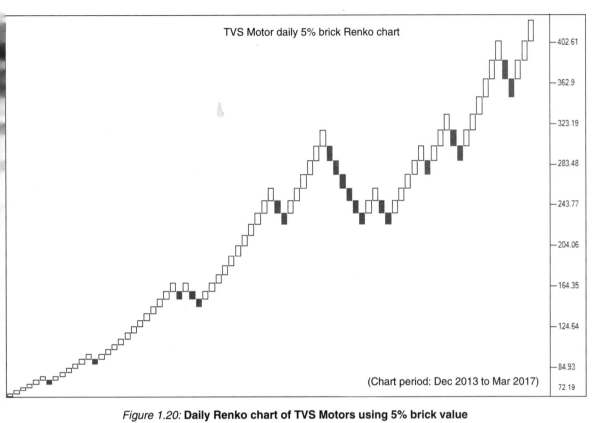

Figure 1.20: **Daily Renko chart of TVS Motors using 5% brick value**

$\sim$

An aggressive trader looking for more trades can opt for a lower brick value. A momentum trader, on the other hand, can increase the brick value in order to ride the trend. This is explained in detail in the subsequent chapters.

Irrespective of what your trading style may be, following Renko charts will certainly help you filter out unnecessary trades and deal better with emotional issues and overtrading.

Brick Reversal Pattern

The change of brick from bearish to bullish, or from bullish to bearish, is called a brick reversal pattern.

- A bullish brick reversal pattern happens when a bearish brick is followed by a bullish brick.

- Correspondingly, a bearish brick reversal pattern is formed when a bullish brick is followed by a bearish brick.

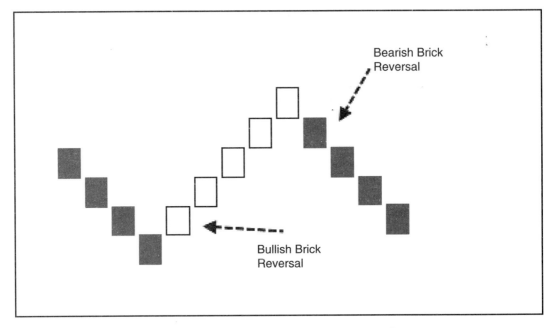

Figure 1.21: **Bullish and bearish brick reversals**

~

Bullish and bearish brick reversals are illustrated in Figure 1.21.

Now, a logical question that arises is: can one trade when the brick colour changes? In other words, can we buy when a bearish brick is followed by a bullish brick, and *vice versa*? The simple answer is yes, but, unfortunately, it is difficult to implement this simple sounding strategy in practice. **The basic injustice rendered to Renko charts is to consider a bullish brick as a buy signal and a bearish brick as a sell signal. Readers must realise that Renko is not a trading system; it's a method of charting akin to candlestick charts or bar charts.**

While a brick reversal does indicate a change, namely a reversal in the trend, the key question from a trading perspective is the significance of the reversal.

A brick reversal is thus just a pattern, and while it can be traded effectively, we need more information and chart analysis to see what caused the brick reversal. We will discuss many other patterns and tools that will help us understand how to deal with brick reversals from a trading perspective.

Brick reversal formations in higher brick value charts are obviously more meaningful. We will come back to this discussion in Part 2 of the book, once we have fully discussed Renko pattern analysis.

Chapter 2

~

Renko Chart Analysis with Conventional Patterns

L ET'S BEGIN OUR DISCUSSION ON RENKO CHART ANALYSIS with conventional methods and patterns.

In this chapter, almost all Renko charts have been plotted with a 1% brick value on daily charts and so they typically capture the medium term price action. The concepts discussed are however, applicable on all brick values and time frames, unless specified otherwise. I have used the same brick value only for the sake of consistency, though the concepts are applicable on all brick values and time frames.

Support and Resistance

The terms support and resistance need no explanation for those who are even somewhat familiar with technical analysis. In simple terms, support is a price level, or range, where the demand is expected to overcome supply, while resistance is a price level, or range, where the supply is expected to overcome demand.

Previous tops and bottoms are important reference points for identifying support and resistance levels — and this concept is applicable on Renko charts, too. If price had earlier faced resistance at a particular level, there is a high probability that the same level would again act as resistance on a subsequent revisit by the price. The situation gets more interesting when the market is either overbought or oversold, or when the broader market trend looks overstretched at the time of a revisit of old resistance or support zones.

All tools and methods of identifying support and resistance used in candlestick, bar and line charts are applicable to Renko charts as well. In practice, you'll observe that analysis becomes simpler in Renko charts due to their noiseless nature. This characteristic helps in easily identifying support and resistance levels.

Previous Peaks and Bottoms

Previous peaks and bottoms are treated as significant support and resistance price levels. We can draw horizontal lines at these pivotal levels to indicate support and resistance.

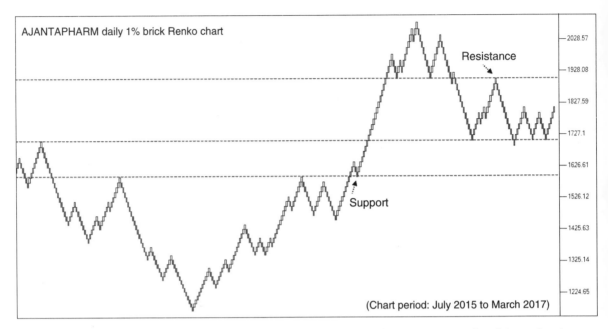

Figure 2.1: **Renko chart of Ajanta Pharma with horizontal at lines drawn support and resistance levels**

~

Let's consider the Ajanta Pharma Renko chart in Figure 2.1, showing some support and resistance levels.

Due to the clarity with which a Renko chart captures trends, it is a visual treat to analyse them. In the chart shown in Figure 2.1, horizontal lines are drawn for major tops and bottoms that acted as support and resistance.

The concept underlying the polarity principle, wherein a previous support, when broken, becomes resistance, and *vice versa*, is also clearly visible in the chart in Figure 2.1. The arrows marked in this chart highlight the polarity principle at play.

Renko Support and Resistance Setup

Double tops and double bottoms are popular chart formations used in traditional chart analysis. A double top is a bearish reversal pattern that is completed when two tops are formed at a similar level and the price falls below the neckline, i.e. the lowest point between the two. Conversely, when price forms two lows in the same zone and goes above the neckline — the highest point between the two lows of the pattern — it's a bullish reversal pattern termed as a double bottom pattern (*see* Figure 2.2).

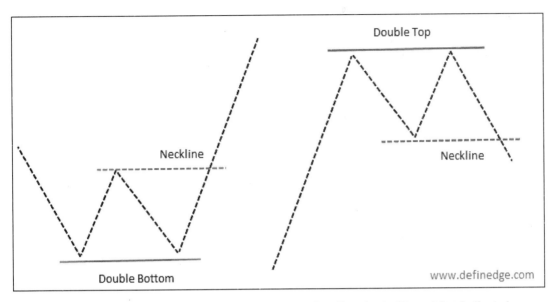

Figure 2.2: **Double bottom and double top patterns in a line chart with neckline indicated**

∼

The double top and double bottom patterns shown in Figure 2.2 can be identified on Renko charts as well. Have a look at the examples in the Renko chart in Figure 2.3.

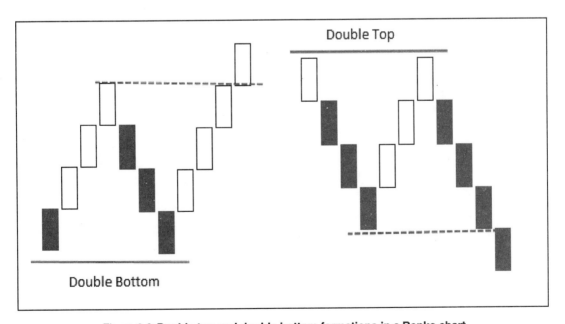

Figure 2.3: **Double top and double bottom formations in a Renko chart**

∼

A double bottom pattern in a Renko chart is characterised by two bearish bricks appearing at a similar level, and a breakout above the neckline of the pattern.

Correspondingly, price going below the neckline after a brick forming a second peak at a similar level as an earlier brick forms a double top pattern in Renko charts. As you can see in Figure 2.3, identification of such patterns is simple and objective in Renko charts.

A double bottom is a bullish pattern which shows that the price has taken support at a previous pivotal point. A double top, on the other hand, is a bearish pattern that shows that the price has seen resistance at the previous peak. Besides the neckline break, a brick reversal formation offers trading opportunity as well. A brick reversal, after taking support or resistance at a previous brick, is the first indication that the price is respecting the support or resistance level concerned. If the brick reversal pattern is traded, it offers an early entry, and with a tighter stop, as illustrated in the examples in Figure 2.4.

- A Renko double bottom support pattern is confirmed when a bullish brick appears after two bearish bricks have formed at a similar level, indicating support. The pattern gets negated if the price then goes below the support brick.

- A Renko double top resistance pattern is confirmed when a bearish brick appears after two bullish bricks have formed at a similar level. This bearish pattern fails if a bullish brick is formed above the resistance brick.

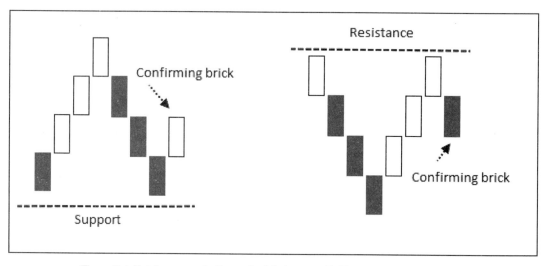

Figure 2.4: **Brick reversal after a double bottom (left) and double top (right)**

~

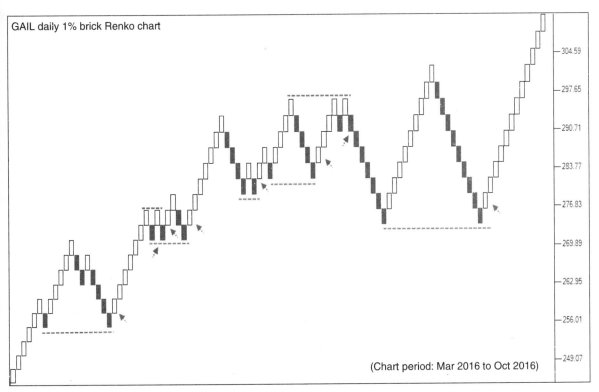

Figure 2.5: **Trade setups based on Renko support and resistance levels in a 1% brick daily Renko chart of Gail**

~

A reversal brick provides confirmation of the support and resistance levels concerned and makes for an effective trade setup.

One can also choose to wait for the neckline break as confirmation, but I recommend using a lower brick value chart in that case. A brick reversal filters out frequently appearing formations, and other methods of analysis help in identifying high probability trading opportunities.

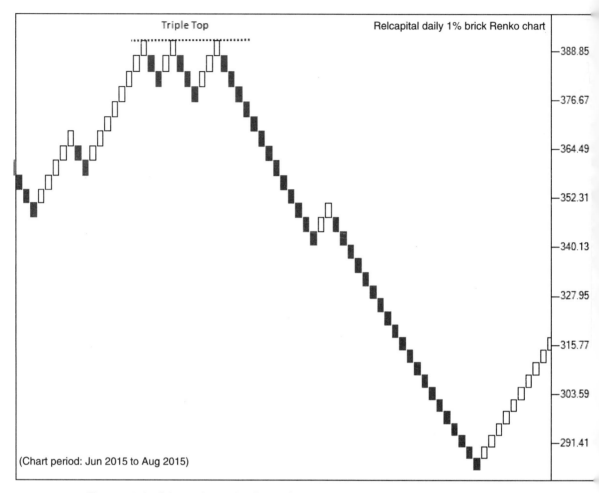

Figure 2.6: **A triple top formation in a daily 1% brick Renko chart of Reliance Capital**

~

Multiple top or bottom patterns such as triple top and triple bottom formations can also be identified in a similar manner. Have a look at Figure 2.6.

Note that in the case of a triple top, the double top also remains active because the top brick has not yet been broken by the price.

There remains the question about targets and exit rules. Here we are restricting the discussion only to patterns and analysis. Trading setups, along with objective rules, will be explained in detail in later chapters.

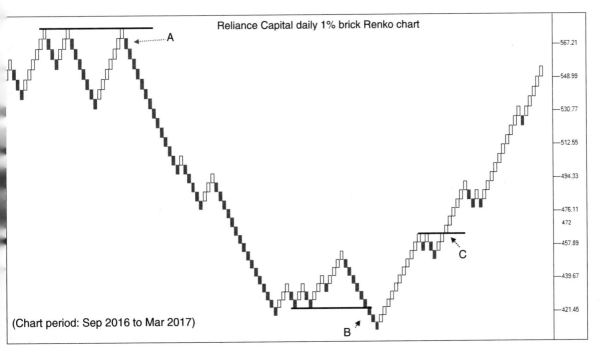

Figure 2.7: **Triple tops and triple bottoms in a 1% brick daily Renko chart of Reliance Capital.**

Pattern A is a triple top confirmed by a bearish brick reversal. Pattern B is not a triple bottom because the brick did not reverse immediately, though it did so eventually. Pattern C is where the brick did not turn bearish and hence it is not a triple top formation; in fact, it is a resistance breakout pattern.

~

Figure 2.7 is a Renko chart of Reliance Capital showing triple tops and triple bottoms.

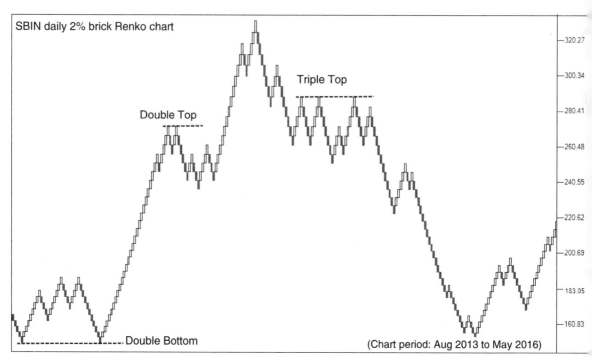

SBIN daily 2% brick Renko chart

Triple Top

Double Top

Double Bottom

(Chart period: Aug 2013 to May 2016)

Figure 2.8: **SBI's round trip from ₹150 to ₹150 had a few Renko support and resistance levels in between which you can observe on this daily 1% brick value chart**

~

Figure 2.8 is a Renko chart of SBI showing support and resistance levels.

Support or Resistance Line

A horizontal trend line is another popular technique where a line is drawn connecting multiple peaks and bottoms to identify demand and supply zones.

Figure 2.9 is a chart of Axis Bank showing horizontal support / resistance lines on a Renko chart.

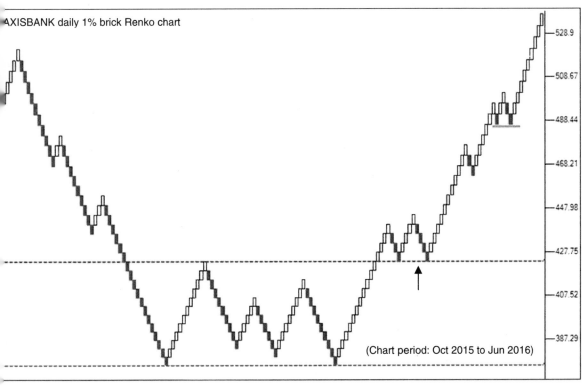

Figure 2.9: **Renko double bottom setup at a support line in a 1% brick daily chart of Axis Bank. Arrow shows where the price took support at a previous resistance line is. Trade can be identified by using these concepts together.**

~

Higher Low, Lower High

When the price forms a low which is higher than the previous low, it is known as a higher low or a rising bottom pattern. This is one of the first indications of a bullish trend reversal to up.

Correspondingly, a lower high is marked when the price forms a high point lower than the previous high. This is considered an early signal of a potential top and a trend reversal to down. Brick reversal formations help in identifying these patterns. Let's see how in the chart featured in Figure 2.10.

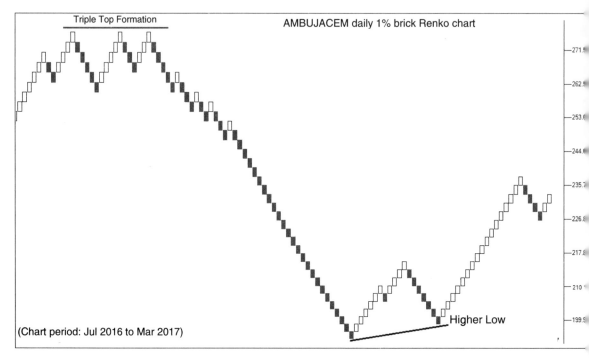

Figure 2.10: **Triple top formation and a higher low in Ambuja Cement**

~

The triple top formation shown in the chart in Figure 2.10 was followed by a significant downtrend. Later, at the right hand edge of the chart, the price formed a higher low at the bottom, signalling an impending reversal of the prior downtrend to up.

Fibonacci Levels

The Fibonacci sequence is named after the Italian mathematician Leonardo Pisa, also known as Fibonacci. He introduced this sequence to the Western world in the 12th century. It is said that this sequence had been described earlier as Virahanka numbers in Indian mathematics.

The Fibonacci sequence is a series of numbers, as follows:

> 0, 1, 1, 2, 3, 5, 8, 13, 21, 34, 55, 89, 144, 233, 377 . . .

Each number in this sequence is simply the sum of its two previous numbers. For example, the number 2 is arrived at by adding the two numbers before it (1 + 1). Similarly, 3 is nothing but the sum of the two numbers before it (2 +1), and so on.

Fibonacci numbers are treated as nature's numbers because it is said that they are found in the arrangement of leaves in plants and florets in a flower, etc.

There are also many natural objects where this ratio is not found, and even if it is found, it is not necessary that it should be applicable to the markets. I am mentioning this to emphasize that this is no magical ratio. However, it is fairly widely used for designing trade setups.

If any number of the series is divided by the number that follows it, the ratio will be 61.8%, which is also referred to as the Golden Ratio. If any number in the series is divided by the number after the next one in the sequence, the ratio we get is 38.20%. Similarly, every number in the sequence is 23.60% of the number after the next two numbers in the sequence.

Fibonacci retracements and extensions are widely followed tools for identifying price support, resistance and target levels. Traders who prefer to trade when prices correct have found Fibonacci ratios useful for calculating support or resistance levels based on the retracement to the earlier trend. Generally, 23.60%, 38.20%, 50%, 61.80% and 78.60% are treated as Fibonacci ratios. Actually, the 50% level has nothing to do with Fibonacci sequence but traders use this level because of the tendency of price to reverse after retracing half of its previous move.

Traders who prefer to initiate trades at the support or resistance levels find Fibonacci ratios a useful tool. The following are the steps to follow.

Step 1

Find a swing or a trend and mark its tops and bottoms. If it is an up move, Point A will be the bottom of the move and Point B its top. For a down move, Point A will be the top and Point B the bottom.

Step 2

Calculate the distance between the two points and apply the Fibonacci ratio to this distance for projecting the price retracement.

For example, in an up move if Point A is at 100 and Point B is at 200, the method to calculate the 50% retracement is as follows:

Distance = Point B – Point A = 200 – 100 = 100 points
50% Retracement = 50% x Distance = 50% x 100 points = 50 points
Retracement Price = Point B – Retracement amount = 200 – 50 = 150

All ratios are calculated in a similar manner. For a bearish retracement, the distance is added to Point A. Though most technical analysis software will automatically calculate these retracement levels, it is useful to understand the underlying method and logic.

Figure 2.11 illustrates a retracement in a bullish price move from Point A to Point B.

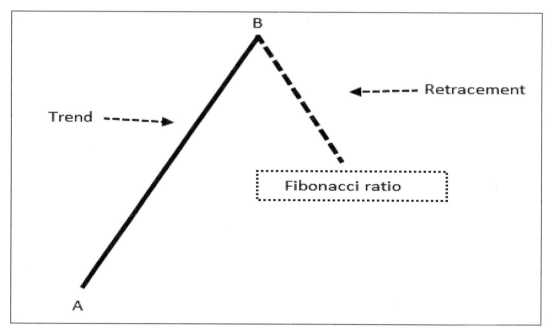

Figure 2.11: **Retracement during a bullish price move from Point A to Point B**

~

Figure 2.12 illustrates a retracement in a bearish price move from Point A to Point B.

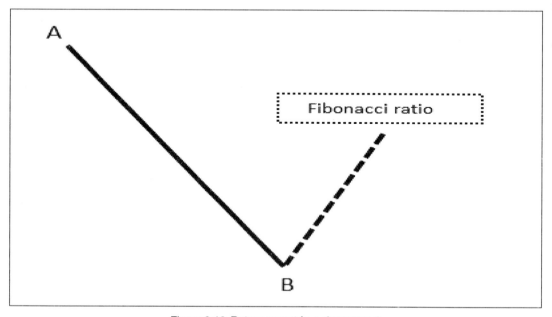

Figure 2.12: **Retracement in a downtrend**

~

Price correction in a strong move is the logical setup for entering a trade. The risk is usually low and there is a sense of psychological comfort of not buying at the high price point — or selling at the low price point, as the case may be.

We can apply Fibonacci retracement to Renko charts as well — by connecting the tops and bottoms of the price bricks. We don't know whether the price will halt at 23.60% or 38.20%; or if it will get into a deeper correction. Equally, there are chances that the price may choose to ignore all retracement levels and get into a bigger counter trend move. Therefore, it makes little sense to take trading decisions based on retracement levels alone. It is always advisable to use other confirmatory tools to trade those levels.

The Renko charts of Grasim shown in Figure 2.13 and Figure 2.14 are very educative.

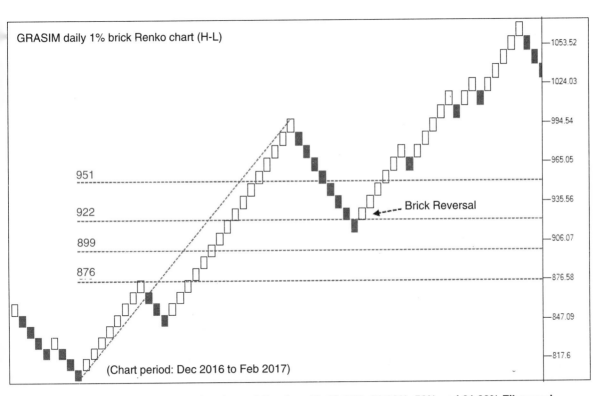

Figure 2.13: **1% brick daily Renko chart of Grasim with 23.60%, 38.20%, 50% and 61.80% Fibonacci retracements applied on it. In this case, the price did not take support at 23.6% retracement but reversed from the 38.2% retracement level. Trading it with a brick reversal becomes a more logical decision.**

~

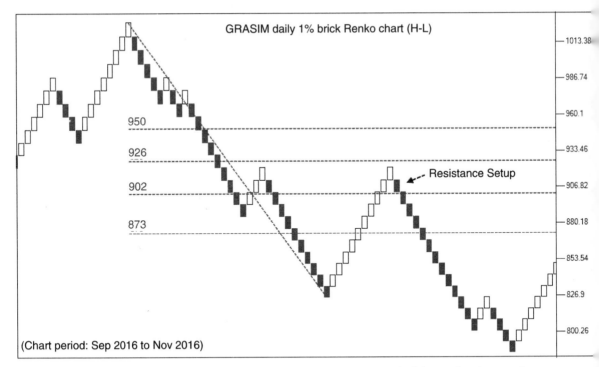

Figure 2.14: **The price of Grasim retraced from 50% retracement level of the earlier down swing move and formed a Renko resistance setup in this 1% brick daily chart.**

~

Other Fibonacci techniques, such as extensions or Fibonacci clusters, can also be used with Renko charts.

Knowledge of Renko formations can be very helpful for those interested in taking trades from these retracement levels. It can help eliminate the guesswork associated with identifying the retracement level that will be respected by the price. This will also result in improving your odds of trading success.

Remember, though Fibonacci retracements are an integral part of the setup, what we trade with this methodology is the Renko pattern and the trade should be exited if the pattern fails. A pattern following approach has the advantage of knowing the risk in advance, at the time of initiating the trade.

Trend Lines

The trend line is another basic and popular tool used in technical analysis. As the name suggests, a trend line is drawn on the chart mainly to identify trends. It is also a useful tool for analysing support, resistance and breakouts. In an uptrend, a rising trend line is drawn by connecting two or more swing lows, while in a downtrend a falling trend line is drawn by

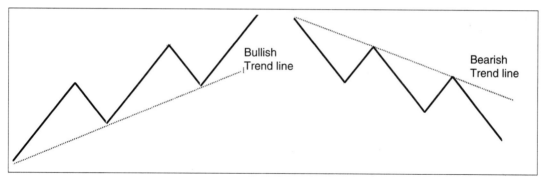

Figure 2.15: **Bullish and bearish trend lines on a line chart**

~

connecting two or more peak highs. These trendlines are used as resistance and support levels, and can also be used as trend filters.

Trend lines can be drawn in a similar manner on Renko charts, too. We connect the price lows of two bricks to draw a rising bullish line; and connect the price tops of two bricks to draw a falling bearish line.

Figure 2.16 is a Renko chart with trend lines drawn on it.

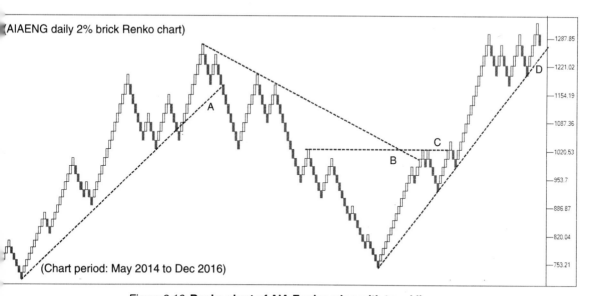

Figure 2.16: **Renko chart of AIA Engineering with trend lines**

The trend line labelled A is a bullish rising line that connects the lows of bearish bricks. Trend Line B is a bearish falling line connecting the top of bullish bricks. Trend Line C is a horizontal line drawn by connecting the highs. It shows a resistance that the price cleared eventually, resulting in a bullish breakout. Trend Line D is relatively steep bullish line drawn by connecting price lows.

~

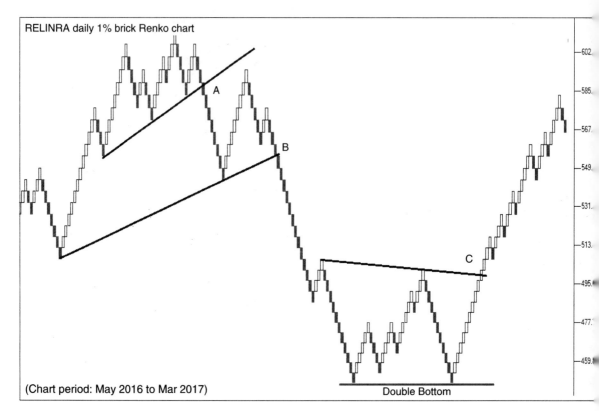

Figure 2.17: **Trend line breakouts on a Renko chart of Reliance Infra. Point A and Point B show a breach of bullish trend lines. Point C is a resistance trend line breakout after a double bottom formation.**

∼

Figure 2.17 is a Renko chart of Reliance Infra showing trend line breakouts.

Channel lines

A channel line is created by drawing a line on the chart parallel to the trend line (*see* Figure 2.18).

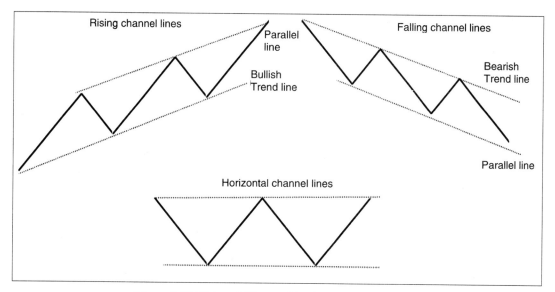

Figure 2.18: **Rising, falling and horizontal channel lines**

~

A line drawn parallel to a bullish trend line is a rising channel line. Correspondingly, a falling channel line is drawn by plotting a line parallel to the bearish trend line (*see* Figure 2.19).

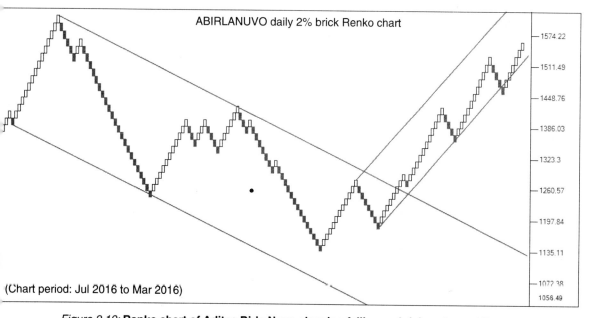

Figure 2.19: **Renko chart of Aditya Birla Nuvo showing falling and rising channel lines.**

~

Patterns with Trend Lines

Traditional chart patterns, such as head and shoulders, cup and handle, rounding tops and bottoms and triangles can be spotted more easily on Renko charts. Attractive visual appearance and the inherent noise filtration characteristics of these charts make identifying and analysing such patterns much simpler and effective on Renko charts.

Take a look at the Renko chart of Tata Steel in Figure 2.20.

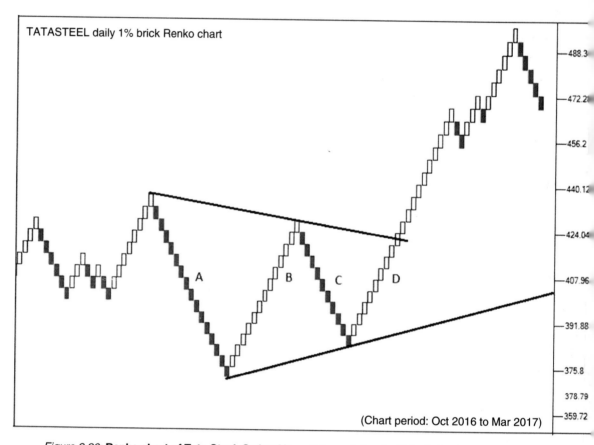

Figure 2.20: **Renko chart of Tata Steel. Swing Move B is contained within Swing Move A, and Swing Move C within Swing Move B. Move D finally breaks out. It is a triangular converging formation where trend lines helped in identifying the breakout.**

~

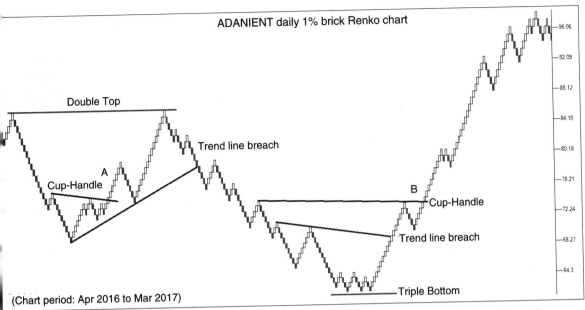

Figure 2.21: **Renko chart of Adani Enterprises. Cup and handle formations at Point A and Point B were effective on this chart. Apart from these, support, resistance and trend line breach formations are also seen on the chart.**

~

Figure 2.21 is a chart of Adani Enterprises that shows price patterns along with trend lines.

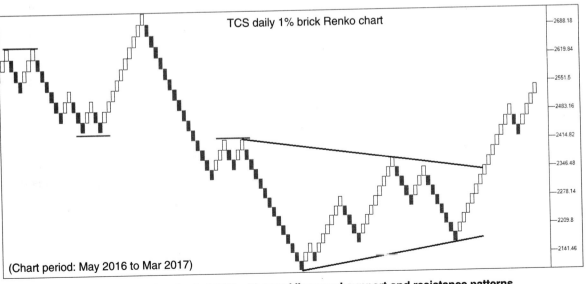

Figure 2.22: **Renko chart of TCS with trend lines and support and resistance patterns**

~

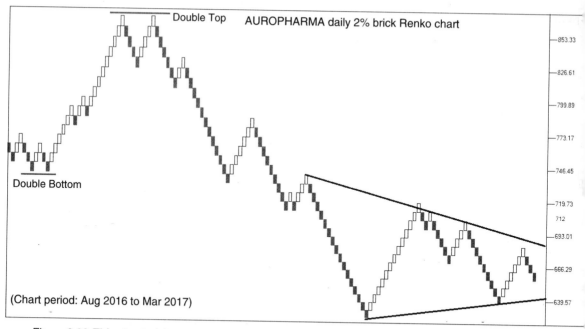

Figure 2.23: This chart of Aurobindo Pharma is another example of support, resistance and trend line breakout patterns on a Renko chart.

~

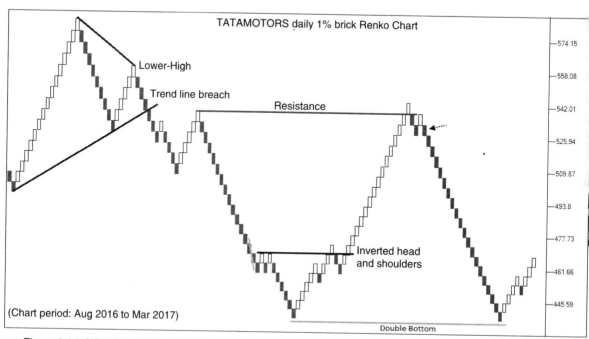

Figure 2.24: A Renko chart of Tata Motors which captures the various concepts discussed in this chapter

~

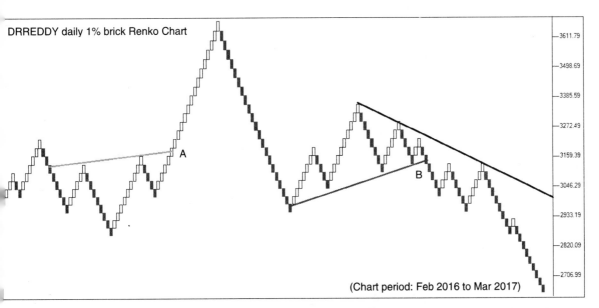

Figure 2.25: **Renko chart of Dr. Reddy Labs. Pattern A is an inverted head and shoulders while Pattern B is a head and shoulders formation. A larger head and shoulders formation is also at play but is not shown in the chart to avoid confusion. As highlighted earlier, traditional price patterns of technical analysis are easier to identify on Renko charts.**

~

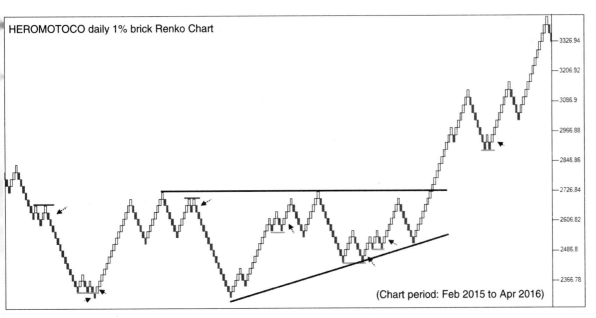

Figure 2.26: **This chart of Hero Motocorp shows Renko support and resistance formations. A rising bottoms formation, followed by a horizontal trend line break, is also seen in the chart.**

~

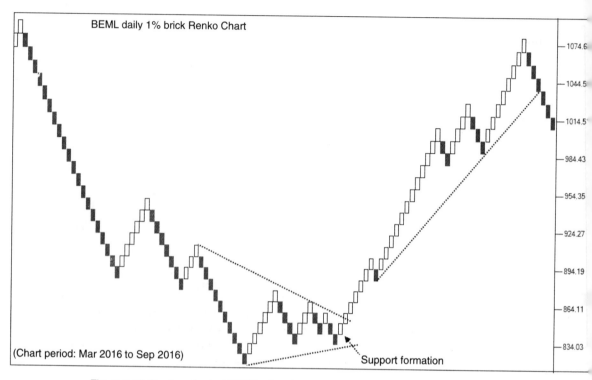

Figure 2.27: **Renko chart of BEML showing trend lines and converging formation**

Higher Brick Value Charts for Assessing Longer Term Trends

As observed earlier, the bigger time frame picture can be analysed by using higher brick values. This helps us in gauging longer term trends and price formations (*see* Figure 2.28).

In figures 2.28 and 2.29, you will notice smaller sized bricks at lower price levels and bigger ones at relatively higher price levels due to the inherent nature of calculating logarithmic brick levels. As explained earlier, it is very important to use log bricks while analysing long term charts.

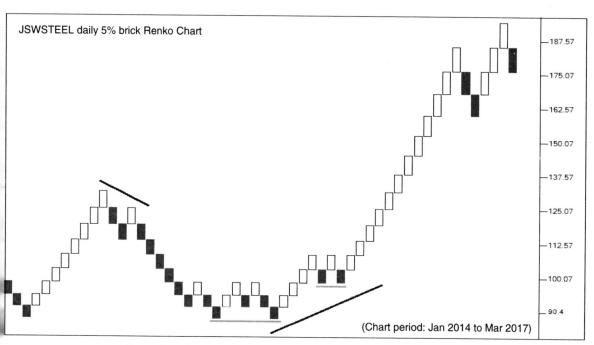

Figure 2.28: **Renko chart of JSW Steel plotted with 5% brick value**

~

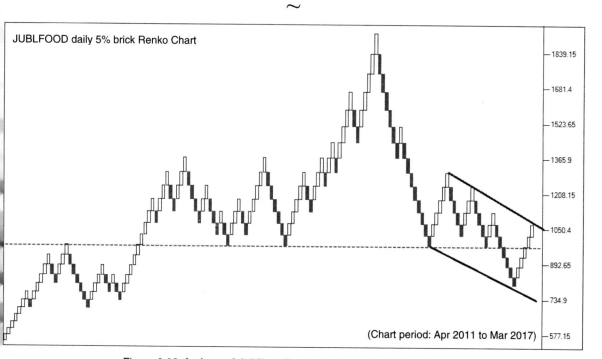

Figure 2.29: **A chart of Jubilant Foods plotted with 5% brick value**

~

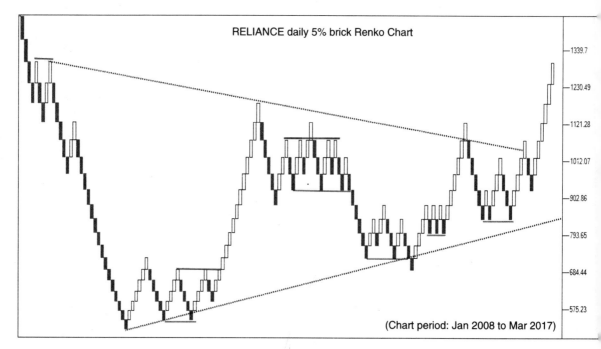

Figure 2.30: **A daily chart of Reliance Industries with 5% brick value which illustrates a difficult phase to trade. The price was in a long convergence formation for about 9 years. Renko support and resistance patterns during this period are shown on the chart.**

~

Figure 2.30 is the daily chart of Reliance Industries with 5% brick value which captures a difficult phase to trade in this stock.

By now, you would have understood how Renko charts are plotted and how traditional methods of technical analysis are relevant in Renko charts as well. To begin with, you can open a Renko chart as per your brick value and look for patterns such as support and resistance, higher highs, lower low formations and draw trend lines. This will help you get accustomed to Renko charts and also help you gain confidence and proficiency in the method.

Truly speaking, however, Renko analysis begins thereafter.

Before we go any further about Renko charts, it is very important for you to spend some time on understanding the construction of these charts. Have a look at Figure 2.31.

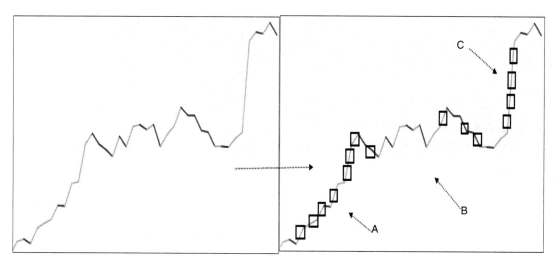

Figure 2.31: **How bricks are formed**

~

Figure 2.31 shows the formation of bricks; it is basically a line chart converted into bricks. Doing so has the follow major advantages:

1. A line chart is converted to fixed size (brick value) boxes, that can be counted.

2. The Renko chart doesn't move so long as the price remains within a particular price range or price zone — in other words, needless noise is eliminated from the chart.

3. You get a series of continuation bricks when there is a significant trend — as you can see at areas A and C in the chart in Figure 2.31.

4. You don't get many bricks when the price is moving sideways (*see* Area B).

5. Size of the bricks can be changed. So if you want to seek more information, you simply reduce the brick value. If you want to see a very large picture, just increase the brick value. Figure 2.32 and Figure 2.33 bring out this point clearly by way of comparison between a line chart and the corresponding Renko chart.

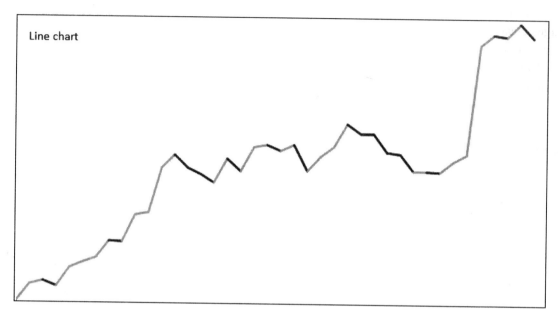

Figure 2.32: **Line chart**

~

The three images displayed in Figure 2.33 are Renko charts, with different brick values, of the line chart in Figure 2.32.

The chart with 0.50% brick value has more information, and we can filter the noise *via* higher brick values to look at the larger picture. We will discuss how we can make the best use of this knowledge in the forthcoming chapters.

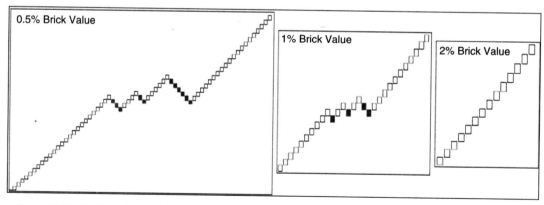

Figure 2.33: **The line chart of Figure 2.32 converted to Renko charts of (1) 0.5% brick value (left), (2) 1% brick value (centre), and (3) 2% brick value (right)**

~

I have great trust in breakouts on closing basis in line charts. The above comparative images clearly illustrate that the Renko charts are much clearer and simpler to analyse than are line charts.

Now, consider the Bajaj Financial Services chart shown in Figure 2.34, which vividly brings out how Renko charts show us the trend in the best possible manner.

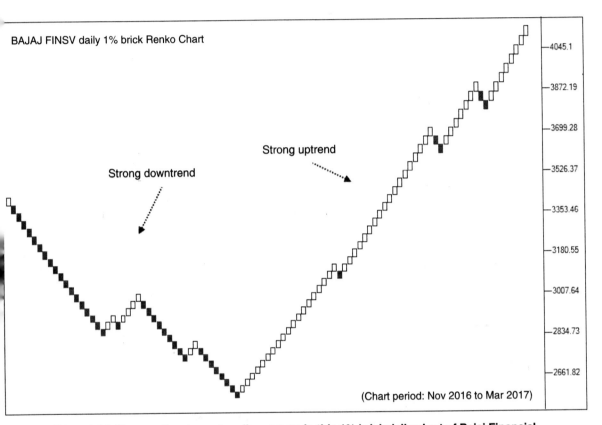

Figure 2.34: **Observe the strong trending moves in this 1% brick daily chart of Bajaj Financial Services, wherein there are very few corrective bricks in between. Riding a profitable position is arguably the most difficult thing to do. But, remember too, the ability to ride trends is essential in order to earn significant returns in trading.**

~

Chapter 3

~

Unique Renko Patterns

I N THE PREVIOUS CHAPTER WE DISCUSSED HOW ALL THE CONVENTIONAL CHART patterns are workable and relevant on Renko charts as well. In this chapter, we will discuss patterns that are unique to Renko charts.

The formation of bricks is a unique feature of Renko charts which no other chart category possesses. Equally, different combinations of bricks can help us in analysing both trends and setups. Over the years, I have explored, researched and analysed numerous possible combinations and come up with a comprehensive list of unique Renko patterns. I have also tried to keep the patterns as objective as possible and kept their names simple so that they are easy to remember.

Swing Breakout Patterns

Renko charts are basically swing charts. A series of bullish or bearish bricks represents a swing move, minus unnecessary noise. So when we see a series of bricks in a Renko chart, it means that the price has moved in a particular direction without a correction of twice the brick size (*see* Figure 3.1).

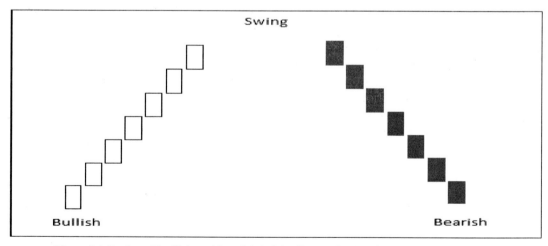

Figure 3.1: **Series of bullish and bearish bricks illustrating bullish and bearish swings**

~

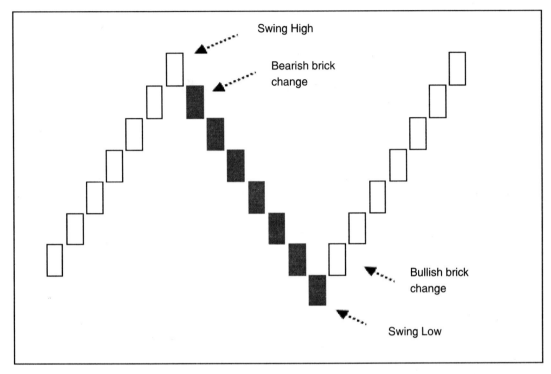

Figure 3.2: **Swing high and swing low on a Renko chart**

~

A series of bricks in one direction is called a swing move. A series of bullish bricks indicates a bullish trend and a series of bearish bricks captures a bearish trend.

As discussed in Chapter 1, a brick reversal occurs only when the reversal criteria is met. Hence, the price in a daily Renko chart can progress in the same brick colour for several days until the brick reversal criteria is met.

Swing breakouts are basic Renko chart patterns. Before we discuss them any further, let us objectively define swing highs and swing lows on Renko charts (*see* also Figure 3.2):

- When there is a brick reversal pattern from a bullish brick to bearish, the high price of the previous bullish brick is a swing high.

- Correspondingly, when there is a flip over from a bearish brick to a bullish one, the low price of the most recent bearish brick is the swing low.

This basically implies that there will be a swing high or swing low at every brick reversal pattern.

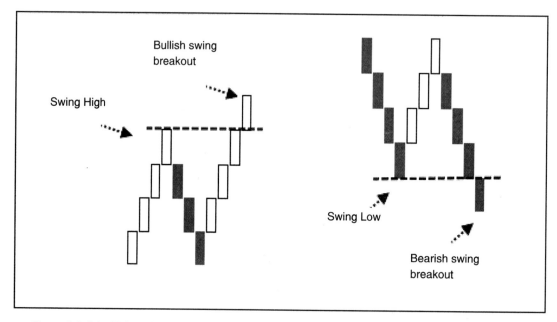

Figure 3.3: **A bullish swing breakout from an immediate previous swing high (left) and a bearish swing breakout from an immediate previous swing low (right)**

~

Figure 3.3 explains swing breakout formations.

A swing high gets formed when a bearish brick appears after a series of bullish bricks. If the next series of bullish bricks goes above the immediate previous swing high, it then triggers a bullish swing breakout. To complete a bullish swing breakout, the price needs to print one brick above the prior swing high.

Correspondingly, if the next series of bearish bricks goes below the low of an immediate previous swing low, and prints one brick below it, the bearish swing breakout is then said to have been triggered at that brick.

Please note that a breakout above — or below — the immediate previous swing high or swing low is necessary to call it a swing breakout. Any swing pivot prior to the most recent one is not considered as swing breakout.

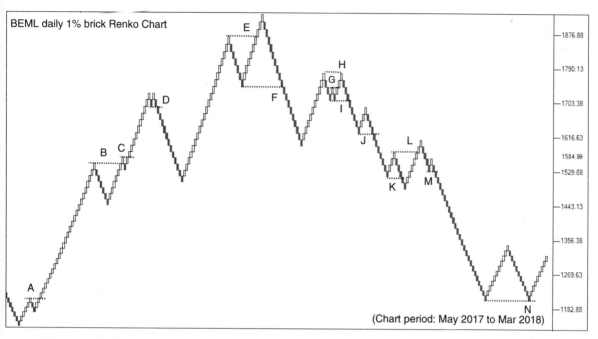

Figure 3.4: **Bullish and bearish swing breakouts in the daily 1% brick value Renko chart of BEML**

A, B, C, E, G and L are bullish swing breakouts while D, F, I, J, K and M are bearish swing breakout patterns. Pattern H is a resistance level and N shows a double bottom support pattern.

~

Figure 3.4 is a chart of BEML illustrating and explaining bullish and bearish swing break-outs.

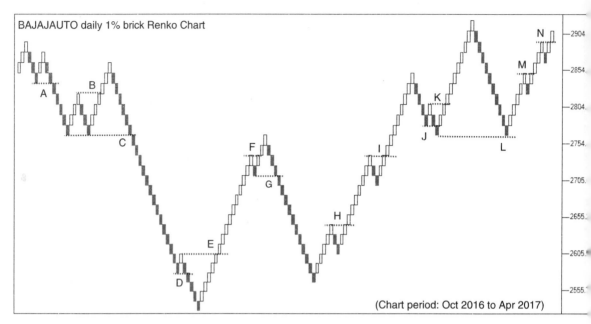

Figure 3.5: **Bullish and bearish swing breakouts in the daily 1% brick value Renko chart of Bajaj Auto**

A, C, D, G and J are bearish swing breakouts, while B, E, F, H, I, K, M and N are bullish swing breakout patterns. Pattern C is also a multiple-swing breakout and L is a double bottom support pattern.

~

Figure 3.5 is a chart of Bajaj Auto showing swing breakouts.

In Renko charts, swing breakouts can also be traded as a system by themselves. Trading a swing breakout is a price or trend following method that doesn't require prediction as regards the direction of the trend. You buy when a bullish swing breakout occurs with a stop loss at the bearish swing breakout level. If the stop loss gets triggered, you exit and reverse by trading the bearish swing breakout with a stop placed at the bullish swing breakout price level. The method comes with clear and pre-defined risk (stop loss) levels, breakout and trend riding technique.

Price going above the previous swing high has bullish implications. As noted, this swing breakout technique comes with a pre-defined rule for risk management, as follows.

- A bullish swing breakout pattern fails if the price falls one brick below the swing low.

- A bearish swing breakout pattern will get invalidated if the price goes one brick above the swing high of the pattern (*see* Figure 3.6).

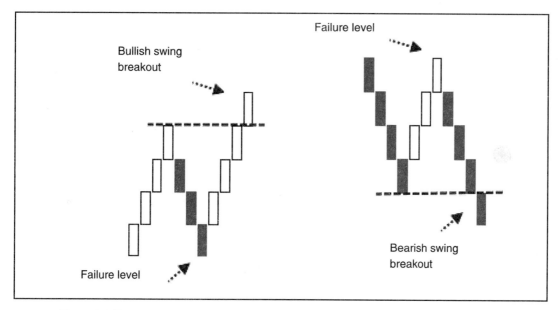

Figure 3.6: **Breakout and failure levels of bullish and bearish swing breakout patterns**

~

The failure levels highlighted in Figure 3.6 can be used as stop loss when initiating trades. This approach has the advantage of objectively identifying the initial risk in the trade. If the risk in a particular trade is unaffordable, you can skip that trade and wait for the next suitable opportunity. Or, you can adjust the position size (explained later in the book) while initiating the trade and add to the position later if the initial stop loss is too wide.

Renko chart swing breakouts can also be effective when it comes to trailing the stops. As you might be aware, the Dow Theory's simple definition of a trend is successive higher tops and higher bottoms, or successive lower tops and lower bottoms. This theory has stood the test of time, and thus I consider Renko swing breakouts to be the best method of trailing a trend.

Let's have a look at the chart of Maruti in Figure 3.7.

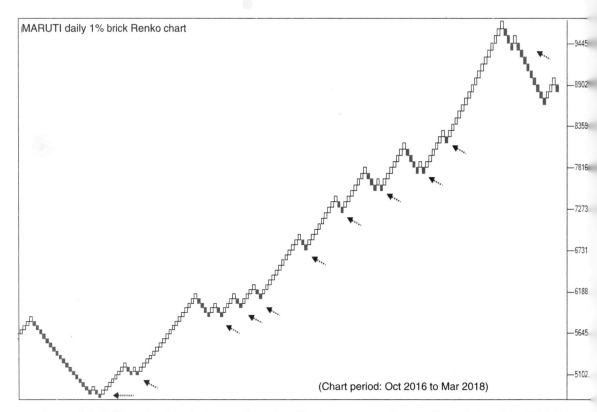

Figure 3.7: **Trailing stop loss technique based on Renko swing breakout patterns in the daily 1% brick value Renko chart of Maruti**

~

Once established, a trend can be analysed, or traded, using continuation swing breakout patterns. But look carefully at all the points shown by arrows in Figure 3.7. The stop could have been trailed at the bearish swing breakout level (one brick below the previous swing low) as the bullish bricks advance. Interestingly, there is no bearish swing breakout pattern in the chart of Maruti in Figure 3.7 from levels of around ₹4,800 in November 2016 to about ₹9,700 in December 2017.

Using an objective trailing stop loss is an effective method of riding a trend and creating wealth by trading. It must, however, be highlighted that it needs a lot of experience to be able to ride a trend with the help of trailing stops. It is very easy to discuss it in hindsight, but very difficult to ride a trend through its intervening temporary drawdowns which hit the paper profits you are sitting on. While noise is removed from the price data in Renko charts, it is very much present between the trader's ears! That's because it has become more difficult to avoid noise in today's world of social media influence and information overload.

The swing breakout is a simple and effective method of trading. It can also be combined with traditional tools of analysis which we discussed earlier in Chapter 2.

Swing breakouts are basic Renko patterns. If one is trading any instruments on a regular basis, then trading based on these simple swing breakouts is recommended. The whipsaws during a consolidation phase will be controlled by the noise reduction feature of the Renko charts, while the strong trends will get captured due to the simplicity and underlying logic behind Renko chart plotting.

Have a look at Figure 3.8. From the chart in Figure 3.8, it can be observed that a bullish swing breakout will occur if the price goes to, or above, 1,100.

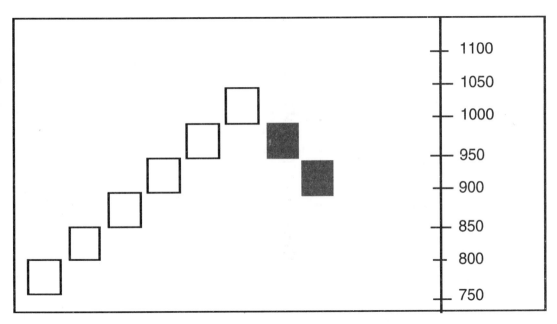

Figure 3.8: **A series of bullish bricks followed by a series of bearish bricks**

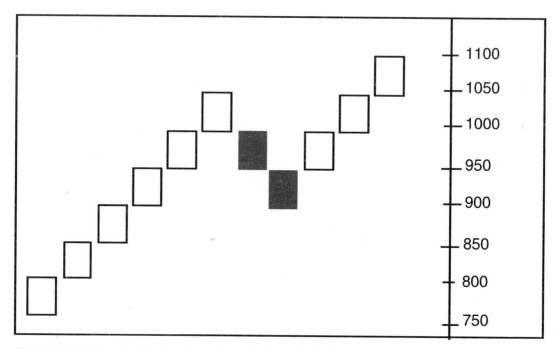

Figure 3.9: **Bullish swing breakout gets formed above 1,100 after a series of bullish bricks triggered a bullish swing breakout pattern when the latest brick got formed at the price level of 1,100.**

~

As you might have noticed, it is possible to know in advance the price level where the swing breakout formation will get triggered. Equally, swing points are easy to define and scan.

Remember this basic rule: a Renko chart is bullish if the last pattern is a bullish swing breakout and it is bearish if the last pattern is a bearish swing breakout.

Extensions from Swing Breakouts

Once a swing breakout is triggered, we can project the extent of the breakout move using the corrective bricks in the following manner.

Bullish swing extension is a method of extending, or projecting, the corrective bricks higher after a swing breakout has occurred. Figure 3.10 explains a bullish swing extension projection.

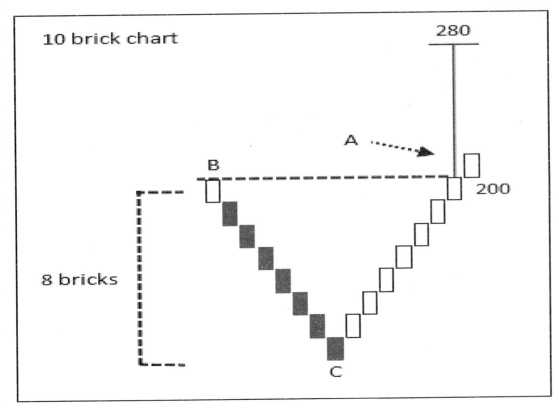

Figure 3.10: **Calculation of a bullish swing extension**

~

Consider a bullish swing breakout pattern formed at Point A in Figure 3.10. Once the breakout gets triggered, one counts the number of bricks from the top of the corrective swing move from Point B to the swing low at Point C, and multiply it with the brick value. You then add the result to the breakout price at point B.

The following is the formula for a bullish extension:

Potential Move = Number of bricks × Brick value
Bullish Extension = Potential Move + Swing high brick price level

In the example of Figure 3.10, the number of bricks from Point B to Point C is 8, the brick value is 10, and the swing high price level is 200. So the calculation of bullish extension would be as follows:

Potential Move = 8 x 10 = 80
Bullish extension = 80 + 200 = 280

A bullish extension gets negated if the price falls below the low of Point C before achieving the bullish swing extension.

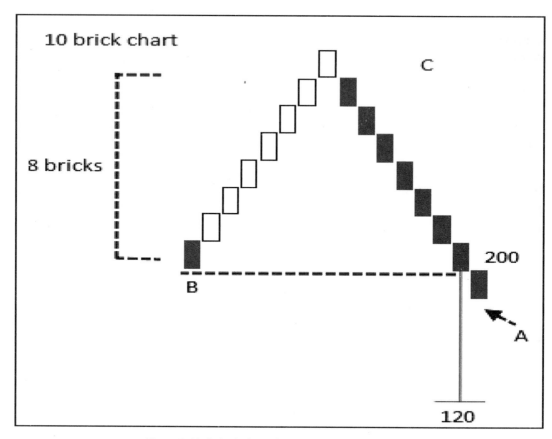

Figure 3.11: **Calculation of bearish swing extension**

~

Let us now consider a **bearish swing extension** (*see* Figure 3.11).

In figure 3.11, the swing breakout happens at Point A, where we can plot a bearish projection. The formula for a bearish swing extension projection is as follows:

Potential move = Number of bricks x Brick value

Bearish extension = Swing low brick price level – Potential Move

In the example in Figure 3.11, the number of bricks is 8, the brick value is 10, and the swing low price level is 200. So below is the calculation of bearish projection, would be as follow:

Potential move = 8 x 10 = 80

Bearish extension = 200 – 80 = 120

This bearish extension gets negated if the price goes above the high of Point C before achieving the target.

These extensions are a method of projecting, or extending, the breakout move. **Remember, a swing extension should be plotted only when a swing breakout has occurred and should be plotted from the swing high, or the swing low, which has been broken and which triggered the swing breakout.**

The construction of Renko charts gives us the opportunity to calculate the projection from the breakout brick. Though this is a projection technique, I'll rate it as an important technical tool that gives you additional information about the price setup. Both achievement and non-achievement of these extensions is equally important information for Renko chart analysis.

As observed earlier, if the price fails to achieve the bullish projection and goes below the bottom of the swing brick from which it was plotted, then the bullish extension stands negated. Correspondingly, if the price fails to reach the bearish projection level and moves above the high brick price from which the bearish extension was calculated, the bearish extension level stands negated.

In the above examples, the price corrected by 8 bricks and then resulted in a swing breakout. We are plotting price extension up to the length of the correction. In other words, we are extending the corrective move. Here are some variants:

- If the breakout is strong, the price will typically move at least up to the length of the previous correction. If the price doesn't move that much, it indicates weakness in the breakout.

- If the bullish extension is invalidated by the price falling below the bottom of the swing move, it is then a very significant bearish event.

- Correspondingly, it is a significant bullish event if the price fails to achieve the downside projection resulting in the extension being invalidated.

As noted earlier, these extensions are not only price projections or targets from a trading perspective, they are also a significant technical tool. When you plot them from different swing breakouts on the chart, you can observe whether the extensions are achieved or not.

In an uptrend, for example, the achievement of extension levels shows the strength of the bullish breakout, and failure indicates underlying weakness since the price could not even travel up to the corrective bricks from the breakout level.

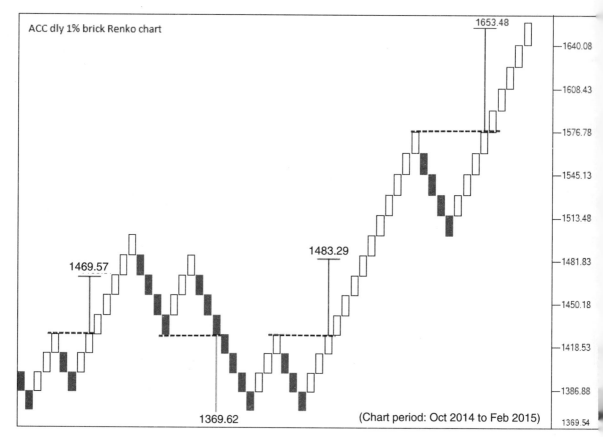

Figure 3.12: **Bullish and bearish extensions in the 1% daily brick value Renko chart of ACC**

~

Multi-Brick Swing Breakout Patterns

Let us now consider multi-brick breakout patterns. We discussed double top and triple top resistance and double bottom and triple bottom support patterns in Chapter 2. Multiple bricks at the same level represent an area or zone of either support or resistance. When the price breaks out from these important levels, it triggers a multi-brick breakout pattern which is a very important event, especially when coupled with confirmation from other technical tools.

Let's consider the chart of Ashok Leyland in Figure 3.13.

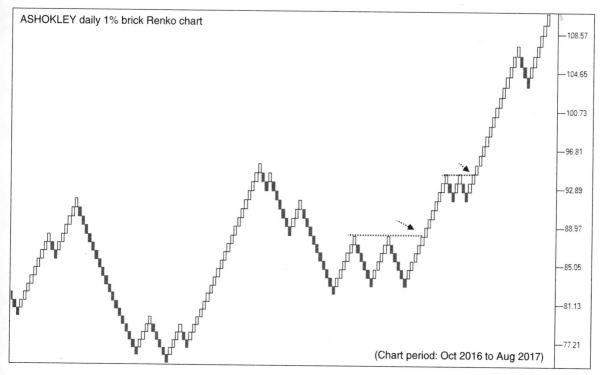

Figure 3.13: **Bullish multi-brick swing breakout patterns in the 1% brick value daily Renko chart of Ashok Leyland. The two arrows highlight price breakouts from multiple bricks showing resistance at a particular level.**

~

Multi-brick breakout is a very important pattern that can be easily spotted in Renko charts. It is very useful on the lower time frame charts for intraday traders. Those who trade midcaps and small caps can use multi-brick breakout as an effective entry strategy by using a higher brick value.

Breakout from tested resistance or support levels is a traditional concept of technical analysis that has stood the test of time. It can be spotted without much difficultly on Renko charts. The breach of an important support or resistance marked by multiple-bricks at the same level is significant information for traders.

A multi-brick breakout pattern shows us that a level that was tested on numerous occasions in the past has been broken. Price witnesses supply, or demand, at a particular level for important reasons. When it faces a supply, i.e. resistance, at the same level on multiple instances, the price should typically fall to new lows and trigger a downtrend. Correspondingly, when demand comes in at a particular level on numerous occasions, the logical expectation is to look for a nice upward move in the price.

Accordingly, if the price breaches an important support or resistance level that has previously been tested on several occasions, it typically sets the tone for the start of a new trend. Hence, multi-brick breakout patterns are important for both intra-day and positional traders.

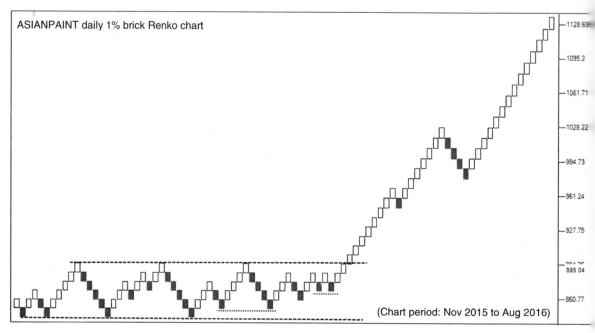

Figure 3.14: **Breakout from multiple bricks at the same level in the 1% brick value daily Renko chart of Asian Paints**

~

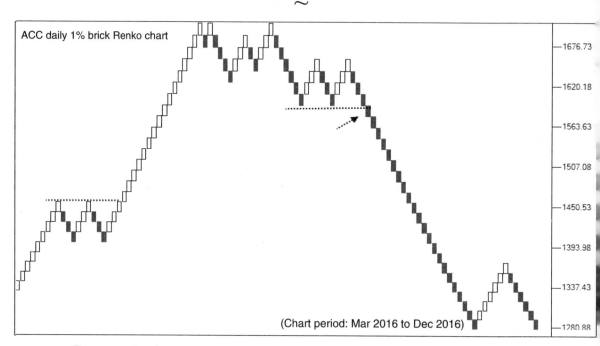

Figure 3.15: **Bearish multi-swing breakout in the 1% brick value daily Renko chart of ACC**

~

In a nutshell, the multiple-brick swing breakout is an important Renko chart pattern. It often creates a base or a range which acts as a launch pad for a future trending move.

Two-Back Pattern

When a trend resumes after a small correction, it indicates that the underlying trend is strong and thus provides an opportunity to initiate a trade with an affordable risk. Two-back is a pattern where a swing breakout occurs after a correction of just two bricks. Figure 3.16 illustrates a bullish two-back pattern.

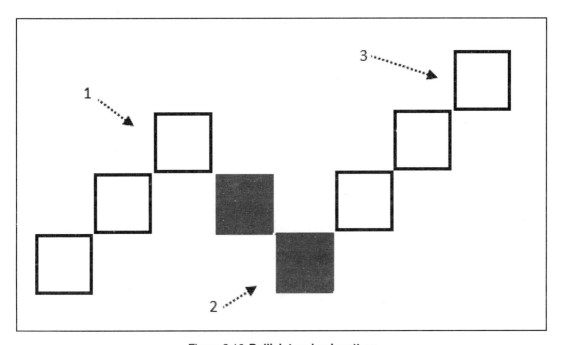

Figure 3.16: **Bullish two-back pattern**

~

As highlighted in the chart in Figure 3.16, a bullish two-back pattern requires:

1. At least three bullish bricks that indicate an ongoing bullish uptrend;

2. Bullish bricks to be followed by two bearish bricks, constituting a correction;

3. The correction of two bearish bricks is followed by three bullish bricks that form a bullish swing breakout pattern.

It is a pattern that suggests the resumption of the uptrend post a two-brick correction (*see* Figure 3.17).

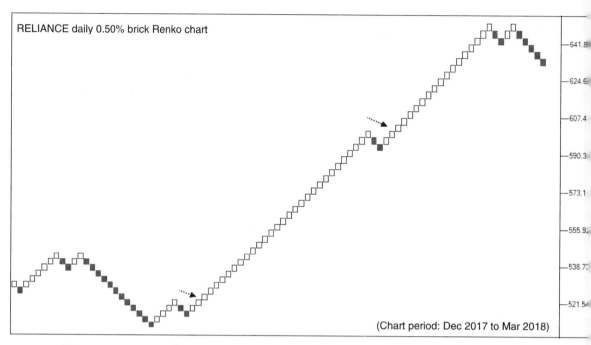

Figure 3.17: **Bullish two-back pattern in the 0.50% brick value daily Renko chart of Reliance**

~

A bearish two-back pattern, on the other hand, shows the resumption of a downtrend after a correction of two bullish bricks (*see* Figure 3.18).

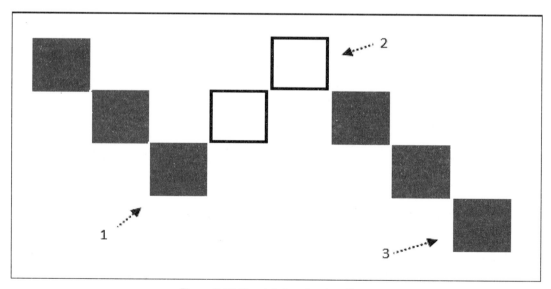

Figure 3.18: **Bearish two-back pattern**

~

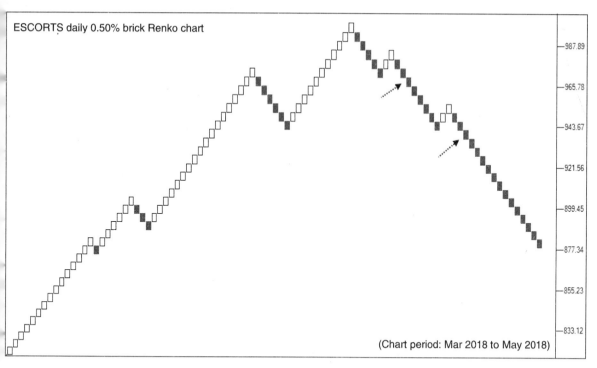

ESCORTS daily 0.50% brick Renko chart

(Chart period: Mar 2018 to May 2018)

Figure 3.19: **Bearish two-back patterns in the 0.50% brick value daily Renko chart of Escorts**

~

As highlighted in the chart in Figure 3.18, a bearish two-back pattern requires:

1. At least three bearish bricks that indicate an ongoing bearish trend;

2. The series of bearish bricks should be followed by a correction of two bullish bricks;

3. The correction of two bullish bricks must be followed by a series of at least three bearish bricks.

That constitute the bearish swing breakout (*see* Figure 3.19).

Two-backs are basically continuation patterns, and you will often find them amidst strong trends. A correction of not more than two bricks indicates immense inherent strength in the ongoing trend.

- A bullish two-back formation shows that bears could not hold the correction for more than two bricks, and the bulls then reasserted their dominance. The small pullback also indicates that the weaker bulls have probably been shaken out and the weak bears might have also taken short positions. The breakout after the two-back pattern will gain momentum owing to short covering by weak bears and breakout buying by new bulls.

■ Correspondingly, a bearish two-back pattern shows that bulls could not oppose the ongoing down trend for more than two bricks and that the bears wrested back control immediately thereafter. Such small pullbacks bring weak bulls into the fray and this gives further opportunity to the strong hands to dump the stock. A move past the bearish breakout level will trigger panic selling by weak bulls who may have entered on the two-back pullback.

Rules for Trading Two-Back Patterns

Renko charts give us the opportunity to trade these continuation patterns with an affordable risk. Figure 3.20 illustrates the rules of trading the two-back pattern.

It is important to note that a two-back pattern doesn't fail if the stop loss is triggered. Instead, a bullish two-back pattern fails only when the price moves below the lowest brick of the first swing and a bearish two-back pattern fails only when the price moves above the highest brick of first swing.

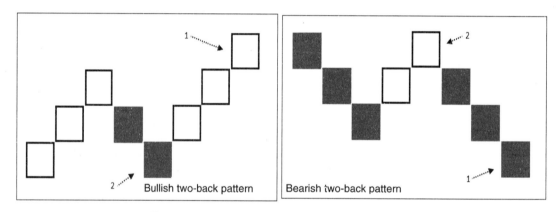

Figure 3.20: **Rules of trading the two-back pattern:**

One can enter a trade in a bullish two-back pattern at Point 1 placing the stop loss at one brick below the bearish brick i.e. at Point 2 (*see* the left hand chart).

Correspondingly, one can short the scrip in a bearish two-back pattern at Point 1, and put a stop loss at one brick level above the bullish brick, i.e. at Point 2 (*see* the right hand chart).

∼

Figure 3.21 shows the breakout and stop-loss levels in a bullish two-back pattern.

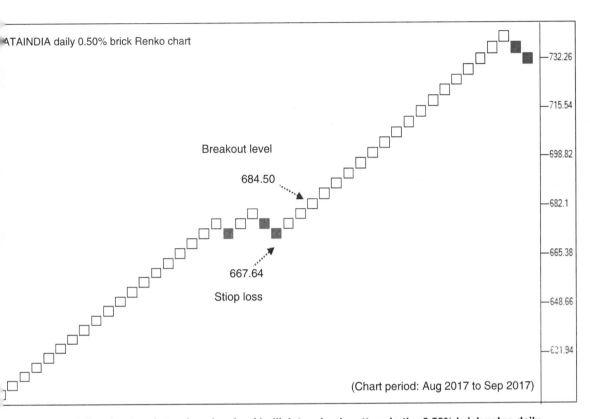

Figure 3.21: **Breakout and stop-loss levels of bullish two-back pattern in the 0.50% brick value daily Renko chart of Bata India. The chart shows the price levels at which the two-back pattern was completed (₹684.50) and where the stop loss might be placed (₹667.64). A series of bullish bricks in the chart shows the strength behind the uptrend — and the bullish two-back formation gives an opportunity to board the trend train.**

~

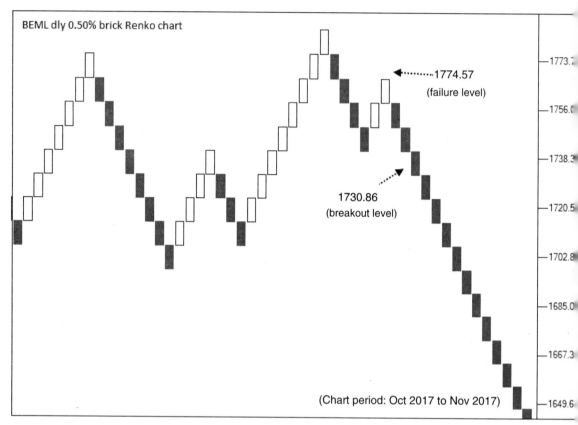

Figure 3.22: **Breakout and stop-loss levels of a bearish two-back pattern in the 0.50% brick value daily Renko chart of BEML**

~

Figure 3.22 is a chart of BEML showing the price levels in a bearish two-back pattern.

It is important to understand that a two-back pattern on a daily chart doesn't signify a two-day correction. The correction might have spanned several days, but the price correction did not last for more than two bricks.

Two-Back Extension Pattern

Readers would realise that a two-back pattern is also a swing breakout. Hence, swing breakout extensions are applicable to two-backs as well. The rules are different, though. A retracement in the case of two-back patterns is not meaningful. Instead, we can plot a bullish extension from the initial price move when the bullish two-back pattern gets triggered. Figure 3.23 explains this.

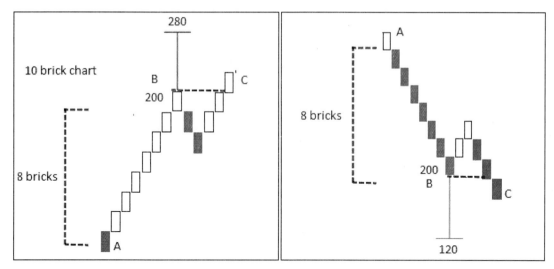

Figure 3.23: **Calculation of extension from two-back patterns. When a two-back gets triggered at Point C, extensions should be plotted from Point B. Instead of plotting the extension from the breakout level, it should be plotted from Point B in the case of two-back patterns.**

~

Formulas for Two-Back Extensions

Bullish Extension

Potential Move = Number of bricks x Brick value

Bullish Projection = Potential Move + Swing high brick price level

In the example in Figure 3.23, the number of bricks is 8, brick value is 10, and the swing high price level is ₹200. Accordingly:

Potential Move = 8 x 10 = ₹80

Bullish Projection = 200 + 80 = ₹280

In Figure 3.23, the bullish extension would stand negated if the price fails to achieve the projected move and falls below the low of Point A.

Bearish Extension

Potential Move = Number of bricks x Brick value

Bearish Projection – Swing low brick price level – Potential Move

In the example in Figure 3.23 (right), the number of bricks is 8, the brick value is 10 and the swing low price level is 200.

Potential Move = 8 x 10 = ₹80
Bullish Projection = 200 − 80 = ₹120

The bearish extension would get negated if the price were to fail to achieve the projected move and instead goes above the high of Point A.

Consider the swing extensions plotted from bullish two-back patterns in Figure 3.24. The trend of the instrument was up, and most of the extensions plotted from two-back continuation patterns were met.

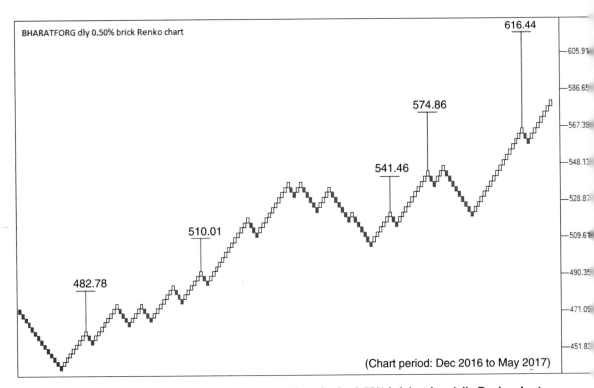

Figure 3.24: **Bullish two-back pattern extensions in the 0.50% brick value daily Renko chart of Bharat Forge**

~

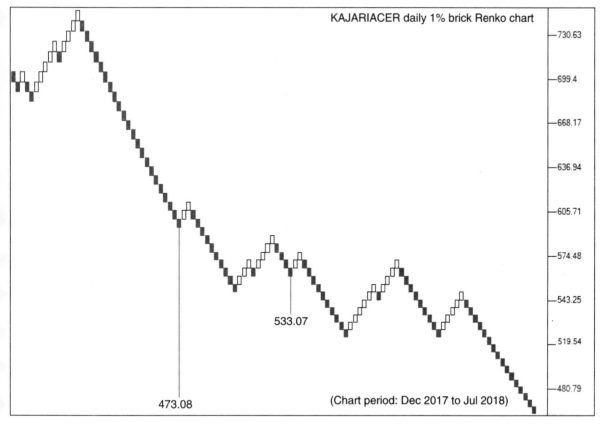

Figure 3.25: **Bearish two-back pattern extensions in the 1% brick value daily Renko chart of Kajaria Ceramics**

~

Extensions can be considered as projections from a two-back pattern. Trading the price setups in direction of extensions is advisable. Also, pay attention to the extension clusters from different swings or setups.

One-Back Pattern

We've discussed that two-brick patterns are swing breakout patterns with a correction of not more than two bricks. Now, what if the correction is just one brick.

One-back is a pattern that gets formed when a swing breakout occurs after a correction of one brick. Figure 3.26 illustrates a bullish one-back pattern.

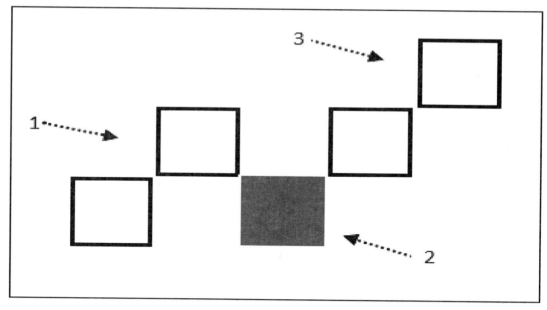

Figure 3.26: **Bullish one-back pattern**

~

In the case of a bullish one-back pattern:

- There must be at least two bullish bricks to begin with (*see* 1 in Figure 3.26);

- The bullish bricks are followed by not more than one bearish brick (*see* 2 in Figure 3.26);

- The correction signified by one bearish brick should be followed by two bullish bricks that trigger a swing breakout (*see* 3 in Figure 3.26).

Figure 3.27 is a chart of Biocon showing a multiple bullish one-back patterns.

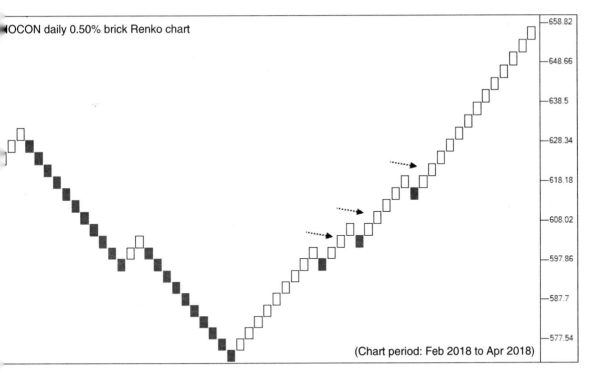

OCON daily 0.50% brick Renko chart

(Chart period: Feb 2018 to Apr 2018)

Figure 3.27: **Bullish one-back patterns in the 0.50% brick value daily Renko chart of Biocon**

~

The bearish one-back pattern comprises:

- At least two bearish bricks (*see* 1 in Figure 3.28);
- Bearish bricks followed by not more than one bullish brick (*see* 2 in Figure 3.28);
- Correction of one brick followed by at least two bearish bricks, thus forming a bearish swing breakout (*see* 3 in Figure 3.38).

Figure 3.28 illustrates a bearish one-back pattern.

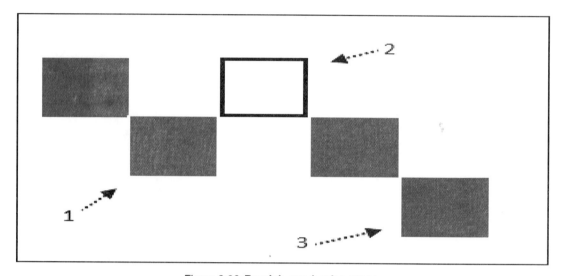

Figure 3.28: **Bearish one-back pattern**

∼

Figure 3.29 is a chart of Axis Bank illustrating bearish one-back patterns.

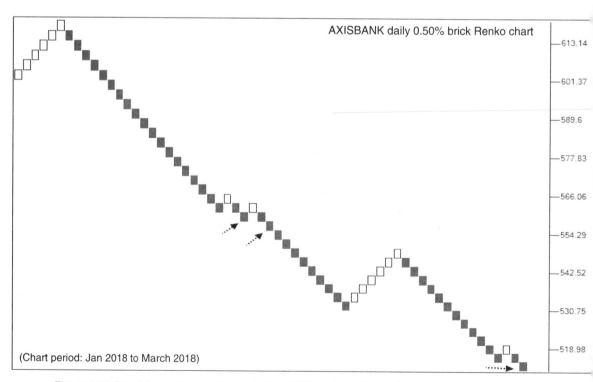

Figure 3.29: **Bearish one-back patterns in the 0.50% brick value daily Renko chart of Axis Bank**

∼

Though both are equally effective, the one-back pattern is conceptually more powerful than the two-back pattern. In the case of a bullish one-back, such is strength of the bulls that bears are unable to initiate a pull-back of more than a single brick. And in case of a bearish one-back, the bulls could not hold on for more than one brick.

Rules for Trading One-Back Patterns

In my experience, the one-back pattern is very reliable, and it can be a significant tool in the trader's arsenal. Figure 3.30 illustrates the rules for trading one-back patterns.

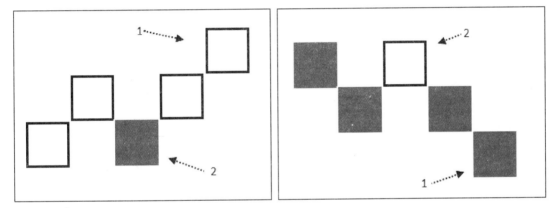

Figure 3.30: **Rules of trading one-back patterns; a bullish one-back on the left, and a bearish one-back pattern on the right.**

One can enter a bullish one-back pattern upon swing breakout at Point 1 and place a stop loss one brick below the bearish brick, i.e. at Point 2.

Correspondingly, short positions can be considered upon bearish one-back at the bearish swing breakout at Point 1, with a stop loss placed at one-brick above the bullish brick at Point 2.

~

A bullish one-back pattern fails when the price moves below the lowest brick of the first swing, while a bearish one-back pattern fails when the price moves above the highest brick of the first swing.

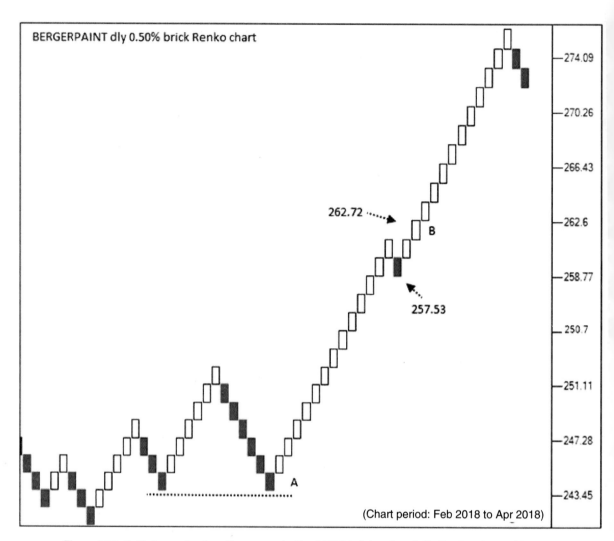

Figure 3.31: **Bullish one-back pattern seen in the 0.50% brick value daily Renko chart of Berger Paints. The price level where the breakout occurred as also the level where a trader should place the stop loss are highlighted in the chart.**

~

A bullish one-back pattern trade is explained with the help of Figure 3.31.

You would notice in Figure 3.31 that a Renko double bottom support pattern occurred at Point A, followed by a complete retracement of the earlier bearish trend. This also resulted in a swing breakout at Point B. A series of bullish bricks thereafter shows strength in the trend. A one-back formation at Point B provides traders the opportunity to participate in the trend.

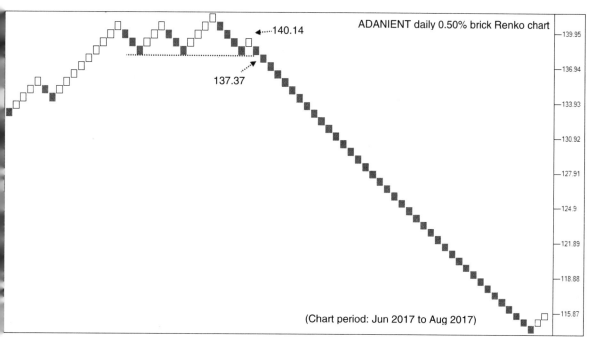

Figure 3.32: **Bearish one-back pattern highlighted in the 0.50% brick value daily Renko chart of Adani Enterprises. The price at which the breakout occurred (137.37), and the stop loss (140.14) level are both highlighted on the chart.**

~

A bearish one-back pattern trade is explained with the help of Figure 3.32.

A bearish one-back pattern shown in the chart in Figure 3.32 also triggered a multi-brick bearish breakout, indicating a breach of the strong support level. The bearish one-back, coupled with the multi-brick breakout, gives an opportunity to trade an important breakout at very affordable risk. One should never miss such a trade when a one-back coincides with, or results in, a multi-brick breakout.

Remember, one-back and two-back patterns remain valid unless the price moves below the low of first swing of the bullish pattern or above the first swing high of the bearish pattern. Else, it's a pattern failure.

One-back and two-back patterns are continuation patterns that occur often during a strong trend.

They offer an opportunity to participate in strong trends at an affordable risk. Affordability is the key highlight of these patterns. Once entered, one can ride the trend either with a brick reversal or a swing breakout criteria.

Have a look at Figure 3.33.

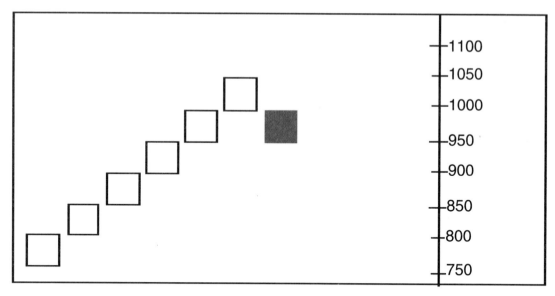

Figure 3.33: **A bearish brick appears after a series of bullish bricks**

~

Can you identify the price level at which a bullish one-back pattern will be triggered in the chart in Figure 3.33?

You would be right if your answer were 1,100. If your answer was different, please re-read this chapter before proceeding further.

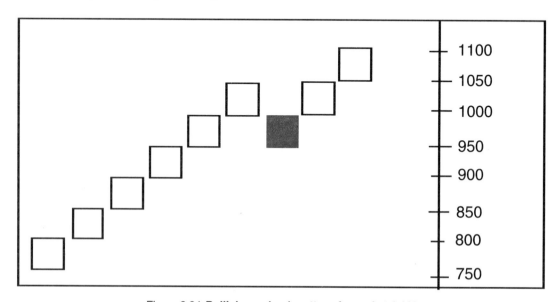

Figure 3.34: **Bullish one-back pattern formed at 1,100**

~

Extensions from One-Back

Like the two-back, the one-back pattern is also a swing breakout and shows the strength of the initial move. We can also plot extensions from one-back patterns the same way as we do in two-backs.

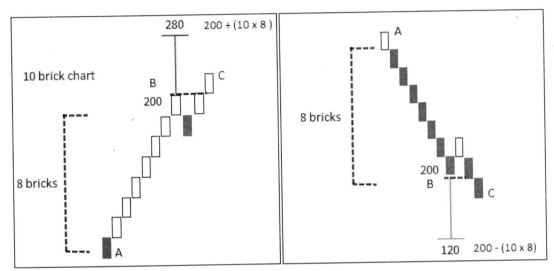

Figure 3.35: **Calculation of extensions from one-back patterns; bullish one-back on the left, bearish one-back on the right.**

The one-back gets triggered at Point C, extensions should be plotted from Point B. The formula and rules of plotting and negation for extending the bricks remain same as for the two-back pattern.

~

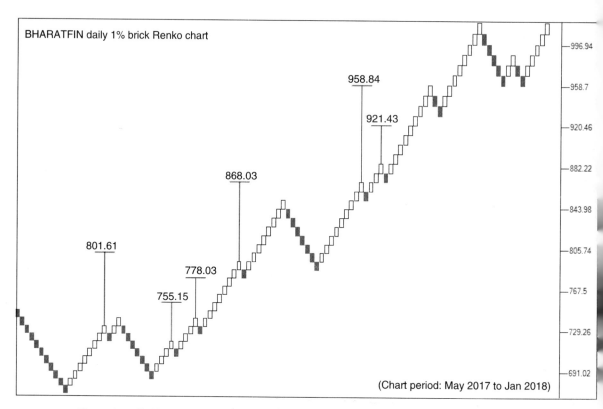

Figure 3.36: **Bullish one-back pattern extensions in the 1% brick value daily Renko chart of Bharat Finance**

~

Figure 3.36 illustrates bullish one-back extensions.

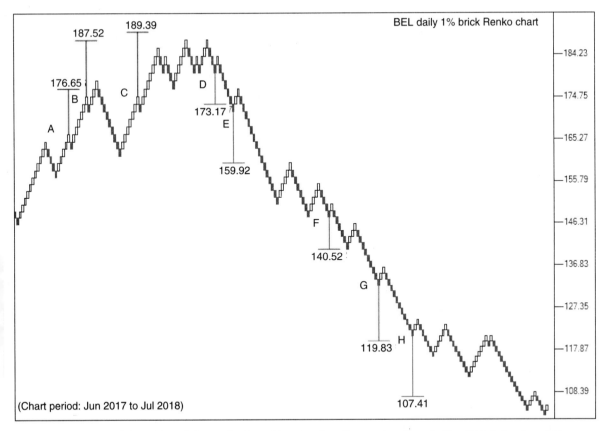

Figure 3.37: **Bullish and bearish one-back and two-back pattern extensions in the 1% brick value daily Renko chart of BEL.**

Points A, B and C are extensions plotted from bullish one-backs. Extension at Point D is from a bearish one-back. The extension at Point E starts from a bearish two-back pattern. Extension at Point F is from a bearish one-back, while extensions at Point G and Point H are from bearish two-back patterns.

~

Figure 3.37 is a chart of BEL showing extensions from one-back and two-back patterns.

Extensions plotted in Figure 3.37 are from one-back and two-back continuation patterns. One-back and two-back breakouts are more significant when the price is in the midst of a strong trend.

Remember, that while we can plot extensions from the price patterns discussed above, it is not necessary to do so. One can as well follow only the price patterns themselves and ignore the extensions. Or, calculate the extensions manually to get an idea about their possible levels.

There is a reason for discussing two-backs and one-backs separately. It is possible for someone to focus and trade only specific patterns on a continuous basis. So one can, say, choose to trade only a one-back or only a two-back chart pattern on different instruments. This is, in fact, the recommended approach.

Every method goes through phases of profitability and losses. During a favourable phase, immature traders often grow complacent and increase their position size, thus sowing seeds of future disaster. In a difficult phase, the pattern is often condemned for not working any more, and the search for something new then begins. A key aspect behind successful trading is being consistent with one's approach.

Anchor Bricks

A series of consecutive bullish or bearish bricks is called anchor bricks. It is difficult to define the number of bricks for such a series, because it depends on the brick value being used. The general rule of thumb is that there should be a relatively high number of bricks in one direction. **For the sake of simplicity, one can consider any series of more than ten bricks in one direction as anchor bricks.** Such a series shows the presence of a strong trend.

One-backs or two-backs, or even simple swing breakouts, that occur after anchor bricks are significant patterns and should be actively traded. They are perhaps the best form of trend continuation trade set-ups. Anchor bricks represent strength, or momentum, and a follow through breakout reinforces the strength of the underlying trend.

Zigzag

Let's now discuss the zigzag pattern which is otherwise a relatively complicated price pattern that gets simplified by using Renko charts.

Zigzag is a pattern that shows indecisiveness. We have already discussed how the Renko chart remains static if the price consolidates for many days without any significant move. If, however, the price action triggers bricks that are frequently changing direction, then it indicates confusion among market participants.

A series of four bricks with alternating colours is known as a zigzag pattern. A breakout from the zigzag pattern indicates the new direction and offers a trading opportunity.

Figure 3.38 explains a bullish zigzag pattern.

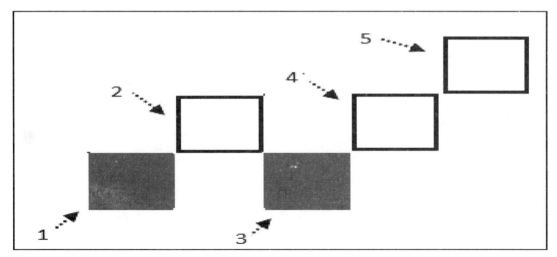

Figure 3.38: **Bullish zigzag pattern: 1 is a bearish brick, followed by a bullish brick 2; followed by a bearish brick, marked 3; followed by another bullish brick, marked 4; and then comes a bullish brick above the highest brick of the pattern forming the swing breakout, namely brick 5.**

~

Figure 3.39 is a chart of Pidilite Industries illustrating a bullish zigzag formation.

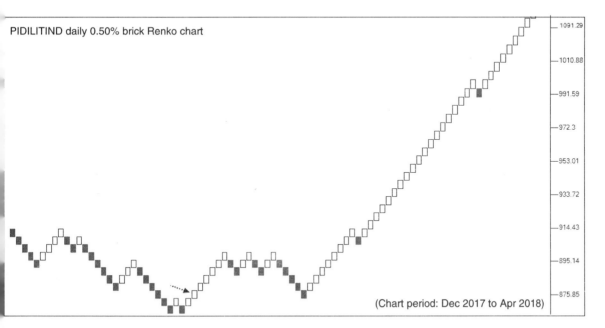

Figure 3.39: **Bullish zigzag formation in the 0.50% brick value daily Renko chart of Pidilite Industries. The arrow shows that a bullish zigzag pattern formed at the bottom of the chart, which was eventually followed by a strong up trend**

~

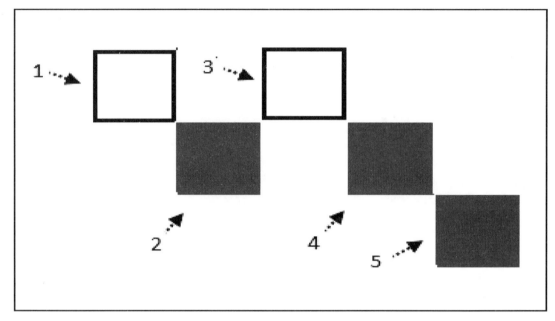

Figure 3.40: **Bearish zigzag pattern: 1 is bullish brick; followed by a bearish brick 2, which is followed by a bullish brick 3, followed by another bearish brick 4, and then a bearish brick below the lowest brick 5 of the pattern, forming the bearish swing breakout.**

~

Figure 3.40 explains the bearish zigzag pattern.

Figure 3.41 is a chart of HDFC illustrating the bearish zigzag pattern.

Unlike one-back and two-back patterns, the zigzag pattern indicates confusion and typically occurs towards the end of a trend. Hence, **a zigzag pattern that occurs after a significant trend is far more important because it indicates indecision and hesitancy among market participants after a strong trending phase**. It could also indicate the possibility that a trend reversal may occur soon and provide a nice trading opportunity.

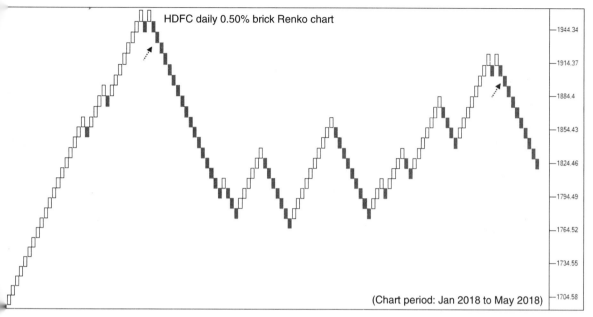

Figure 3.41: **Bearish zigzag formation in the 0.50% brick value daily Renko chart of HDFC**

~

Rules for Trading Zigzag Patterns

Figure 3.42 explains the rules of trading a zigzag patterns.

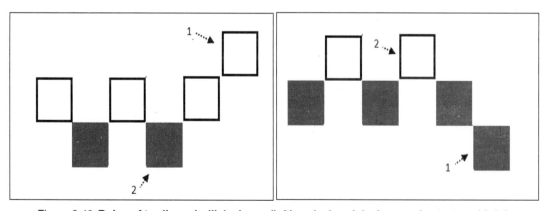

Figure 3.42: **Rules of trading a bullish zigzag (left) and a bearish zigzag price pattern (right).**

The bullish zigzag breakout can be traded at Point 1, with the stop placed one brick below the bearish brick, i.e. at Point 2. The bearish zigzag pattern can be traded at Point 1, with the stop placed ono briok above the bullish brick at Point 2.

~

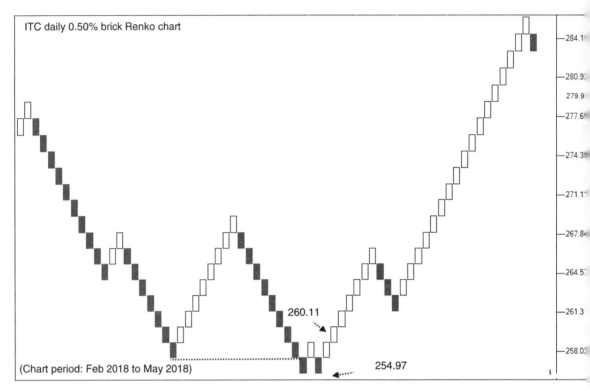

Figure 3.43: **Bullish zigzag pattern levels in the 0.50% brick value daily Renko chart of ITC**

The price formed a bearish swing breakout at the bottom but failed to progress any lower. It then formed a zigzag pattern indicating confusion or indecision. The bulls subsequently struck back and triggered a breakout from the zigzag formation giving an opportunity to traders to take long positions with an affordable stop.

~

Figure 3.43 is a 0.50% daily chart of ITC showing bullish zigzag pattern levels.

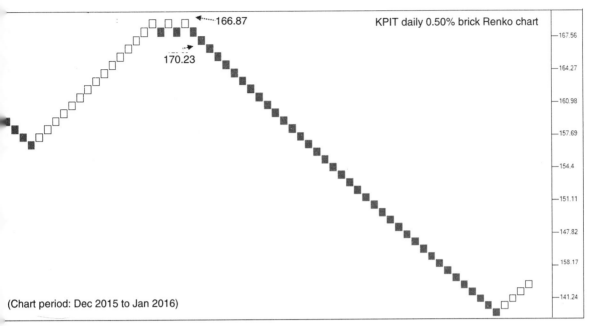

Figure 3.44: **Bearish zigzag pattern in the daily 0.50% brick value Renko chart of KPIT**

~

Figure 3.44 is a chart of KPIT showing a bearish zigzag pattern.

The zigzag pattern in Figure 3.44 comprises of a series of six alternating bricks, which indicated indecisiveness among market participants. There was relatively prolonged confusion that eventually leading to a bearish zigzag breakout.

This is an example of an extended zigzag where the zigzag has prolonged and lasted for more than four bricks. It is not important to remember the name but it's important to understand that it indicates serious indecision which often results in a trend reversal.

Zigzag is a consolidation breakout pattern. It is also a swing breakout pattern but it occurs post a price consolidation and that is what adds more information to the simple swing breakout pattern.

The zigzag pattern is a very important formation from an analysis perspective, too. This pattern suggests confusion among participants at a particular price zone. The zigzag price zone often acts as an important reference area on a subsequent revisit by the price. Quite often, it turns out to be a reversal area on the revisit.

Zigzag pattern zones are also important support and resistance levels on the charts.

~

Now that you are familiar with Renko patterns, Let's once again review the earlier Figure 3.4 of BEML and Figure 3.5 of Bajaj Auto chart in the swing breakout section. In Figure 3.4, Pattern A on the BEML chart is a bullish two-back, Pattern C is a bullish one-back, Pattern D is a bearish zigzag, Pattern G is a bullish zigzag, and Pattern M is a bearish one-back.

In Figure 3.5, Pattern A in the Bajaj Auto chart is bearish two-back. Pattern H and Pattern I are bullish two-back patterns. Pattern D and Pattern J are bearish one-backs, Patterns F, M and N are bullish one-back patterns. I recommend going back to the charts of previous sections and try to identify one-back, two-back and zigzag patterns.

~

All the patterns discussed thus far are simple to identify and understand. They are objective in nature and there are simple trading rules associated with their use. As we have been emphasizing right through, objectivity and noiselessness are two major advantages of Renko charts. Using Renko, then, the entire focus can be directed toward the most important aspect of trading, which is execution.

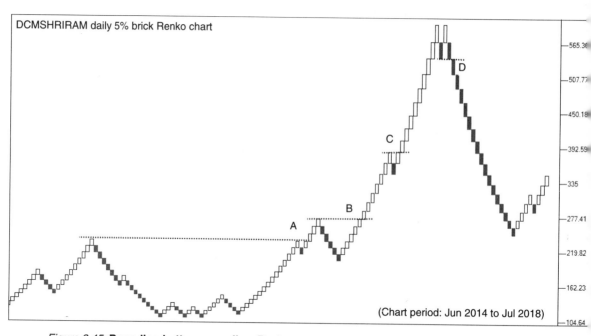

Figure 3.45: **Rounding bottom as well as Renko patterns in the 5% brick value daily Renko chart of DCM Shriram.**

There is a rounding bottom / cup-handle breakout at Point A, which is also a bullish one-back Renko pattern. There is bullish continuation swing breakout at Point B, and a bullish one-back at Point C. One can ride the trade with trailing stop losses at the swing bottom of every brick, or keep booking profits and trading the continuation breakouts so long as the chart is bullish. A bearish swing breakout was triggered at Point D, which is also a bearish zigzag.

~

The amalgamation of the above patterns with conventional analysis or other tools is another important aspect. The Renko pattern following a major swing breakout, especially from a rounding bottoms, cup-handle, or head and shoulders pattern, etc. can offer an important trading setup.

Let's consider Figure 3.45.

You can easily identify important pivot points or reference zones in a Renko chart. A prior zigzag pattern or a swing breakout level often acts as support or resistance.

~

When a trader trades a chart formation across various instruments on a consistent basis, it helps the trader focus more on execution than analysis, which is a very logical way of trading the markets. Though pattern trading may come across as a relatively simple approach, it is very difficult to implement on a consistent basis. Our emotions are the major impediment and often make us over analyse and deviate from objective pattern trading.

~

Chapter 4

Reversal and Pullback Patterns

M OST PEOPLE VIEW RENKO AS A BREAKOUT AND TREND following trading system, forgetting that it is primarily a charting method. The beauty — and the major advantage — of Renko charts is that they plot price as fixed boxes. This feature is most important to grasp as it is very useful from a trading perspective.

Each charting method has a unique ingredient which should be understood and explored. Renko's uniqueness is the fixed price diagonally plotted boxes.

So far, we have discussed only continuation patterns — and they happen to be my favourites ones. But that doesn't mean reversal patterns are not applicable on Renko charts. This chapter deals with reversal patterns that can be traded on Renko charts.

Breakout patterns discussed so far were relatively simple to identify. A proper understanding of those setups will help you to better grasp the concepts and patterns explained in this section, which are relatively more advanced.

Before considering reversal patterns, it is important to understand the difference between continuation patterns and reversal patterns. Continuation patterns are those that indicate the underlying trend's strength and which result in the continuation of a prior move. Typically, these are breakout patterns. Reversal price patterns, on the other hand, are patterns that indicate a reversal of the current trend.

Those continuation setups that are in sync with the underlying trend would have a higher probability of being successful. Trend lines and / or indicators may be used to identify the trend and the trades that are not in sync with the trend may be ignored.

Reversal setups occur against the trend. When found in the direction of the trend, reversal setups are pullback patterns, and they are very effective. In fact, they are among the most productive price setups of all.

In this context, I recall that a prominent analyst was sitting beside me at a conference. When I told him that I would be speaking about Renko charts, he instantly said, "Oh, that's a trend following method." I wasn't shocked but was certainly disappointed to hear this from an experienced analyst.

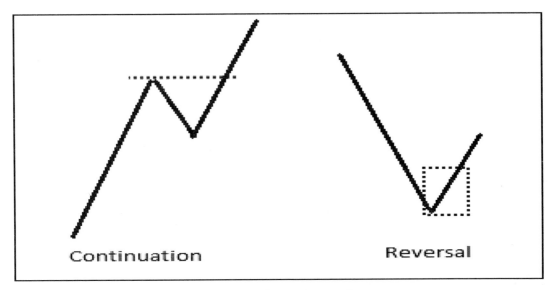

Figure 4.1: **Continuation and reversal patterns**

~

I politely clarified that Renko was a charting technique. According to him, one can only see breakouts in Renko charts. This is quite a widespread misconception because Renko charts are often associated only with trend following.

Similarly, people also associate Renko charts with simply throwing up buy opportunities on a bullish brick and selling opportunities on a bearish brick, making Renko more of a trading system rather than a charting method.

Renko is a charting method in which any trading strategy can be applied.

Strike-Back Patterns

We discussed the swing breakout pattern in Chapter 3. Now, in the case of reversal patterns when the price moves back into the swing breakout territory, it is an early sign of a potential trend reversal. When bulls or bears strike back, it is an early indication of a potential reversal. A little further research helped me formulate trading rules based on this observation. Let us first understand the rules associated with the strike-back formation.

Bullish strike-back is a pattern that takes the price back above the level from where the bearish swing breakout pattern was triggered (*see* Figure 4.2).

Figure 4.3 explains the bearish strike-back pattern.

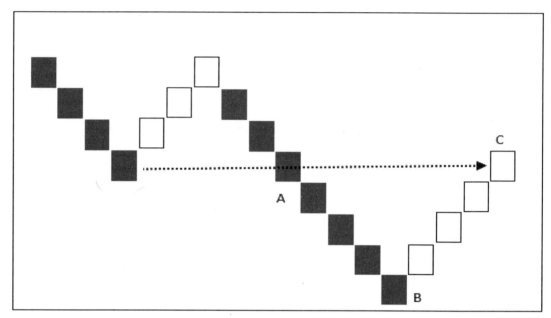

Figure 4.2: **Bullish strike-back pattern: Point A shows the bearish swing breakout; Point B shows the bullish brick reversal that forms the swing low; and Point C shows the price moving back above Point A, the level at which the bearish swing breakout pattern was completed.**

~

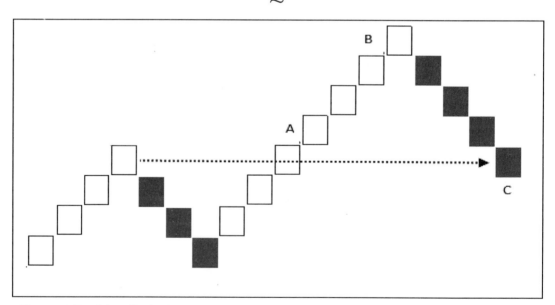

Figure 4.3: **Bearish strike-back pattern: Point A is the bullish swing breakout; Point B is the bearish brick reversal that forms the swing high; and Point C kicks off the price moving back below Point A, the level where the prior bullish swing breakout pattern was completed.**

~

When the price moves back to the level of the swing breakout brick, it triggers the strike-back pattern, indicating that the other side is trying to regain their territory. But it is not advisable to trade simply on this to much formation. The win rate and risk-reward of the trades will increase if we wait for follow through price action. This is illustrated and explained in the charts in Figure 4.4 and Figure 4.5.

It is important to grasp that only a follow through activates the strike-back pattern. Strike-backs without follow through are not significant.

The follow through requirement ensures that there is strength behind the strike-back pattern. The correction that holds the low of the brick at Point B in Figure 4.4 results in a higher low pattern (Point D) and indicates that bulls have wrested control to strike back and a potential price reversal setup is in place.

Figure 4.4 illustrates and explains a bullish strike-back.

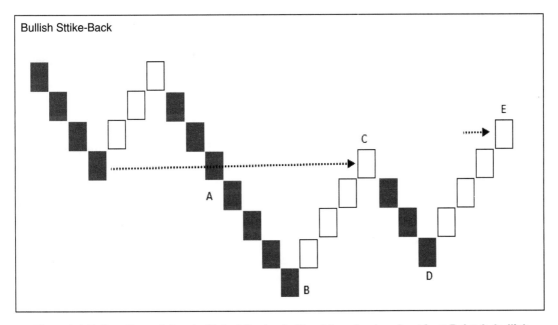

Figure 4.4: **Follow through to a bullish strike-back: Bearish swing breakout is at Point A; bullish strike-back gets formed at Point C; Point D is a correction that doesn't go below the low of Point B; and Point E is the bullish swing breakout at Point E. One can buy at Point E with stop loss placed below the brick at Point D.**

∼

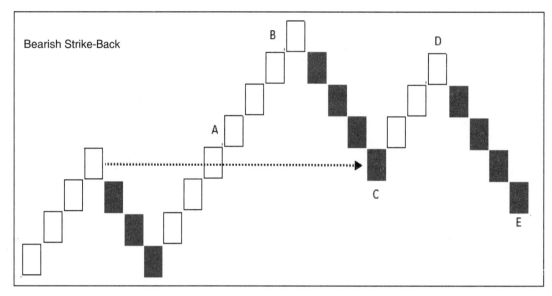

Figure 4.5: **Follow through to a bearish strike-back: Bullish swing breakout is at Point A; a bearish strike-back gets formed at Point C; Point D is a correction that doesn't go above the high of Point B; bearish swing breakout at Point E. You can sell at Point E with the stop placed above the brick at Point D.**

~

Figure 4.5 illustrates and explains a bearish strike-back.

Note that in Figure 4.5 the brick above or below Point D will trigger the stop loss for the trade but that doesn't invalidate the strike-back pattern. The pattern remains valid so long as the swing low at Point B of the bullish strike-back, and the swing high at Point B of the bearish strike-back, are maintained.

The follow through rule for trading strike-backs comes with twin advantages. The primary advantage being a strong indication of the strength behind the move. The advantage is that this pattern offers a trading opportunity at a very affordable risk.

Let's now have a look at Figure 4.6.

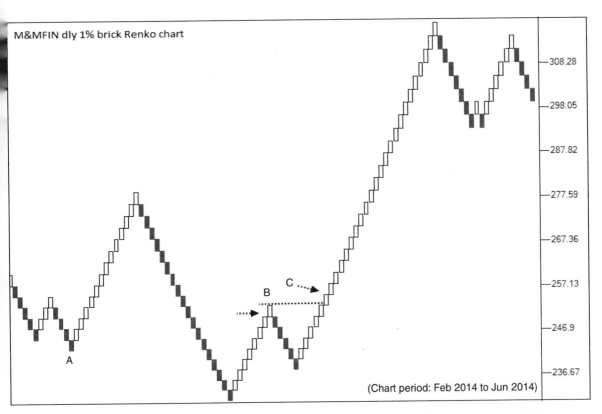

Figure 4.6: **Follow through to a bullish strike-back in a 1% brick value daily Renko chart of M&M Finance. The bullish strike-back was completed at Point B when the price moved above the previous low of Point A. The follow through to the strike-back occurred at Point C, when the price went back above Point B after a correction. The price went much higher thereafter.**

~

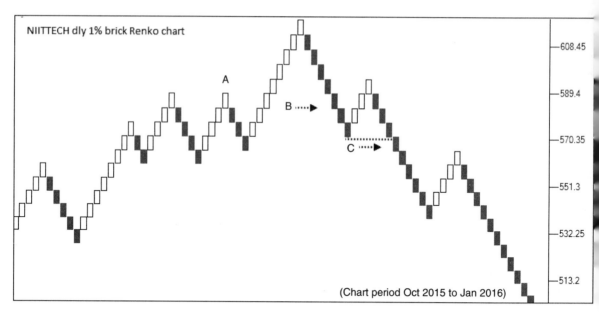

Figure 4.7: **Follow through to a bearish strike-back illustrated in this 1% brick value daily Renko chart of NIIT Technology. Point B is where the price fell below the previous swing high of Point A. Point C triggered the follow through to the bearish strike-back. The price fell significantly thereafter.**

∼

The follow throughs illustrated in Figure 4.6 and Figure 4.7 were both triggered in the immediate series of bricks post the strike-back patterns. A strike-back pattern follow through can, however, occur either immediately or even after a little while, but it remains valid so long as the strike-back pattern is not negated.

Extension from Strike-Back

A strike-back pattern indicates a possible trend reversal. If there is strength in the potential reversal move, the price is expected to travel the distance that is at least equal to the length of the first wave.

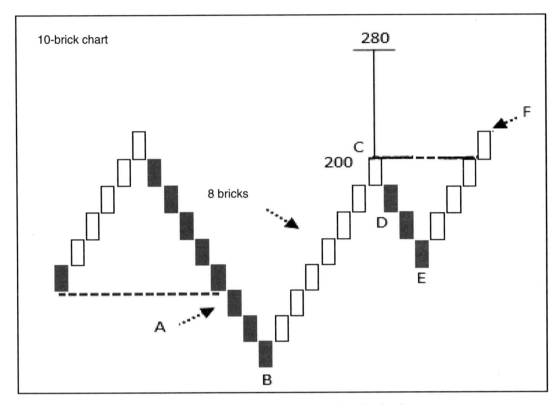

Figure 4.8: **Extension from a bullish strike-back**

Bearish swing breakout is at Point A; the first wave is marked from Point B to Point C upon the formation of a bearish reversal brick at Point D; the correction doesn't go below the low of the first wave; Point E is the swing low above Point B; Bullish swing breakout at Point F; Extension can be plotted from Point C.

~

The formula for calculating the bullish extension is as follows:

Bullish extension = High price of the first wave + (The number of bricks in the first wave x Brick value)

In Figure 4.8, there are 8 bricks in the first wave, the brick value is 10, and the high price of the first wave is 200. Here is the calculation for the bullish extension:

Bullish extension = 200 + (8 x 10) = 280

The extension gets negated if the price doesn't achieve the extension target price and falls below the lowest brick of the first wave at Point B.

The bearish extension has similar rules and can be plotted from a bearish strike-back pattern.

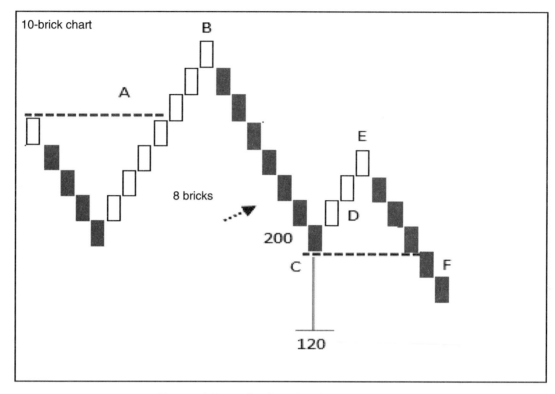

Figure 4.9: **Extension from bearish strike-back**

Bullish swing breakout is at Point A. The first wave is marked from Point B to Point C upon the formation of a bullish reversal brick at Point D. The correction doesn't go above the high of first wave; Point E is swing high below Point B. Bearish swing breakout at Point F; and extension can be plotted from Point C.

~

The formula for calculating a bearish extension is as follows:

Bearish extension = Low price of the first wave − (Number of the bricks in first wave x brick value)

In the case of Figure 4.9, the number of bricks in the first wave is 8, the brick value is 10, and the low price of the first wave is 200. Below is the calculation of the bearish extension:

Bearish extension = 200 − (8 x 10) = 120

If the price fails to achieve the target extension price but, instead, moves above the highest brick of first wave at Point B, the extension then stands negated.

The charts of M&M Finance and NIIT Technologies shown in Figure 4.10 and Figure 4.11, respectively, show extensions plotted from strike-back patterns.

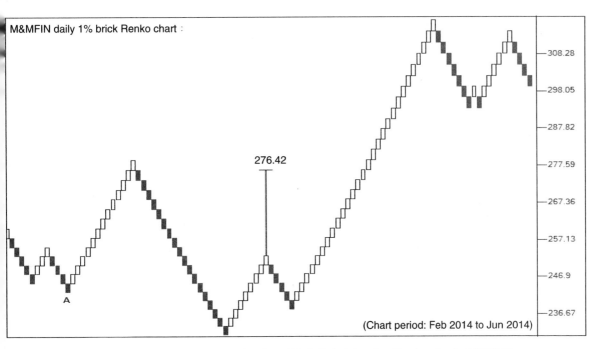

Figure 4.10: **Strike-back bullish extension in a 1% daily brick value Renko chart of M&M Finance**

~

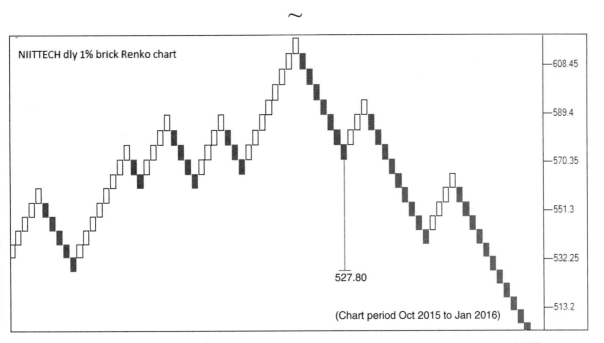

Figure 4.11: **Extension from a bearish strike-back in a 1% daily brick value Renko chart of NIIT Technologies**

~

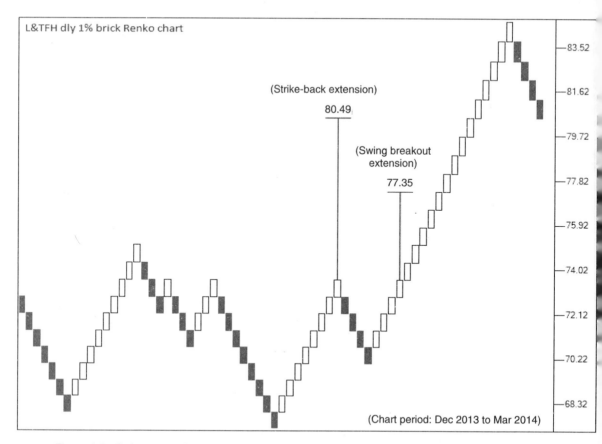

Figure 4.12: **Swing extension and strike-back extension in a 1% daily brick value Renko chart of L&T Finance Holdings Ltd**

~

By now you would have understood that two extensions can always be plotted from every strike-back follow through. One is a strike-back extension and the other is a swing breakout extension, which you can see in Figure 4.12.

These can be viewed as first and second targets or projection levels. We will discuss more about this in Chapter 6 which is wholly devoted to extensions.

Strike-Backs with the Trend

A reversal pattern that occurs in the direction of the major trend is known as a pullback. When the trend of an instrument is up, bearish swing breakouts offer an opportunity to buy. But we don't know whether the price will bounce from those levels or form a major reversal. A strike-back pattern on such occasions works as a confirmation and provides an opportunity to participate in the trend at affordable risk. It is the best mix of continuation and reversal setups.

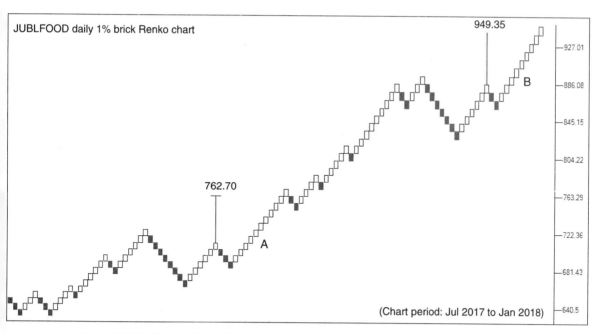

Figure 4.13: **Bullish strike-back patterns in an uptrend in a 1% brick value daily chart of Jubilant Foods**

~

Figure 4.13 is a chart of Jubilant Foods showing bullish strike-back patterns during an uptrend.

We will discuss trend identification indicators in Chapter 7, but an uptrend with higher lows is visible in the chart in Figure 4.13. Point A and Point B in Figure 4.13 are the bullish strike-back follow through patterns. Observe that the bullish strike-back pattern shown at Point A was followed by a series of bullish continuation one-back and two-back patterns.

Swing Engulfing

I have borrowed this concept of engulfing from candlestick chart patterns. Readers would recall that a bullish engulfing candle is one where the current price completely engulfs the body of the previous candle. With Renko charts, we plot a series of bricks which show price swings. **When a swing move completely retraces the previous move, which was a swing breakout, then it is known as swing engulfing.**

Swing engulfing is, in effect, an extended strike-back pattern. It is explained and illustrated in Figure 4.14 and Figure 4.15.

Bullish Swing Engulfing

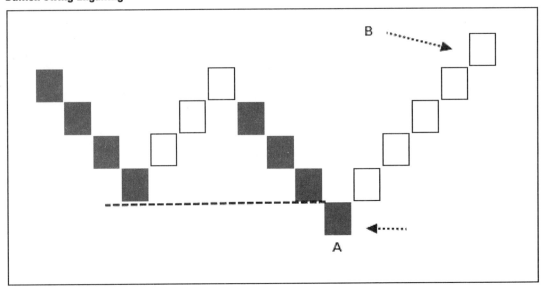

Figure 4.14: **Bullish swing engulfing: Point A — Price forms a bearish swing breakout here. Point B — Bullish swing breakout is completed in the immediate next move.**

~

Bearish Swing Engulfing

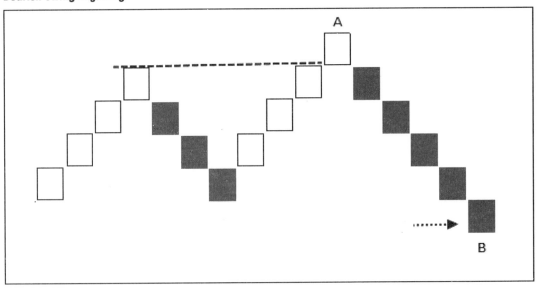

Figure 4.15: **Bearish swing engulfing: Point A — The price forms a bullish swing breakout here. Point B — Bearish swing breakout is completed in the immediate next move.**

~

Figure 4.14 and Figure 4.15 illustrate strike-back patterns but the price move at Point B in each case completely engulfs the previous move at Point A.

Though the name and appearance are like those of an engulfing candlestick pattern, or an outside day bar reversal pattern, the concept of swing engulfing is slightly different. Unlike candlestick or bar charts, it doesn't imply the engulfing of either the body or the entire previous candle. Renko swing engulfing engulfs the entire previous swing, and this makes it more powerful and far more significant.

Like with the strike-back pattern, waiting for a follow through is the best approach for trading these swing engulfing patterns, as illustrated in Figure 4.16..

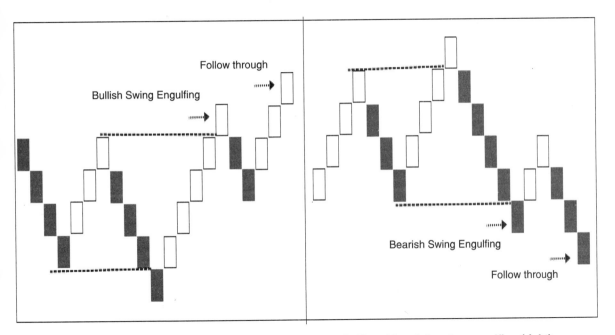

Figure 4.16: **Follow through to bullish swing engulfing (left) and bearish swing engulfing (right)**

~

Trading Swing Engulfing Patterns

Once there is swing engulfing on the chart, the subsequent swing breakouts can be traded. Figure 4.17 shows you how.

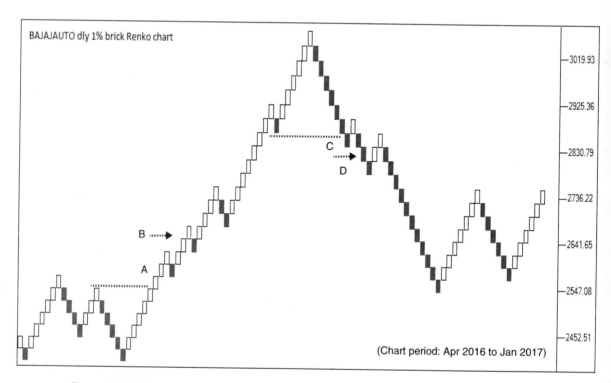

Figure 4.17: **Swing engulfing follow through patterns in a 1% brick value daily Renko chart of Bajaj Auto**

Pattern A is a bullish swing engulfing pattern with a follow through breakout at Point B, which also happens to be a bullish one-back. Pattern D is a follow through to a bearish swing engulfing pattern at C, which happens to be a bearish one-back.

∼

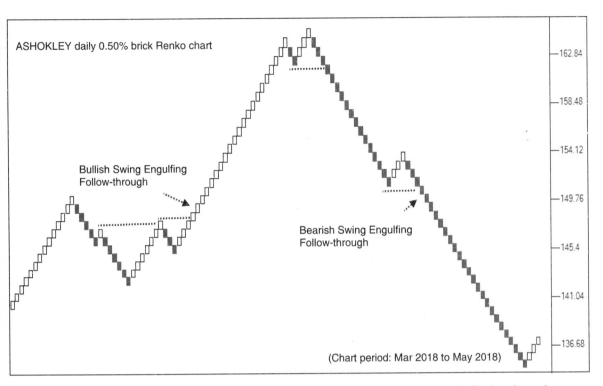

Figure 4.18: **Swing engulfing follow through patterns in a 0.50% brick value daily Renko chart of Ashok Leyland**

~

Figure 4.18 is a chart of Ashok Leyland showing another example of the swing engulfing follow through pattern.

You would have noticed that swing engulfing is also a strike back pattern. In fact, it is an extended version of the strike back pattern.

There is, however, greater bullishness associated with bullish swing engulfing than with bullish strike back patterns. The logic being that in the case of swing engulfing, the price not only moves above the previous breakout brick but also manages to retrace the entire previous swing move and registers a breakout in the same swing.

Similarly, bearish swing engulfing is more bearish than the bearish strike-back pattern. *Strike-back and swing engulfing patterns are nothing but a failure of the prior swing move. While the strike-back represents a partial excursion into the prior swing, swing engulfing represents a complete retracement of the prior swing. Hence, both these patterns have an ingredient of failure embedded in them.* Swing engulfing has got the additional flavour of a breakout that can lend momentum to the price. The concept of follow through to swing engulfing pattern is a logical setup that strengthens the case for a reversal and offers a more affordable trade set up as well.

The rules relating to applying extensions associated with the strike-back pattern are relevant to swing engulfing, too.

Extensions from Swing Engulfing

When the price makes a bullish swing engulfing pattern and reverses from a bearish swing breakout, we can treat it as a first wave. Post correction to the first wave, when the price forms another swing breakout, we can project the first wave as explained in the case of the strike-back pattern.

Figure 4.19 is a 1% brick Renko chart of Jet airways, illustrating the extensions plotted from swing engulfing patterns.

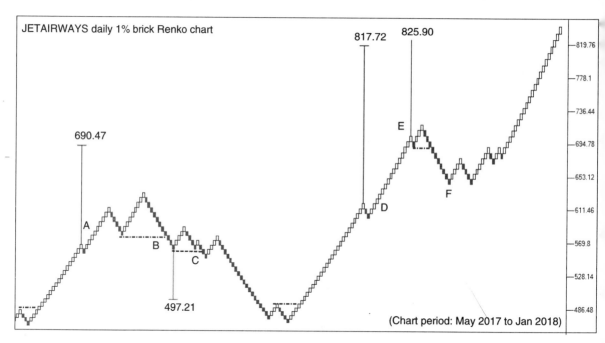

Figure 4.19: **Swing engulfing pattern extensions in a 1% brick value daily Renko chart of Jet airways**

Point A is a bullish swing engulfing follow through pattern and also a bullish one-back pattern. Point B is a bearish swing engulfing pattern that witnessed follow through at Point C. Point D is a bullish engulfing pattern and a bullish two-back pattern. Point E is a bullish one-back pattern extension. Point F is a bearish swing engulfing pattern that did not see a follow through and hence did not get activated.

~

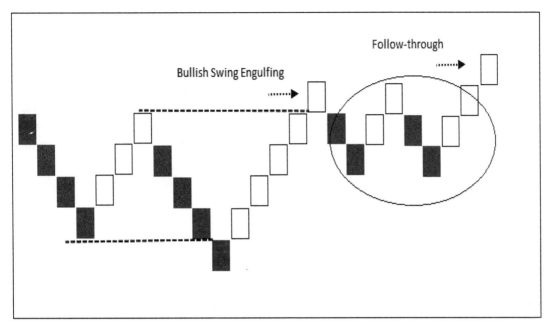

Figure 4.20: **Bullish follow through breakout is not necessary in the immediate swing move, and the pattern remains valid as long as the bottom of the bullish swing engulfing pattern is protected.**

~

One-back and two-back patterns can offer good follow through trades post swing engulfing. You would have noticed that if the follow through to a swing engulfing pattern happens also to be a one-back or a two-back pattern, the extension will be plotted from the same brick.

Like with the strike-back, it is not necessary that the follow through should occur immediately. The swing engulfing follow through pattern can even occur in subsequent swings. The pattern will remain valid if the swing high formed by a bearish swing engulfing pattern — or the swing low formed by a bullish swing engulfing pattern — is not breached. Figure 4.20 illustrates this for a bullish swing engulfing follow through.

The tops and bottoms marked by swing engulfing patterns are very important reference points from the perspective of chart analysis.

Weak Breakout Patterns

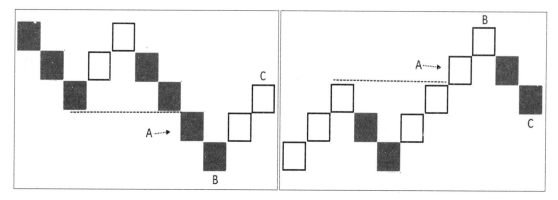

Figure 4.21: **Bullish weak breakout (left) and bearish weak breakout (right).**

When the price forms a bearish swing breakout (A), but fails to record more than two bearish bricks thereafter (B), and instead again turns back above the swing breakout brick (C), it is considered a bullish weak breakout pattern.

Correspondingly, after a swing breakout (A), if the price fails to form more than two bullish bricks (B) and instead moves below the swing breakout brick (C), it is a bearish weak breakout pattern.

~

We have discussed swing breakouts in Renko charts. At times, the price changes direction immediately after a breakout. We usually call that a failed breakout, or a whipsaw. These are very important occurrences to spot because they provide key information about the price setup. When the price reverses after a breakout, it indicates that the breakout traders are trapped, namely caught on the wrong side of the trade.

In Renko charts, when a swing breakout fails to last more than two bricks, and if the price reverses back to the breakout level, it is considered a weak breakout pattern (*see* Figure 4.21).

If you think about it carefully, a weak breakout is nothing but a strike-back pattern. Only the requirement of not more than two bricks after a breakout is the key variation and it highlights the weakness of the camp which could not take the price any further in the direction of the breakout. I have often seen that important tops and bottoms are marked by these weak breakouts. The weak breakout strike-back adds to the information and strength of the top, or the bottom, so formed.

Trading Weak Breakouts

- Aggressive traders can trade bullish weak breakout patterns with a stop loss placed one brick below the bearish brick that produced the false breakout.

- Bearish weak breakout patterns can be traded with a stop placed at one brick above the bullish brick that produced the false breakout.

- Follow through to this pattern can be utilised for adding to the positions.

Readers would have realised that the concept of a false breakout is converted into an objective pattern in a Renko chart that gives us the opportunity to take rule based contra trades with an affordable risk.

Let's consider Figure 4.22, which shows a 0.50% brick chart of Amara Raja Batteries Ltd.

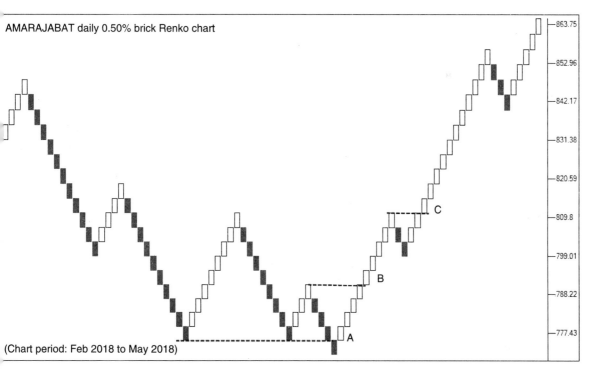

Figure 4.22: **Bullish weak breakout in the 0.50% brick value daily Renko chart of Amara Raja Batteries**

Pattern A is bullish weak breakout pattern. Notice that there was a double bottom formation which was breached at Point A. But the down move did not last more than a single brick and it turned bullish thereafter, signifying a bullish weak breakout pattern. This resulted in a bullish swing engulfing breakout pattern at Point B and follow through to it, which is also a bullish two-back at Point C.

~

This formation also gives us an opportunity to position size[*] the trade. I recommend entering 50% quantity when the weak breakout is completed and adding the remaining 50% when the swing breakout pattern occurs. This way one adds to the position once the strength is confirmed by the price.

Let us consider Figure 4.23, which is a 1% brick chart of DHFL.

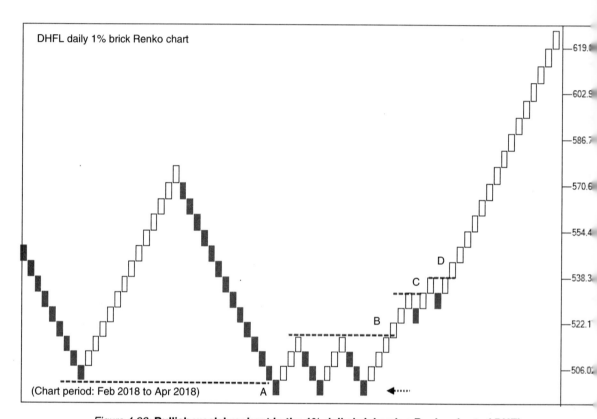

Figure 4.23: **Bullish weak breakout in the 1% daily brick value Renko chart of DHFL**

A bullish weak breakout pattern occurred at Point A. The price then reversed and tested the weak breakout level multiple times. Eventually, a bullish swing breakout, which is a also a multi-brick breakout, occurred at Point B. Continuation bullish one-back patterns occurred at Point C and Point D, providing confirmation of the swing breakout.

~

Typically, the price is expected to test the last swing high post a bullish weak breakout pattern and the last swing low post a bearish weak breakout pattern.

There is a phase in every instrument or market when breakouts fail. This typically happens in sideways price action. You will find many weak breakout formations during such a phase.

Let's now take a look at the chart of Equitas in Figure 4.24, which captures almost a year's price action.

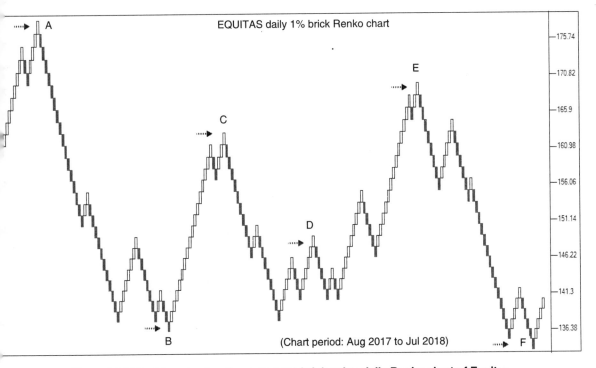

Figure 4.24: **Weak breakout patterns in a 1% brick value daily Renko chart of Equitas**

Patterns A, C, D and E are bearish weak breakouts. Patterns B and F are bullish weak breakouts. You may notice a few one-backs and two-backs that worked during the same period.

~

Let's now have a look at Figure 4.25.

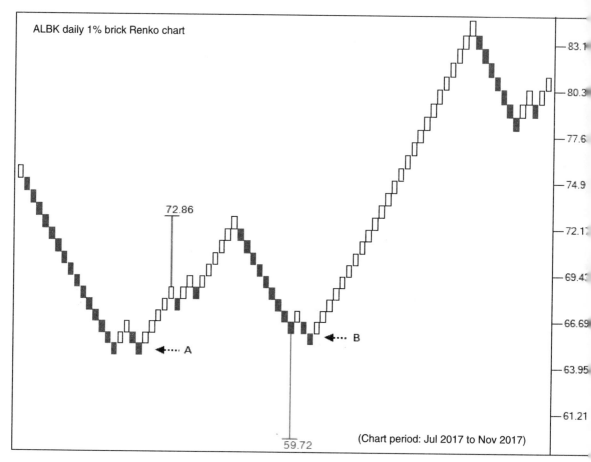

Figure 4.25: **Renko chart patterns in a 1% brick value daily Renko chart of Allahabad Bank. The price completed a Renko double bottom pattern at Point A, followed by bullish one-back patterns. The price corrected and took support around the same levels at Point B, which was a bearish one-back formation but resulted in a bullish weak breakout.**

~

Figure 4.26 is a chart of REC Limited showing reversals triggered by a weak breakout and zigzag patterns.

The weak breakout is one of my favourite reversal setups. Especially, when there is confirmation from other technical tools, or when it occurs in the direction of the major trend.

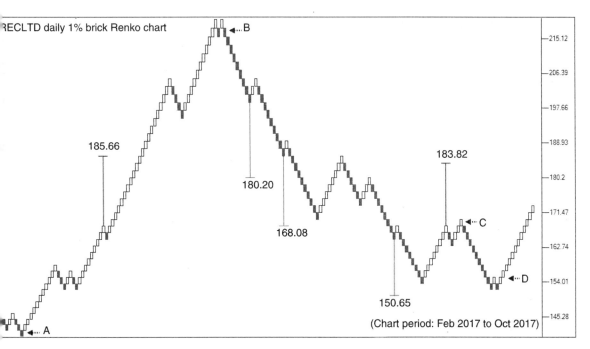

Figure 4.26: **Weak breakout reversal patterns and one-back, two-back extensions in a 1% brick value daily chart of REC Ltd.**

Pattern A is a bullish weak breakout followed by continuation patterns. Point B is a bearish zigzag at the top, followed by bearish continuation patterns. Point C is a bearish weak breakout and Point D is a bullish zigzag pattern that marked the reversal. Extensions from one-back and two-back patterns are plotted on the chart for your observation.

~

Renko ABCD

Harmonic patterns are popular reversal patterns. One can refer to the 3-volume book *Harmonic Trading* written by Scot M. Carney for a more detailed study of harmonic patterns. **ABCD is a popular harmonic pattern for trading reversals.** I have incorporated it into Renko, considering the advantage of objectivity offered by Renko bricks.

ABCD is a three-leg pattern, with AB being first move, BC the second, and CD the third. Rules of the Renko ABCD pattern are explained below with the help of Figure 4.27.

In the bullish Renko ABCD pattern in Figure 4.27:

- There is a series of 6 bearish bricks in the move AB.

- BC is a corrective move having fewer bricks than the move AB, and the high at Point C is lower than Point A.

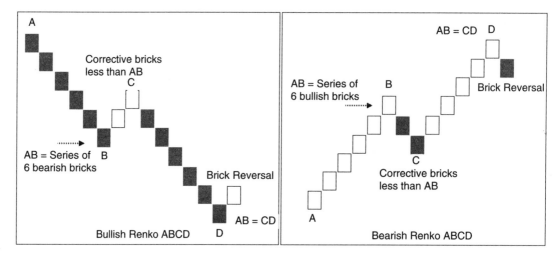

Figure 4.27: **Bullish Renko ABCD (left) and bearish Renko ABCD (right) patterns**

~

- CD is also a series of 6 bearish bricks which is exactly equal to the number of the bricks in AB series.

- CD is followed by bullish brick reversal.

From a trading perspective, one can buy at the bullish brick reversal with stop loss placed below Point D.

In the bearish Renko ABCD pattern of Figure 4.27:

- There is a series of 6 bullish bricks in the move AB.

- BC is a corrective move with fewer bricks than AB; and the low at Point C is higher than Point A.

- CD is also a series of 6 bullish bricks which is exactly equal to the number of bricks in AB.

- CD is followed by bullish brick reversal.

From a trading perspective, one can go short at the bearish brick reversal with the stop loss placed above Point D in Figure 4.27. The series of six bricks each in the two images in Figure 4.27 are just an example; the point is that the number of bricks in AB should be equal to number of bricks in CD.

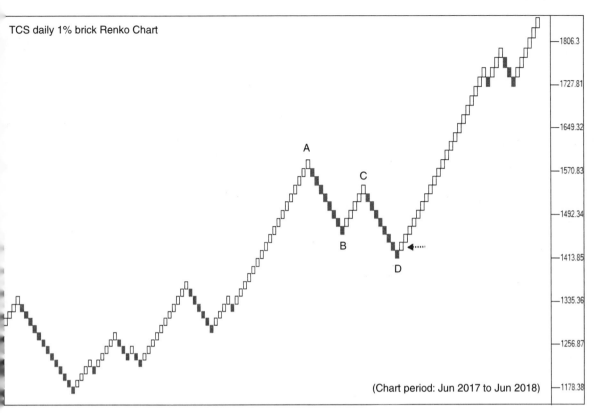

TCS daily 1% brick Renko Chart

(Chart period: Jun 2017 to Jun 2018)

Figure 4.28: **Bullish Renko ABCD pattern in a 1% brick value daily Renko chart of TCS which was in an up trend but witnessed a three-leg correction from April to May 2018. The price resumed its uptrend post the ABCD corrective pattern. Can you spot the four one-back patterns earlier in the up trend?**

~

Figure 4.28 which is a chart of TCS showing a bullish ABCD pattern.

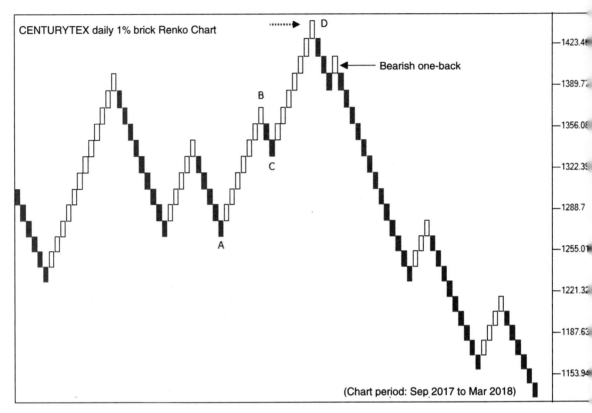

Figure 4.29: Bearish Renko ABCD pattern in a 1% brick value daily Renko chart of Century Textile. The ABCD pattern that got formed at the higher prices was followed by a bearish one-back pattern after which we witnessed a sharp fall in price. Yes, ABCD was also a bullish two-back pattern.

~

Figure 4.29, which follows, is a chart of Century Textile showing a bearish ABCD pattern.

Going by the ABCD theory, we can expect a reversal up to Point C of the pattern in Figure 4.29. But I would recommend riding the trade using Renko swing patterns, or trading the subsequent Renko breakout patterns. For example, the bearish one-back post the bearish ABCD in Figure 4.29 was a tradable and a high probability formation.

Note that like all other Renko patterns, Renko ABCD too is objective in nature which can be scanned or back tested.

Can there be a move in the opposite direction during AB or CD? Can there be a variation of a couple of bricks or should the counts of AB and CD be exactly the same? All these questions might occur in your mind. I have, however, deliberately kept it simple and objective. I prefer that a trader be as rigid as possible with pattern rules to begin with. You can move on to flexibility and variations, once you understand the essence and logic of the pattern. It is important to look at the broader perspective while applying variations. For example, if you have some other pattern or indicator for the reversal's confirmation, you can be a little flexible in such instances. We will discuss more about this in Chapter 7 where we look at indicators in move detail.

A word of caution relating to the variations: Use variations only once you are fully aware of what you are doing. You shouldn't become flexible with risk, or treat stops casually, or keep tinkering with them illogically. Even professional and experienced traders need to be conscious about not having rigid views on the likely price action, especially if that makes you treat your stops casually.

A reversal pattern in a lower brick value chart is a nice pullback formation when the higher brick value chart is in a strong trend. When we get a bullish ABCD on lower brick value charts at a time when the higher brick value chart and overall formations are also bullish, then it is an opportunity to trade long with affordable risk. When patterns are traded in the direction of the higher degree trend, they pay rich dividends.

Don't limit this learning of designing objective price patterns in Renko charts to ABCD. You can try and take this logic of designing objective price patterns further in a similar manner on Renko charts. To be able to count the number of bricks in each swing gives us the opportunity to design different price patterns. You will start enjoying the objectivity of Renko charts that allow you to innovate in this manner.

Principle of Polarity

The polarity principle is a very popular concept in technical analysis. The phenomenon of a prior support turning into resistance when broken — and *vice versa* — is the essence of the polarity principle. Polarity is applicable on Renko charts, too.

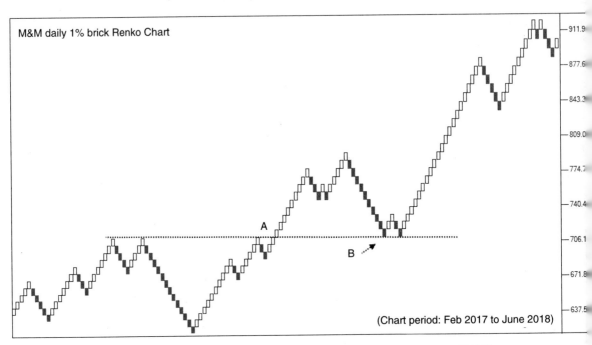

Figure 4.30: **Polarity pattern in a 1% brick value daily Renko chart of M&M**

The price was facing resistance before completing a multi-brick breakout at Point A, which comes across as an inverted head and shoulders pattern. The price then duly corrected and took support at Point B. The previous resistance now acted as support as per the polarity principle, and the price formed a Renko support pattern at that level.

~

The polarity principle provides an effective pull back trading method and Renko brick reversal provides the necessary confirmation that makes it tradable. Have a look at Figure 4.30.

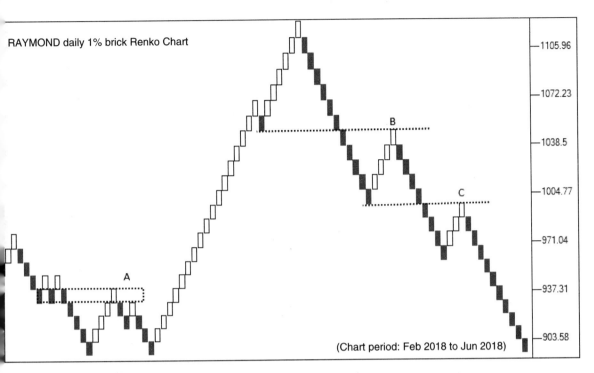

Figure 4.31: **Polarity principle at work in a 1% brick value daily Renko chart of Raymond**

Price encountered resistance at Point A where it had earlier witnessed support. Later, it also witnessed resistance at points B and C, where earlier there had been demand — the previous support acting as resistance as per the principle of polarity. Renko brick reversal formations can help us in seeking confirmation and trading them.

~

Let's now consider the chart of Raymond in Figure 4.31.

Though applicable on all brick values, the principle of polarity is clearly seen and very effective on higher brick value charts.

Retracement Pullback Zone

Fibonacci is a popular theory for retracements. We discussed Fibonacci ratios in Chapter 2. There are multiple theories to calculate retracement. Retracement ratio varies from 25% to 66%. We can refer to retracements between 25% and 66% as a retracement zone. It's important to remember that in order to infer retracement there has to be a significant trend to start with. A strong trend is defined as anchor bricks; recall that a series of bullish or bearish bricks are known as anchor bricks. Hence, after an anchor brick move, which indicates the presence of a strong trend, if the corrective bricks enter the retracement zone, we can then trade that retracement when a brick reverses from that zone.

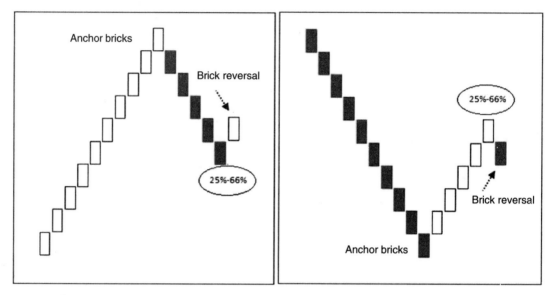

Figure 4.32: **Bullish retracement pattern (left) and bearish retracement pattern (right)**

~

A word of caution here: never initiate a trade unless there is a brick reversal pattern after a retracement. This is an important ingredient of the pattern, and one which indicates the completion of the retracement and gives an opportunity to find affordable trades.

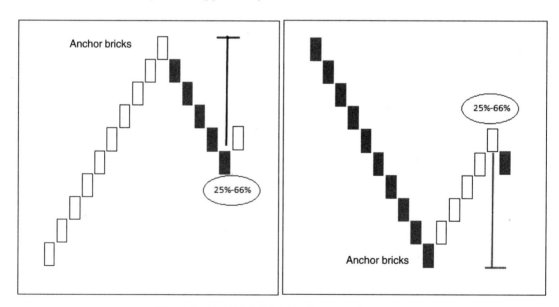

Figure 4.33: **Extension from retracement patterns**

~

I am keeping it very simple here. Once we identify a brick reversal in a retracement zone, we can expect the price to move back to the previous high or low. Refer Figure 4.33.

From a trading perspective, one can trade with the stop placed at the level of the bottom, or top, of the swing brick. If the price achieves the previous swing point and breaks out, it will mark a swing breakout and will throw open projections based on swing extension.

Retracement zone reversals in the same direction as trends in the higher brick value chart are more powerful and offer interesting trading opportunities.

Figure 4.34 is a chart of Grasim showing bullish retracements.

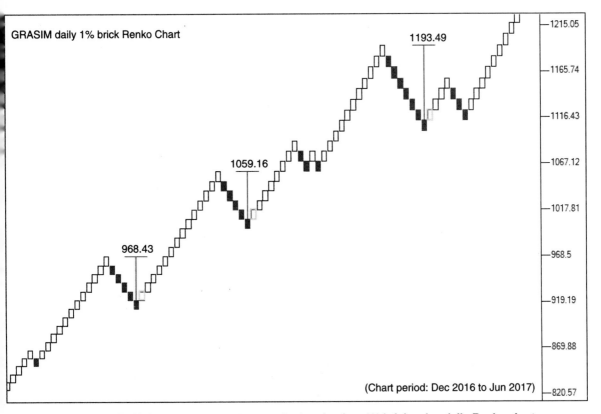

Figure 4.34: **Bullish retracement pattern and extension in a 1% brick value daily Renko chart of Grasim**

~

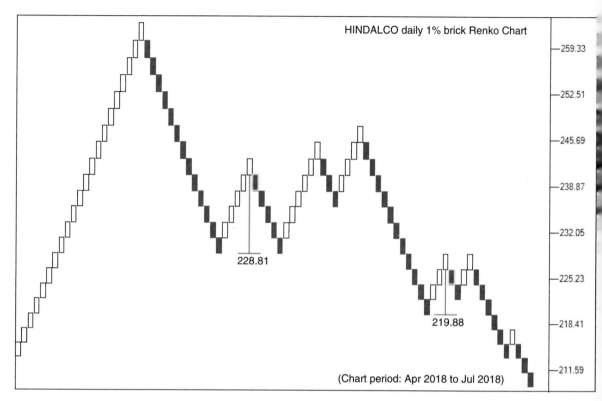

Figure 4.35: **Bearish retracement pattern and extension in a 1% brick value daily Renko chart of Hindalco**

~

Figure 4.35 is a chart of Hindalco showing bearish retracement patterns.

123 Pullback Pattern

Bullish 123 Pullback

During an uptrend, if the price retraces below the previous bullish swing breakout zone and then forms a reversal, it is a bullish 123 pullback pattern (*see* Figure 4.36).

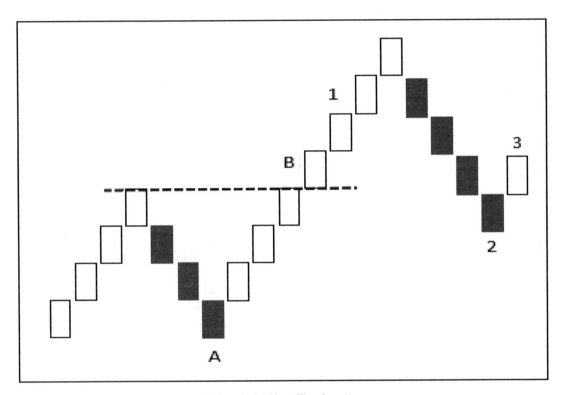

Figure 4.36: **123 pullback pattern**

The bullish swing breakout at Point B is followed by at least three bullish bricks. A subsequent series of bearish bricks was then formed indicating the while price retraced back below the swing high breakout point at Point 1 but it did not falling below the low of the bullish swing at Point A. Then there is a bullish brick reversal at 3.

~

Bearish 123 Pullback

In a down trend, when the price moves back up above the previous bearish swing breakout zone and forms a reversal, it is called a bearish 123 pullback pattern (*see* Figure 4.37).

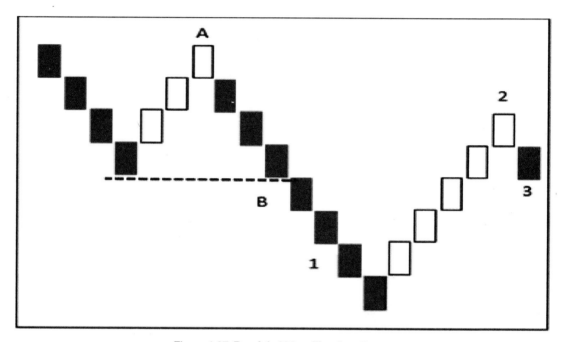

Figure 4.37: **Bearish 123 pullback pattern:**

1 — Bearish swing breakout at Point B is followed by (at least) three bearish bricks;

2 — A series of bullish bricks that indicates the price retracing back above the swing low breakout brick at Point 1, without going back above the high of the bearish swing at Point A;

3 — Bearish brick reversal complete.

~

You must remember to let the brick reversal actually happen before you enter a trade. Don't pre-empt. Many a time the price will reverse the entire previous swing move and not give any trade.

It is also important to keep in mind that this pattern has a higher probability of success if traded with the trend. Patterns against the trend need greater confirmation before a trade is initiated.

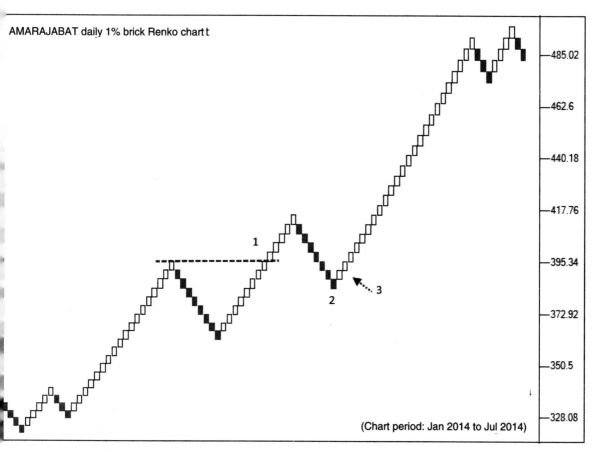

Figure 4.38: **Bullish 123 pullback pattern in a 1% brick value daily Renko chart of Amara Raja Batteries. The arrow mark shows a bullish 123 pullback pattern. Price tested the swing breakout pattern and formed the bullish brick reversal.**

~

Figure 4.38 is a chart of Amara Raja Batteries Ltd illustrating a bullish 123 pullback pattern.

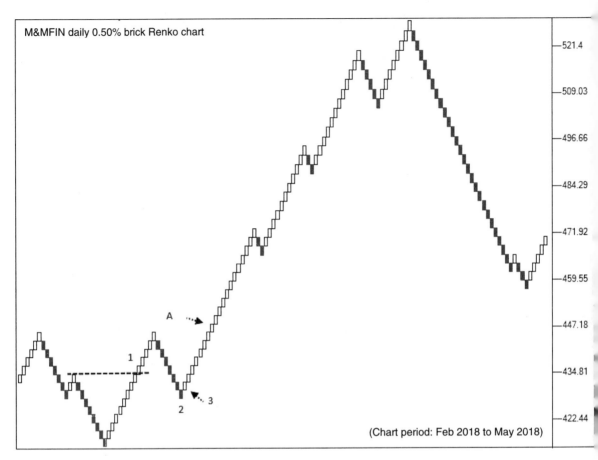

Figure 4.39: **Bullish 123 pullback pattern in a 1% brick value daily Renko chart of M&M Finance. This bullish 123 pattern occurred against the trend. With reversals, one can wait for confirmation. Here, a follow through breakout to the bullish swing engulfing formation got triggered at Point A. It was followed by bullish two-back continuation patterns.**

~

Figure 4.39 is a chart of M&M Finance illustrating a bullish 124 pullback pattern which occurred against the trend.

The price is expected to test the previous swing high in the case of bullish 123 pullback patterns. In both Figure 4.38 and Figure 4.39, the swing breakouts were also bullish swing engulfing patterns. And post the 123-pullbacks, the price triggered follow through to the swing engulfing patterns.

You would have noticed that the 123 pullback pattern retraces back to the previous swing high or swing low and forms the brick reversal pattern. When in sync with trend, it offers an interesting pullback trading opportunity with affordable risk.

Let's now have a look at Figure 4.40.

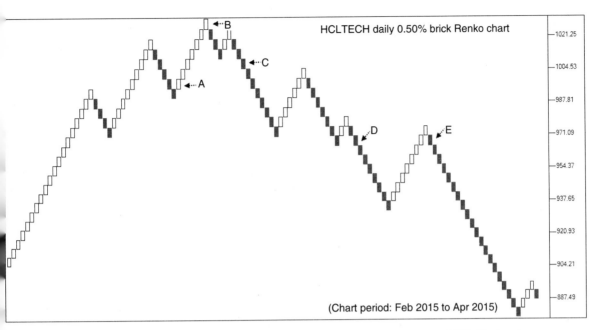

Figure 4.40: **123 pullback patterns in a 0.50% brick value daily Renko chart of HCL Technology**

The price formed a bullish 123 pullback pattern during the uptrend at Point A. The swing breakout pattern at Point B turned out to be a bearish weak breakout. It was followed by a bearish two-back at Point C, followed by anchor bricks that set the bearish tone. Point D is a bearish two-back pattern. Point E is a bearish 123 pullback pattern in the downtrend.

~

Renko support and resistance patterns discussed in Chapter 2 and Chapter 3 are also reversal setups. Even a simple brick reversal is also a reversal setup, but that alone cannot be traded. It becomes tradable when the chart is analysed by observing different price patterns.

Aggressive Trade Enteries — or Pre-empting Patterns

You may think that trades can be taken with the stop placed at brick reversal after a strike back or swing engulfing, especially if it is supported by other technical factors. Such an approach is not nesessarily wrong, and it can certainly be attempted, especially if the price has breached an important price level, or when there is confirmation from other tools. There is nothing completely wrong or right in the markets. But being aware of what you are doing is extremely important. Mastering the rules is an essential step before you can successfully hope to break them.

For example, now when you know about one-back and two-back patterns, it is possible to pre-empt them and buy at the corrective phase, as shown in Figure 4.41.

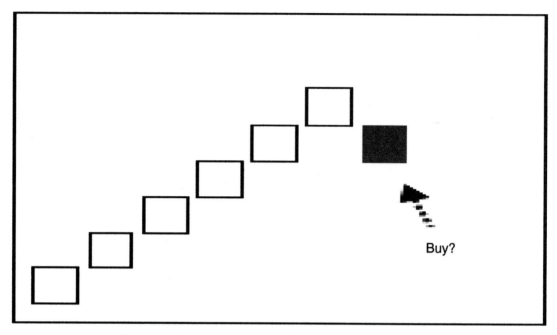

Figure 4.41: **Buying at the corrective brick after anchor bricks**

~

When the price corrects by one box post anchor bricks, one can buy with a stop of two bricks. Why two bricks? Because that will also factor in the possibility of a two-back. If you find the pattern at a two-back, you can buy with a stop of one box. This is pre-empting the pattern but may work well, especially when the broader market or sector concerned is trending.

One can also position size by buying some quantity at pre-empting — and then adding more upon breakout. I have added this point to the pullback list because I have noticed that we get one-backs and two-backs during strong trends. Go for pullbacks over anchor bricks when you are trying to pre-empt. Due to the strong momentum displayed by anchor bricks, the chances of the trade working out in your favour are bright and the initial risk is low. But pre-empting and applying variation needs more confirmation and experience. It's best to begin by trading breakout rules, and only later think of pre-empting.

M and W Patterns

M and W patterns can be easily identified and effectively traded on Renko charts. The plotting of the price action in a diagonal format in the Renko Chart makes it easier to identify and trade these patterns.

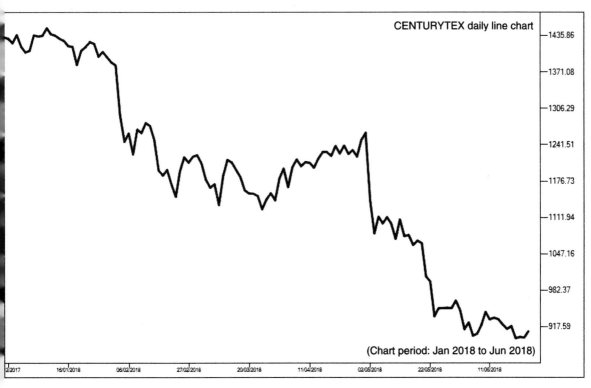

Figure 4.42: **Daily line chart of Century Textile**

~

Have a look at Figure 4.42, which is a daily line chart of Century Textile.

Now, have a look at Figure 4.43, which is a 0.50% daily Renko chart of Century Textile covering the same period as Figure 4.42. The bricks are connected by a line and shown for your observation.

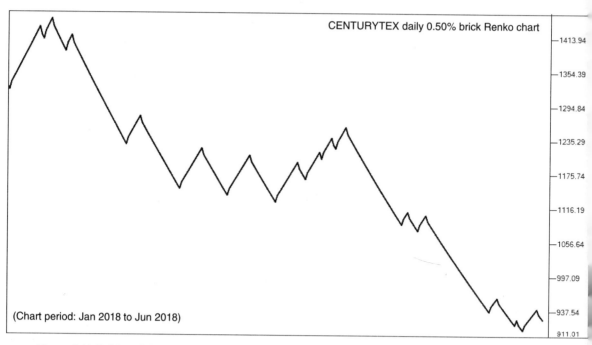

Figure 4.43: **Bricks of the 0.50% brick value daily Renko chart of Century Textile connected by a line**

~

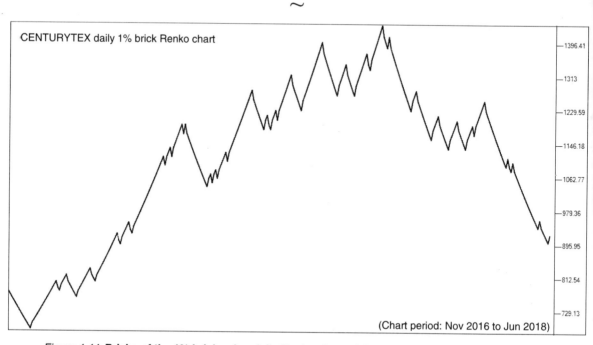

Figure 4.44: **Bricks of the 1% brick value daily Renko chart of Century Textile connected by a line**

~

Figure 4.44 is a line connecting the bricks in the 1% brick value Century Textile chart.

You can observe the steady line curves and noiseless data in Figure 4.43 and Figure 4.44. If you observe closely, you will find many small and large "M" and "W" price patterns in these charts. Such patterns are comparatively easier to find in Renko charts than in other type of charts.

Figure 4.45 is a Renko chart covering the same period as Figure 4.44 to help you observe the same "M" and "W" patterns.

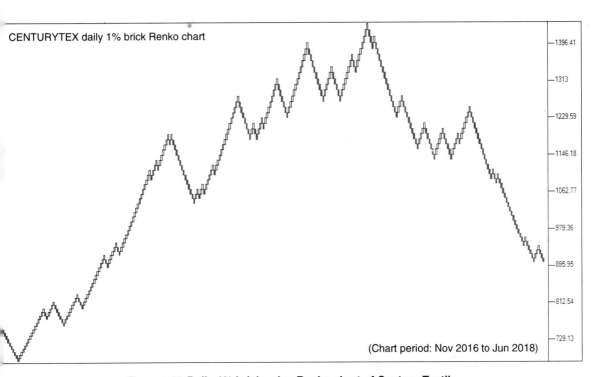

Figure 4.45: **Daily 1% brick value Renko chart of Century Textile**

~

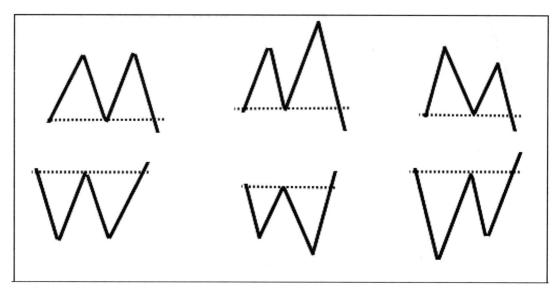

Figure 4.46: **"M" and "W" price patterns**

∼

Broadly speaking, Figure 4.46 shows how the "M" and "W" patterns look.

The breakout from "M" and "W" patterns is completed upon the horizontal neckline breakout, one brick below the neckline in the case of an M pattern and one brick above the neckline in the case of a W pattern. If you notice, the high of the second leg of M exceeds the previous high in the pattern in the middle of Figure 4.46. Similarly, in the W pattern featured in the middle of Figure 4.46, the low of the second leg of the W pattern breaches the previous low. These two patterns will be more significant if they turn out to be weak breakouts wherein the price does not travel more than two bricks post the breakout.

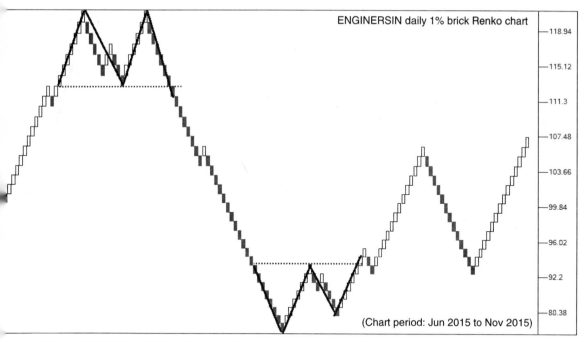

Figure 4.47: **"M" and "W" patterns in the 1% brick value daily Renko chart of Engineers India**

~

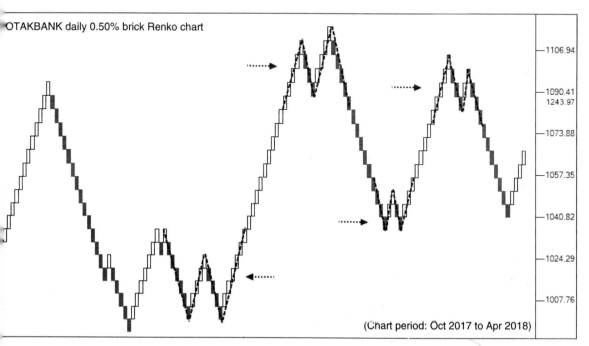

Figure 4.48: **"M" and "W" patterns in the 0.50% brick value daily Renko chart of Kotak Bank**

~

Multiple Swing Extensions

The M or W pattern gets qualified when the price goes above, or below, its neckline. Often, this could be a swing breakout. Whenever that happens, we can project the pattern with multiple swing extensions, or multi-swing extensions, as illustrated in Figure 4.49.

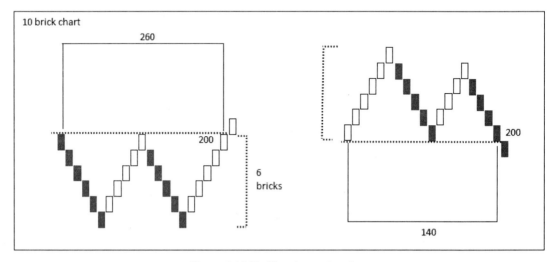

Figure 4.49: **Multi-swing extension**

~

Bullish multi-swing extensions can be plotted from W patterns, while bearish multi-swing extension can be plotted from M patterns.

The brick from which we start the projection is called the projection brick. It will be the brick above the neckline in the case of W patterns, and the brick below the neckline in case of M patterns.

The pattern's height can be calculated by counting the number of bricks from the projection brick to the lowest brick of the pattern. Below is the formula for bullish extension.

Bullish Multi-Swing Extension = Projection brick + (Height of the pattern x brick value)

In Figure 4.49, the brick value is 10, the height of the pattern is 6 bricks, and the projection brick value is 200.

Hence, the calculation would be as follows:

Bullish Multi-Swing Extension = 200 + (6 x 10) = 260

The height of the M pattern can be calculated by counting the number of bricks between the highest point of the pattern and the projection brick.

The formula for bearish projection is as follows.

Bearish Multi-Swing Extension = Projection brick – (Height of the pattern x brick value)

In Figure 4.49, the brick value is 10, the height of the pattern is 6 bricks, and the projection brick value is 200. Hence, the calculation would be as follows:

Bearish Multi-Swing Extension = 200 – (6 x 10) = 140

A bullish extension gets negated when the price falls below the lowest point of the W pattern, while a bearish extension gets negated when the price goes above the highest point of an M pattern.

Figure 4.50 is a chart of Engineers India showing extensions plotted from M and W patterns.

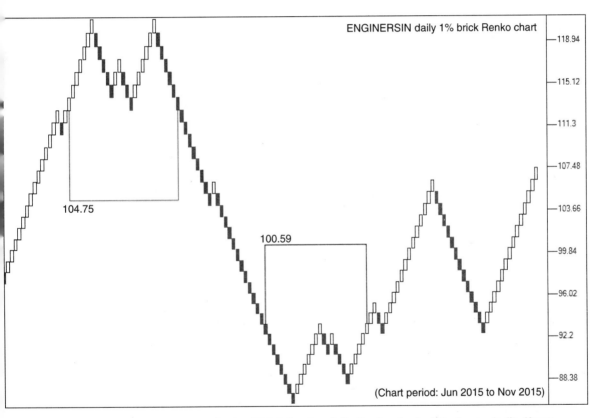

Figure 4.50: **Multi-swing extension in the 1% brick value daily Renko chart of Engineers India. If you notice carefully, a bearish one-back formation occurred after the M pattern while there occurred a bullish two-back formation after the W pattern.**

~

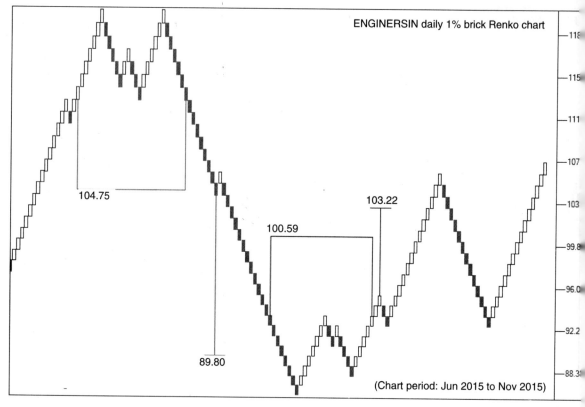

Figure 4.51: **Extensions** in the 1% brick value daily Renko chart of Engineers India

~

Figure 4.51 is a chart showing extensions plotted from the continuation patterns after M and W patterns in Figure 4.50.

A combination of patterns and extensions can help you to design trading setups. When multiple extensions coincide, it becomes a high probability area. We will discuss more about extensions in Chapter 6.

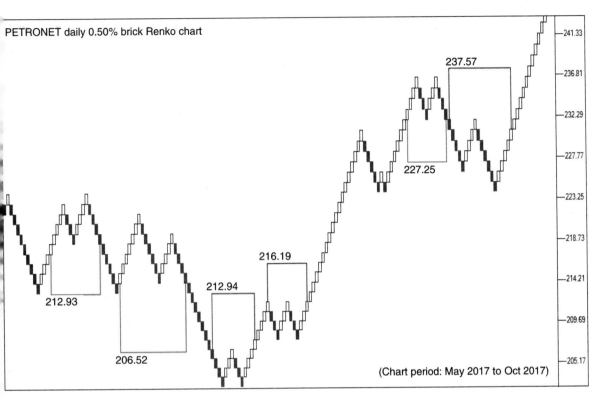

Figure 4.52: **M and W pattern extensions in the 0.50% brick value daily Renko chart of Petronet**

~

Figure 4.52 is a chart showing M and W patterns, and extensions from those patterns.

Multi-swing extensions can be plotted in all time frames, all brick values and all instruments. These are particularly useful and relevant in the high brick value charts. It is important to caution here that the identification of M and W patterns can be subjective in some cases.

Multi-swing extensions can be applied to horizontal patterns of accumulation or distribution as well. As discussed earlier, we can see price patterns such as head and shoulders, cup handle, triangles, etc. on Renko charts. We can plot multi-swing extensions from all such patterns.

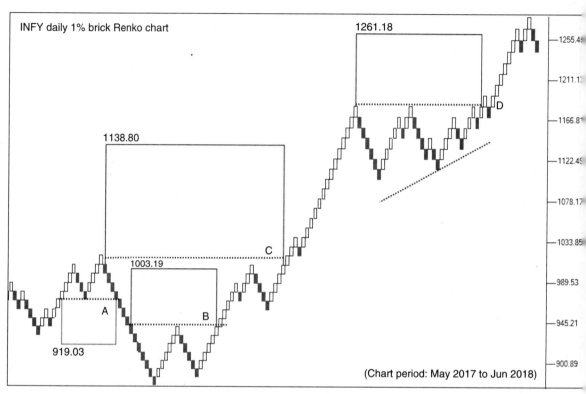

Figure 4.53: **Multi-swing extensions in the 1% brick value daily Renko chart of Infosys**

The extension at Point A is plotted from an M pattern. Extension from Point B starts from a W pattern. Extension at Point C is plotted from a horizontal cup handle pattern. Multi-swing extension at Point D is plotted from a horizontal multi-brick breakout and ascending triangle breakout pattern.

~

Have a look at Figure 4.53.

Unlike other extensions that we have discussed, multi-swing extensions are a bit subjective in nature. Let's have a look at the accumulation and distribution range that can be used for multi-swing extensions.

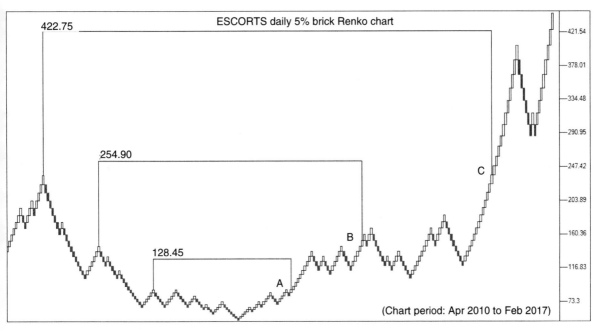

Figure 4.54: **Multi-swing extension in the 5% brick value daily Renko chart of Escorts**

The first breakout showing extension of ₹128 is a two-year pattern breakout that occurred above ₹89 at Point A. The second extension of ₹254 is a 3.5-year pattern breakout that occurred, at Point B (₹152). The third extension of ₹422 is more than a 6-year pattern breakout that occurred at ₹236, at Point C.

~

Examples of Renko Pattern Analysis

While explaining the various patterns, I have clearly discussed the entry and exit rules for each pattern, pattern failure levels, and even extensions. Trade setups can be easily designed based on this information. Also, it is not necessary that you need to apply extensions from all the patterns that we have discussed.

What follows is a summary of all the patterns explained on charts along with an analysis of the chart.

From an analysis persepctive, a combination of patterns can help in analysing any Renko chart. A Renko chart tells us a lot about the price action and the prevailing sentiment among market participants. The probable accumulation or distribution phase can be analysed effectively, too.

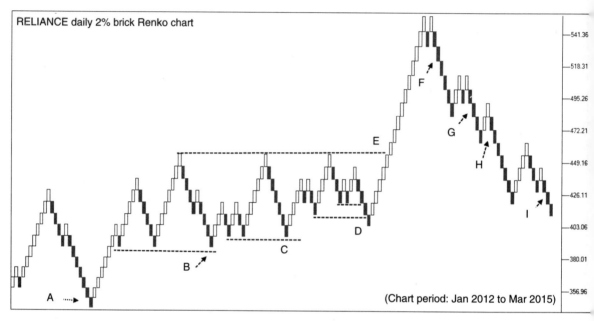

Figure 4.55: **2% brick value daily Renko chart of Reliance Industries**

Point A is a bullish weak breakout when the brick reversed to bullish. Point B is a bullish ABCD and triple bottom support Renko pattern, indicating strong demand level at that price zone. Pattern C is again a triple bottom support pattern around the same levels, confirming the demand zone. This indicates that the price is range bound, but forming a base at lower levels. Pattern D again confirms holding the support zone, but a bullish weak breakout when the brick turned positive adds the flavour of pattern failure. Triple-top resistance breakout at Point E confirms that the price has broken out from the accumulation phase.

Point F is a bearish zigzag breakout that indicates confusion at higher price levels. Point G is also a bearish zigzag pattern, while Point H is bearish two-back pattern and Point I is bearish one-back pattern which drags the price back into the previous demand zone.

~

Figure 4.55 is a 2% brick value chart of Reliance covering price action for more than three years.

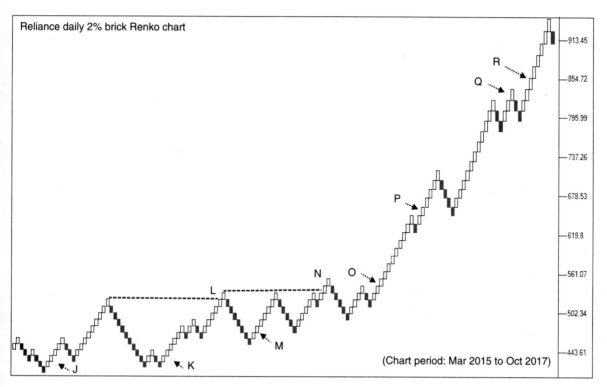

Figure 4.56: 2% **brick value daily Renko chart of Reliance Industries**

Point J turned out to be a bullish ABCD at the previous demand zone. Point K formed a double bottom support around the same price levels. Point L is a weak bearish breakout at the same price level as the bearish zigzag pattern at Point F (refer to the chart in Figure 4.55). Point M is a bullish weak breakout at the support zone. Point N is a bearish weak breakout at a previous resistance zone. Point O is a bullish two-back breakout, and the price is above the previous resistance zone thus offering a trading opportunity. Point P is a bullish one-back continuation pattern. Points Q and R are bullish two-back continuation price patterns. Notice that there is no bearish swing breakout since Point O in the chart. This is a simple and effective price action analysis that needs no special analytical skills.

~

Figure 4.56 is a continuation of the Figure 4.55 and covers the price action of the subsequent two years.

Now, let's have a look at Figure 4.57.

The chart in Figure 4.57 shows how continuation patterns can be traded with affordable stops when a strong trend is established. Identifying significant pattern breakouts and trading continuation patterns that follow is an effective method of trading the markets.

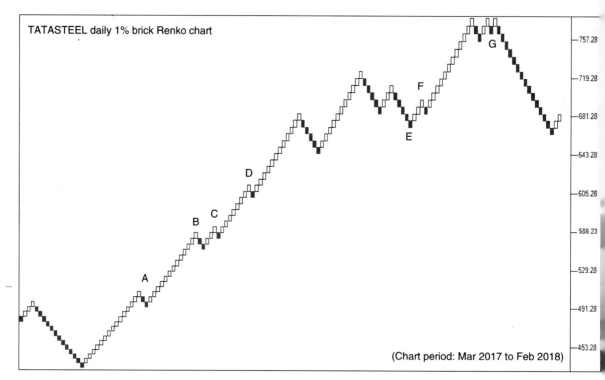

Figure 4.57: **1% brick value daily Renko chart of Tata Steel. Point A is a bullish two-back and also a swing engulfing follow through pattern. Point B is a bullish two-back. Points C and D are bullish one-back continuation patterns. Point E is a bullish ABCD, and Point F is a bullish one-back. Point G is bearish zigzag breakout at top.**

~

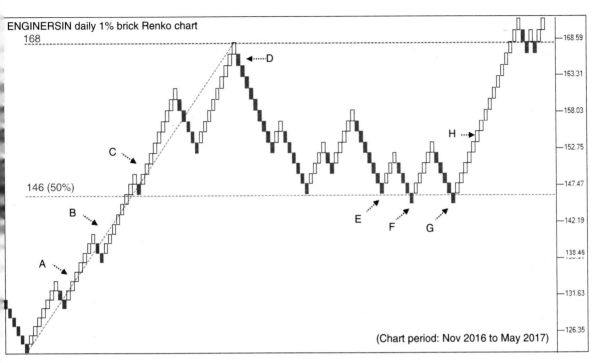

Figure 4.58: **Fibonacci retracement in a 1% brick value daily Renko chart of Engineers India**

Patterns A and B are bullish two-backs while Pattern C is a bullish one-back continuation pattern. Pattern D is a bearish ABCD. The price is taking support at the earlier swing low brick at Pattern E, which also coincides with 50% retracement of the earlier upswing. Pattern F is a bullish weak breakout at the same level indicating strength of the buyers. Pattern G forms Renko support pattern at same levels, highlighting the stubbornness of the bulls. This is followed by swing engulfing follow through pattern at Point H.

~

Figure 4.58 is a chart of Engineers India with Fibonacci retracement.

Figure 4.59 is a 0.50% brick value chart of Raymond highlighting swing breakouts and chart pattern analysis.

Renko price action method is suitable for every type of trader and investor. The analysis above is shown on a particular brick value just as an example. The same approach can be applied on any brick value, any time frame and any instrument. You need to focus on understanding the concepts clearly.

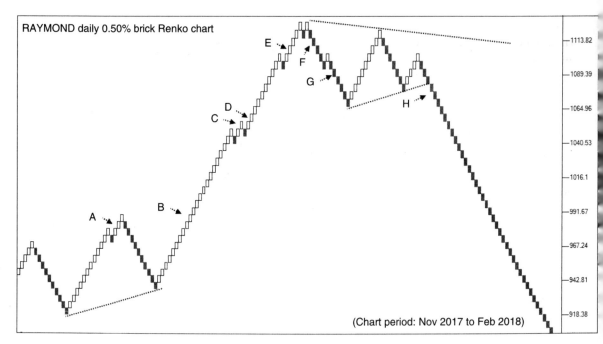

Figure 4.59: *Swing breakout and chart pattern analysis in a 0.50% brick value daily Renko chart of Raymond*

Pattern A is a bullish one-back and also a bullish swing engulfing follow through. Pattern B is a swing breakout which is also a swing engulfing pattern triggered after forming a higher low. Patterns C, D and E are bullish one-back continuation patterns. Pattern F is a bearish zigzag breakout which occurred post a significant rally, followed by bearish one-back at G. Pattern H is a bearish swing breakout post a triangular formation.

~

There can be additional observations on the preceding charts, but I am keeping the discussion to the point. We have already discussed entry and exit levels in the case of various patterns, so you know how to plan trades at each price pattern. I have avoided price and stop levels because the intention is not to show how well a trade worked, but to guide you in chart analysis. The point to convey is that any chart can be analysed if objective pattern rules are practiced and kept in mind. You can decide trade setups and position sizing using these rules.

Pattern Based Trading

Renko patterns that we have discussed can help us in analysing various markets and instruments. A trading approach can also be developed using these patterns. This is known as pattern based trading. Thus, you can take a trade based on a bullish pattern and exit when a bearish formation is formed, or take a short position based on a bearish formation and exit when a bullish pattern is formed. We can shortlist candidates to trade based on our own analysis, or even based on information from trusted sources. But instead of blindly taking such trades, it would be prudent to trade if there is some recognizable Renko pattern in those instruments. The advantage of using a pattern based trading approach is the objectivity it brings in determining entry, exit and failure levels. In effect, we trade following patterns any instrument, and utilize all other things as complementary tools.

Accordingly, you can prepare a list of patterns that you are most comfortable with and follow them on the charts. Concentrating only on major continuation patterns will also suffice; the rest will come handy eventually.

You can begin by practising swing breakouts, one-backs and, two-backs from among the continuation patterns, and weak breakouts for reversal patterns, and then gradually move to the other patterns covered in this chapter. Renko patterns are specific and objective in nature and thus can be practised easily. Ignore unaffordable signals and wait for patterns with follow-through.

All the patterns that we have discussed have definite entry and stop loss rules. Profit booking upon brick reversal can also be initiated if a series of bricks exceeds a particular number. A trade can then be re-initiated upon a fresh breakout. There can be many such ideas that will come to mind when you practiced pattern based trading. You can try out experiments, as long as you know when to exit a trade and keep the potential loss to the minimum. Pattern following imbibes the art of booking losses, which makes one the winner in the long run.

I have seen many accurate and brilliant predictions. There are great minds who can foresee things based on a variety of methods and their experience. They should always be listened to and followed but it is not prudent to blame them when they go wrong. Trade execution and management should always be under your own control. Adopting an objective, pattern based trading approach is the best way of dealing with the different types of analyses, emotions and assumptions.

The key is to wait for a low risk entry after a pattern confirmation. So if a friend asks you to buy something based on this or that news, just consider the friend as a scanner who has identified a possible trading opportunity for you. Trade only the patterns you see in the chart. That way you end up making money when the information you get is correct and you can exit early with minimal loss if the information turns out to be false. Most importantly, you don't need to ask the friend what you should do next!

We have learnt that Renko charts do not plot unwarranted data, a large amount of price data is compressed and captured in just a few bricks. Following objective Renko patterns effectively controls the issue of overtrading which is one of main problems that adversely affect trading performance and profitability.

~

Renko charts allow us to define setups using various combinations of bricks. The advantage of Renko charts is that because the plotting of a brick itself is not frequent, they allow us to keep our heads clear and enable us to ride the trade longer. Accordingly, I tried to present setups which make Renko charts as objective as possible so that one can understand the logic behind the different formations, remember the associated rules — and trade them effectively. So, for example, rather than saying arbitrarily that there should be a "good move before small retracement," or "price reversed immediately post breakout," etc, I discussed rules pertaining to the numbers of bricks and also designed setups using combinations of numbers of bricks to qualify a set-up or pattern. For example, rules with number of bricks were predefined to call it a weak breakout pattern, one-back, two-back, zigzag pattern etc. This can simplify decision making process and thereby makes trading far less stressful.

If a pattern's essence is understood, its variations can also be used. For example, if you have understood that swing engulfing is the overcoming of a previous move, you will know that a simple brick reversal in between is fine. The essence of the pattern remains the same. But this needs much more understanding and experience. And you would gain by keeping things objective with fixed rules to begin with.

~

Chapter 5

~

Pattern Failure

SINCE ONE TRADES IN ORDER TO MAKE MONEY, it is not unnatural for traders to want every trade to be profitable. This is, however, not possible in practice. In fact, if you ask any successful trader he'll tell you that the number of his losing trades is much higher than the number of his winning trades. The reason for success lies not in how may trades are profitable but whether the money made in the winners is much bigger than the money lost in losing trades. With a desire to be successful in every trade, we inadvertently develop a fear of failure, which is not a healthy sign from a trading perspective.

The key is to accept that there will be failures while trading any system or pattern. It is also quite natural that there will be occasions when you will not be comfortable while riding the trend. Not trying to predict or anticipate a reversal is the key aspect for successfully riding the trend.

Come to think of it, a stop loss being triggered can be a significant piece of information. An indication of a pattern failure is another key information that conveys a lot about the underlying trend. The failure of a pattern is a pattern by itself and may offer a trading opportunity with a better probability of success. Once this is understood, a trader can overcome the fear associated with failure. The failure represents a potential trend reversal and may offer a high probability trading opportunity soon.

By wanting a price pattern, an observation, or some news to work, we indirectly impose our opinion on the market. The job of a trader is to listen to what the market is saying and accept what the market wants to do. A pattern failure tells us that the market wants something else. And we should change our stance accordingly.

Strong trends are those that can be easily viewed on any type of chart. Why, then, do so many traders find it difficult to ride them? Breakouts can also be easily identified on a chart using any of the methods available. But not all of them always work, and this fear of failure is the key reason for a trader's inability to ride trends.

Traders either miss breakouts, or exit trades early, because of this fear of failure. Every chart looks great in hindsight. Also, quite often traders feel uncomfortable buying something that has already gone up a lot, or selling something which has already fallen considerably. And if the price continues moving in the same direction, one feels remorse at having missed a strong move.

Once a trade is exited, getting back again is a tough task because there is a fear of giving back the profit already earned. Actually, this is a mindset problem. It should be looked at as just a new trade rather than re-entering an old one. Every trade, irrespective of the scrip, price level or market trend has equal chances of success and failure. This understanding will help you to look for the right things. Ask yourself when is it that you feel tempted to book profits — and what will you do after booking them. You will most likely trade something else, right? Then why not hold on to an already well-timed and successful trade?

Earlier we have discussed price levels where a particular pattern gets negated or fails. Irrespective of the price movement after the pattern, if the top of a bearish pattern or, correspondingly, the bottom of a bullish pattern is broken, it is called as invalidation. *The pattern invalidation level can be different from the stop loss level set while initiating the trade. There will be instances where the pattern invalidation level will be some distance away from the stop loss level. It is important to understand the distinction between pattern invalidation level and the stop loss level.*

Let's consider Figure 5.1.

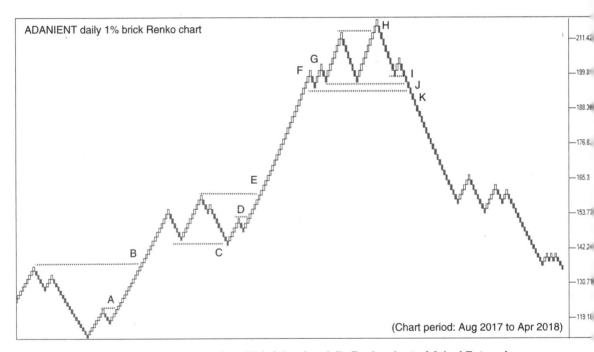

Figure 5.1: **Renko patterns in a 1% brick value daily Renko chart of Adani Enterprises**

Point A is a bullish swing breakout and a higher bottom formation. Point B is where the price went above — and thus invalidated — the previous bearish swing breakout pattern. Point C is a bullish weak breakout, and Point D is a bullish two-back breakout pattern. Point E is where the price went above the previous bearish one-back pattern, and is followed by bullish continuation patterns at points F and G.

The price formed a bearish weak breakout at Point H, followed by bearish two-back at Point I. The price then went below its previous supports and formed a multi-brick bearish breakout at Point J and went below the low of its previous bullish two-back at Point K. Note that points B, E, J and K are breakout patterns that also invalidated previous bullish or bearish patterns.

~

Along with the bearish breakout, the invalidation of previous bullish breakouts in Figure 5.1 was a warning of a serious impending weakness in price. Remember that for a trader the failure of a pattern may lead to the birth of another possible trading pattern. The failure of a bullish pattern indicates weakness while the failure of a bearish pattern indicates strength. The failure of a pattern accompanied by a breakout pattern is key information. In other words, the failure of a bearish pattern along with a bullish breakout patterns shows strength, while the failure of bullish patterns along with bearish breakout patterns is a sign of weakness.

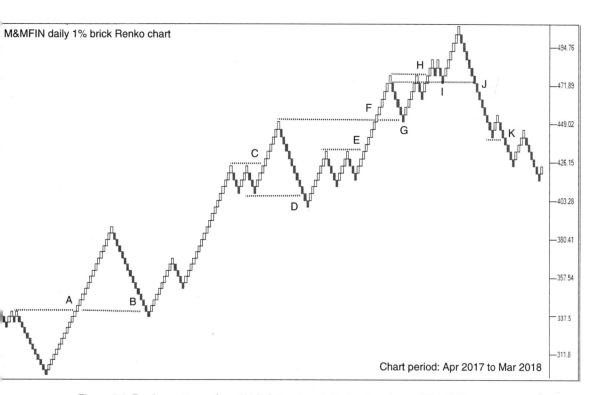

Figure 5.2: **Renko patterns in a 1% brick value daily Renko chart of M&M Finance**

Pattern A is a failure of the bearish zigzag pattern. The price witnessed support at a previous resistance and bounced from the same levels at Point B, which is a 123 pullback, followed by multi-swing breakout at Point C. There is a bullish weak breakout in up trend at Point D, which is followed by a multi-swing breakout at Point E. The bearish swing breakout at Point D got negated at Point F and the price witnessed support at the same levels at Point G. Point I tested the multi-swing breakout of Point H and the price bounced back from those levels. The multi-swing breakout got invalidated at Point J, which also marked a bearish swing engulfing and was followed by a continuation bearish two-back pattern at Point K.

~

So when a pattern fails, or gets invalidated, it can tell you more about the strength of the other side. I am not suggesting that every pattern failure necessarily suggests a stop and reverse (SAR) strategy. What I wish to highlight is that a pattern failure is very important information and reverse trades can sometimes be taken if there is confirmation from other tools. I have witnessed sharp price moves after pattern invalidations, which is why this could be very important information for traders. In fact, it becomes an interesting trade setup when a pattern gets invalidated accompanied by breakouts.

Knowing that "anything can happen" brings a lot of maturity to your trading. Even the strongest and the best tested patterns can fail. Equally, the price can continue to generate unimaginable moves and even achieve "irrational" targets. Market phases can change suddenly when nothing is apparently wrong.

Accepting invalidation will prepare you for shocks and surprises in the market. As a trader, it is important to develop the ability to adapt to such sudden moves or shocks. In such instances, the emotion and extremes are difficult to handle, and the biases built by subjective analysis are difficult to overcome. We can do all types of analysis on the chart — yet that can still fail. But such failure tells us about the strength of the other side. The invalidation must be viewed as a message — and a breakout pattern to the other side can be considered as a possible trading opportunity.

Entrenched opinion is a graveyard of traders. On the other hand, the ability to embrace failure as an opportunity will bring success. Exiting the trade when a pattern fails will result in a losing trade, but it can turn out to be an opportunity to generate bigger returns. Once you realise this, you will be able to overcome the stress and worry of pattern failure. Any such loss should be considered temporary and it comes with an opportunity to succeed in upcoming trades. I recall a dialogue from the Hindi movie, *Baazigar:* "*Kabhi kabhi jeetney ke liye kuch harna bhi padta hai* (In order to win, you have to lose, too, sometimes)." I relate this to trading. I believe money in the markets is made by booking losses, not profits! If losses are cut short, profits will be made.

When a pattern fails, or gets invalidated, the trader's job is to listen to what the price is saying and follow its voice. Many traders, especially newer ones, attempt to prove that they know better — a mindset which is a road to persistent losses in trading. As they say in Gujarati — *Bhav Bhagwan che* (Price is God). By the way, another meaning of *Bhav* in Gujarati is "feeling" or "affection." So, I truly believe that both in life and markets — *Bhav Bhagwan che!*

~

Chapter 6

~

Extensions

W<small>E DISCUSSED EXTENSIONS FROM PRICE PATTERNS EARLIER AS WELL</small> in Chapter 3 and Chapter 4. The logic, rules and calculations of extensions from various patterns were also set out while discussing various patterns. Simply put, extensions can be treated as targets or price projections from those patterns. I studied and researched numerous theories of technical analysis to arrive at targets in Renko charts. To a great extent, extensions in Renko charts are derived from the concepts in point and figure charts. I applied my experience of trading and working with traders over the years to derive rules for plotting extensions, and I want you to understand their logic. Actually, extensions are much more than targets. To be more realistic, there is no precise method of calculating targets. Extensions can be utilized as targets during sideways phases.

Extensions are reference points derived by extending breakouts from different types of patterns. Thus, for example:

- If there is strength in a swing breakout, the price will travel at least up to the length of the retracement.

- If there is a sharp bounce retracing the entire move, as in the case of swing engulfing, the price is expected to move at least up to the first subsequent wave.

- When there is a small retracement, such as comprising of one or two bricks, we extend the entire earlier swing to see if the price moves up to that length.

Thus, there will be extensions from breakout patterns, failures, retracements and follow-throughs. Such extensions give us a picture of open reference points from different price points and structure. Their achievement or non-achievement tells us more about the price setup. Our discussion of invalidation in Chapter 5 is applicable to extensions as well. The achievement, non-achievement or invalidation of an extension, tell us a lot about the strength of the prevailing trend.

There are three types of extensions in a chart:

1 *Open Extensions*: Extensions which have neither yet been achieved nor yet negated.

2 *Negated Extensions*. Extensions which were not achieved and got negated.

3 *Achieved Extensions*: Extensions which are achieved by the price.

Let us have a look at some charts with different extensions.

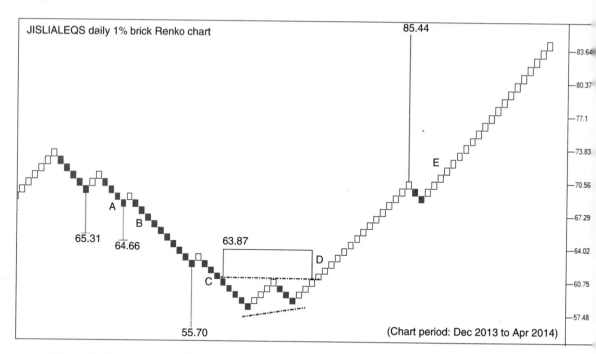

Figure 6.1: **Renko price pattern extensions in a 1% brick value daily Renko chart of Jain Irrigation**

Points A, B and C are bearish continuation patterns that opened up lower extensions. The price formed a higher bottom, and a W formation, at Point D, followed by a bullish continuation pattern at Point E. Note that extensions plotted from points A, B and D are achieved extensions. The extension plotted from Point C got negated, white the extension from Point E is still open.

~

From the perspective of positional and momentum trading, patterns and extensions on the chart in Figure 6.1 can be useful as entry and exit points.

Figure 6.2 is a chart of L&T showing a swing breakout, and one-back and two-back extensions.

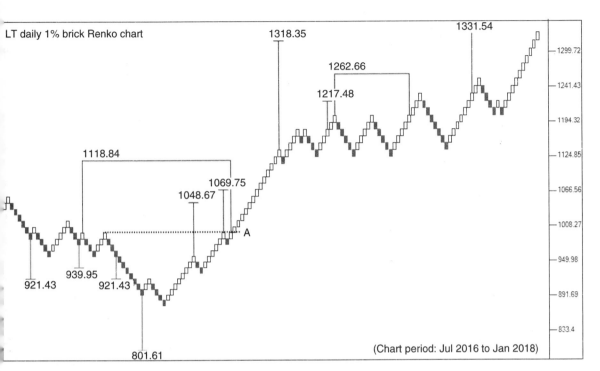

Figure 6.2: **Renko price pattern extensions in a 1% brick value daily Renko chart of L&T. The bearish extensions of ₹801.61 was negated at Point A, where a bullish one-back pattern also got formed.**

~

Do we need to plot all extensions on a chart? The answer is no. You should only plot extensions from patterns that you have understood, or which you can easily identify. But do follow the rules of extensions while plotting them. It is okay if you don't understand a particular pattern and can't plot extensions from it, or if you don't want to follow it. It is perfectly fine if you decide to follow only a few patterns and ignore the rest. Or, say, if you want to trade only continuation patterns and ignore reversals, you can then refer to extensions from those patterns alone.

The idea behind plotting extensions from different patterns is to read the price points which are open on the chart by extending the length of different swing moves — and gather evidence from these patterns to decide the next trading setup.

Extensions plotted from swing engulfing and strike-backs are very dependable because the major ingredient of these patterns is a failure of one side. In essence, then, they mark the victory of the other side which has regained of control. I prefer to plot such extensions, particularly when lower brick value charts are being analysed.

Non-achievement and negation of extensions are equally important events for identifying and understanding the underlying trend and emerging patterns.

As an example, let's review the extensions in Figure 6.3.

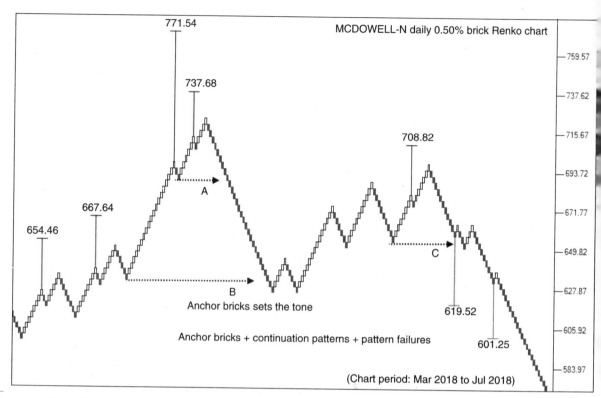

Figure 6.3: **Renko price pattern extensions in a 0.50% brick value daily Renko chart of McDowell-N.**

Swing breakouts have been plotted from one-backs and two-backs. The invalidation of the one-back pattern and extension at Point A indicated an important reversal. The same swing eventually resulted in an invalidation of another bullish extension and pattern at Point B. This series of bearish bricks or anchor bricks sets the bearish tone. The price then witnessed some pullback; the invalidation at Point C of a bullish one-back and extension indicates the strong reversal that was followed by bearish continuation patterns.

~

Figure 6.4 is a one year chart of Bharat Finance showing extensions from different patterns as per the rules we have discussed earlier.

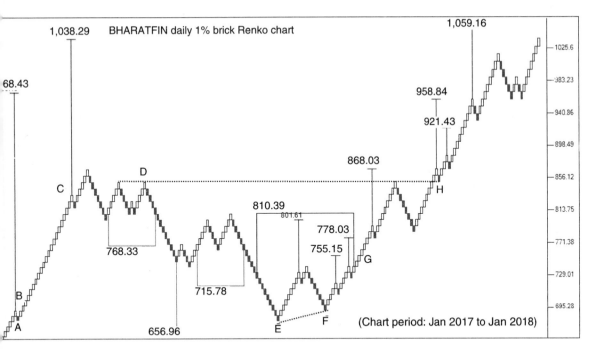

Figure 6.4: **Renko price pattern extensions in a 1% daily brick value Renko chart of Bharat Finance**

Swing breakout retracement extensions are not plotted on this chart. You can observe the one-back, two-back and multi-swing extensions which are plotted. You would notice that bullish extensions got activated at points B and C. The extension plotted from Point C is valid so long as the low at Point A is maintained. Price corrected during the February-May 2017 period and tested the bottom of the brick marked A at Point E. There was a bearish extension that was open at ₹656.96 which was not achieved and instead the price formed a higher bottom at Point F. The price did not produce any bearish swing breakout post that, and the horizontal formation at Point G indicated that the price retracement upto the earlier uptrend was over and that the price had created the base for a further up move.

The bearish extension got negated at Point H when the high price of brick D was broken. Notice that multiple bullish extensions were being achieved by the price before that — a bullish event. Interestingly, I can see a bullish inverted head and shoulders pattern at Point H when the bearish extension got negated. But price patterns at the bottom were early indications of the eventual breakout.

~

Consider the price patterns from point E to H in Figure 6.4. When you see such kind of a base established in any chart, you can plan trade strategies based on continuation price breakouts and extensions post that. There are many achieved extensions on this chart of Bharat Finance in Figure 6.4. Bullish extensions of around ₹968 and ₹1,038 and bearish extension of ₹657 were open at Point E. They remain open on the chart till negated. The subsequent price formations, activation of more extensions, or negation of previous extensions give us hints about the direction of the price. Simple swing breakouts in the direction of the indicated trend can be traded.

Price reversal setups post a negation of the previous bullish extension for bearish reversal pattern, and negation of the previous bearish extension for bullish reversal pattern is an important setup for traders. You can remove achieved extensions from the chart, though I prefer to retain them in order to be able to refer to past price extensions and read the price setup. At times, multiple extensions will open up either from different swings or the same swing. When multiple extensions on the chart point to the same level, it is called an extension cluster. A trader should always give greater importance to these clusters.

Figure 6.5 is a chart of Ceat Ltd.

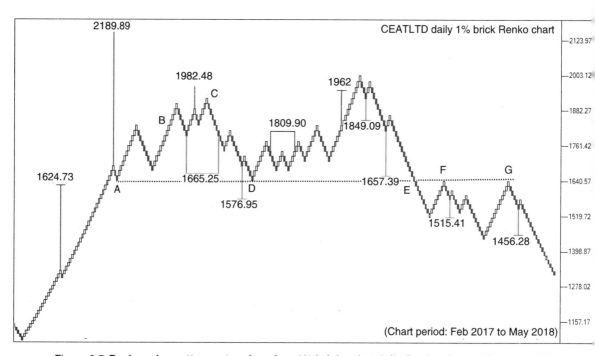

Figure 6.5: **Renko price pattern extensions in a 1% brick value daily Renko chart of Ceat Ltd. All extensions are fairly self explanatory.**

Point A is a bottom of the swing breakout triggered at Point B. Point C is a W pattern which ended up being a bearish ABCD and a bearish weak breakout pattern. This was followed by an M formation and a bearish swing engulfing. Price took support at the bottom of brick A, i.e. at Point D. This became the bottom of a bullish swing engulfing pattern, which got broken at Point E; a major negative event. The price again tested that level at Point F and Point G (polarity principle) but was unable to breach it.

~

If you start noticing these major formations and events on the chart, short-term patterns and extensions can then be traded.

Notice that all the projection technique rules are objective in nature. Hence, once understood, they will not be difficult to implement. The rules of extensions are designed to make the method objective. I don't wish to impose rigid rules for extensions. Once you understand the logic, you can tweak the rules based on your approach. In other words, as well once you understand the logic of these rules, you can design your own rules. Remember, there is no magic in rules; but having a rule does the magic.

Extensions to 123 Pattern

We have discussed extensions from different swing breakout patterns. Let's explore this concept further.

Have a look at Figure 6.6.

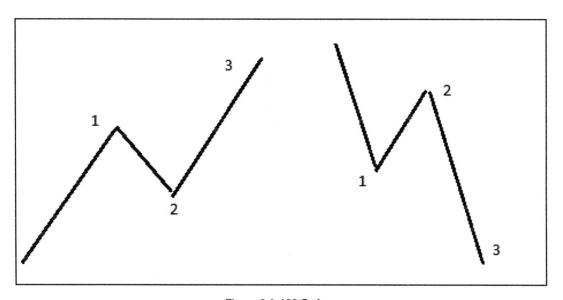

Figure 6.6: **123 Swings**

~

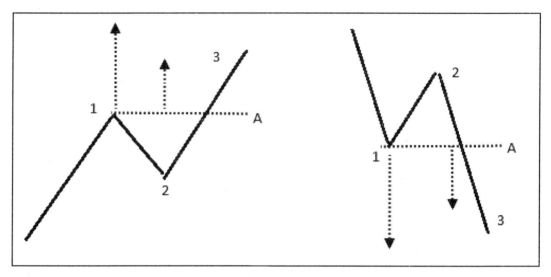

Figure 6.7: **123 formation breakouts**

All price swing breakouts consist of three swings. Since there is a breakout in the third swing, Swing 1 and Swing 3 in Figure 6.6 are impulsive in nature, while Swing 2 is corrective. Or, to keep it simple, all price breakouts are basically 123 formations.

~

We have discussed that we can extend the retracement of a swing breakout. If there is strength in the breakout, the length of Swing 3 should be up to the length of Swing 1. So we can plot the extension from Swing 1, which is an impulse extension while the extension from the retracement is the corrective extension.

Here, again, the achievement or non-achievement of the impulse and corrective extensions from a swing breakout tells us about the strength of the breakout.

Note that it is not necessary for Swing 2 to remain above the bottom of Swing 1 in the case of a bullish swing breakout, or below the top of Swing 1 in the case of a bearish swing breakout because they show the strength of Swing 3 (*see* Figure 6.8).

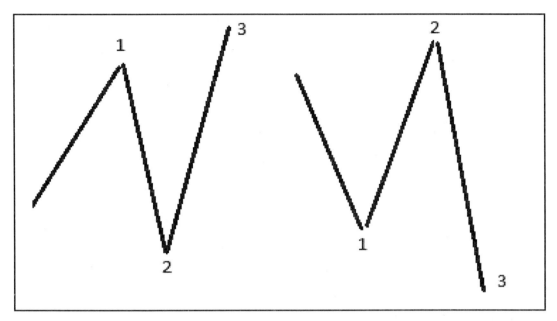

Figure 6.8: **Bullish breakout (left) and bearish breakout (right) on a 123 formation**

The extension from the bullish breakout gets negated if the price falls below the bottom of the pattern that is the lowest point of Swing 1 or Swing 2. Simply, the extension from the bearish breakout gets negated if the price goes above the highest point of Swing 1 or Swing 2.

It is not necessary that Swing 3 has to move up to the Swing 1 extension in the immediate series of bricks. There can be many 123s within a 123, and so there can be many extensions open at one time. This is a tool to read strength and weakness of the markets. In strong trends, extensions of Swing 1 will get achieved. In a sideways trend, there will be more failures. The price will fail to achieve extensions when there is exhaustion in the markets.

~

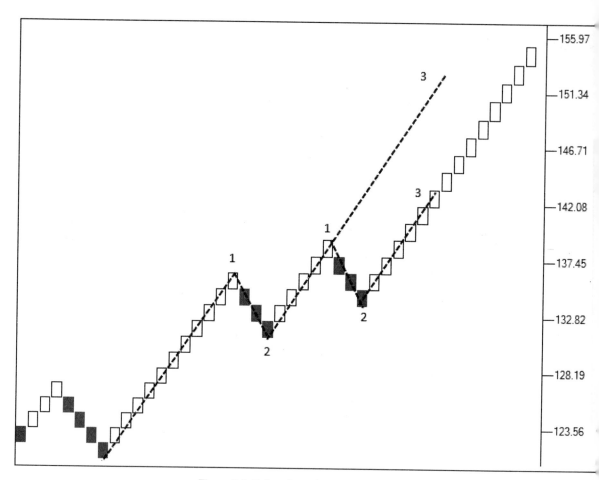

Figure 6.9: **Extensions from 123 patterns**

There are two 123s here. The third swing is on. There is another small 123 within the same larger 123. And every bullish 123 remains active unless the price moves below the bottom of Swing 1, while every bearish 123 will remain active unless the price moves above high of Swing 1.

~

With reference to Figure 6.9, it is not necessary that price move up to Swing 1 in an immediate series of bricks. You can even plot it from a breakout that doesn't get immediately triggered. But to keep it simple and objective, we will plot extensions only from the immediate swing breakouts. Also, there is no point in plotting an extension when the swing move is not significant enough. So as a rule, we will not plot an extension when the breakout or retracement swing move is of less than two bricks.

Basically, then, 123 is a swing breakout pattern. To keep it simple, apply impulse and corrective extensions from swing breakouts. One-back, two-back and swing engulfing are also 123 swing breakout patterns.

Figure 6.10 shows extensions from the patterns shown in Figure 6.9.

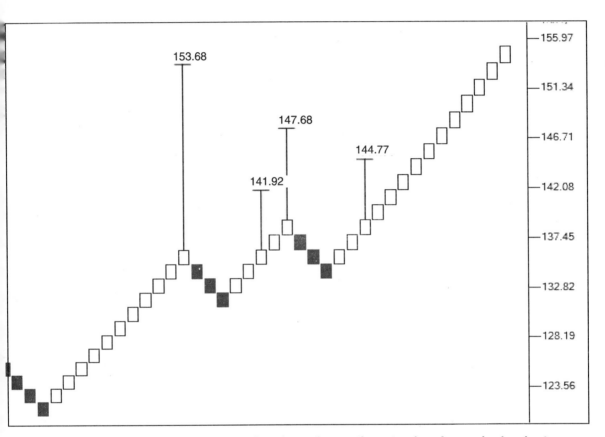

Figure 6.10: **Extension from 123 patterns: Impulse and corrective extensions from swing breakouts are applied on this chart. We discussed corrective extensions from swing breakouts in the Chapter 3. There is no meaning in plotting an extension when the series of bricks comprises less than two.**

∼

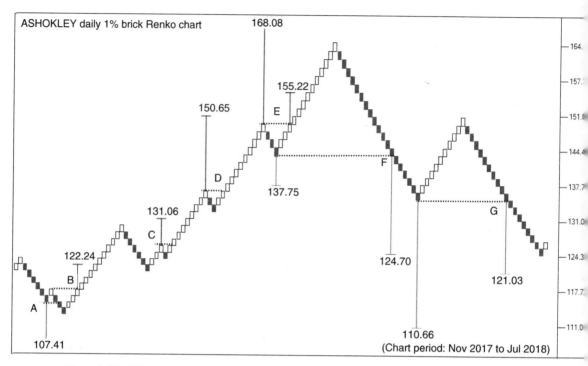

Figure 6.11: **123 pattern extensions in a 1% brick value daily Renko chart of Ashok Leyland**

Pattern A is bearish and is also a one-back swing breakout. Pattern B is a bullish swing breakout but only the corrective extension is plotted from it since the bullish swing is less than two bricks. Pattern C is a bullish one-back and Pattern D is a bullish two-back swing breakout. As the retracement bricks are two or fewer, hence extensions from them are not plotted on the chart. Pattern E is a bullish swing breakout, and impulse and corrective extensions are plotted from it. Patterns F and G are bearish swing breakouts showing both types of extensions.

~

The charts in Figure 6.11 and Figure 6.12 explain 123 pattern extensions.

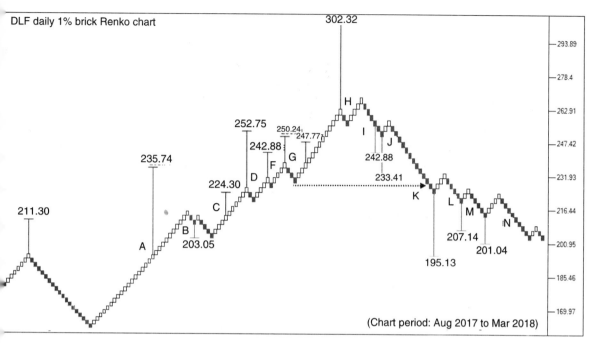

Figure 6.12: **123 pattern extensions in a 1% brick value daily Renko chart of Ashok Leyland**

Pattern A is a bullish swing breakout. The corrective extension is higher than the breakout extension because of a deep retracement. Pattern B is a bearish one-back swing breakout. Pattern C is a swing breakout formation but the impulse extension is not plotted from it because the breakout swing had fewer than two bricks. Pattern D is a bullish two-back and Pattern F is bullish one-back swing breakout showing swing breakout extensions. Pattern G is a bullish swing breakout showing both the extensions. Pattern H is a bullish two-back swing breakout opening an extension of 302+ but it turned out to be a weak breakout and triggered a bearish swing breakout at Point I. Pattern J is a bearish two-back. The extension of 302+ gets negated at Point K that fails the earlier bullish pattern, followed by a bearish swing breakouts at points L, M and N.

~

We had discussed the invalidation of patterns in Chapter 5. Non-achievement of extensions and a reversal pattern is an interesting setup for traders. In essence, what happens is the first time is the failure of a pattern when the price fails to achieve the extension plotted from the pattern and then invalidates the extension going further. People looking for an exhaustion can look for non-achievement of extensions.

This scenario coupled with, or followed by, another breakout pattern are strong trading setups. We plot extensions from the various patterns to check whether the price achieves, a fails to achieve, or negates the extensions. These are important reference numbers on the chart.

For me, 123 is a most simple and effective formation in technical analysis. There must be a reason why the price is breaking the previous swing high or low. There must be a reason why the price could not travel at least up to the first swing. All bullish extensions should get achieved in an uptrend and bearish extensions in a downtrend. If the extensions are not achieved, then there is a reason why they could not be achieved.

You can choose to follow only swing breakout extensions, or extensions from specific patterns. You should form your rules — and then remain consistent. You should also remain sceptical about extensions plotted from large brick values because they are often exaggerated, and have limited practical use.

You can also opt to not plot extensions on the Renko charts. So long as you know that we expect the price to move up to the length of the impulse and corrective swings of the pattern, that's sufficient.

~

Chapter 7

Using Indicators on Renko Charts

THERE ARE NUMEROUS INDICATORS THAT ARE PLOTTED in bar and candlestick charts. All those indicators can equally be used on Renko charts. Technical indicators are calculated on raw price data. With Renko charts, the calculation is applied on Renko brick data and not on the OHLC data. Thus, while the formulae for calculating various indicators remain the same, the logic differs. Remember, there is a difference between ten candles and ten bricks. Ten candles on a daily chart will consist of the prices of ten days, but ten bricks in a Renko chart doesn't necessarily mean that. This makes indicators on Renko charts very interesting.

When you apply indicators, you don't need multiple time frames or brick values. One time frame and a chart with short or medium term parameters would suffice. The more important and popular indicators are explained in this chapter to help you understand the idea and logic of their application on Renko charts. Keep in mind that any type of indicator can be plotted on Renko charts in the same manner and their usual interpretation is applicable to Renko charts as well. I have avoided discussions about their formulae and other basic explanations because these are very popular indicators and tons of literature is available on them online.

Moving Average

Moving average is the most commonly used indicator on all types of charts. It can be applied on Renko charts, too. A 20-day moving average on a bar or candlestick chart calculates the average of the latest prices, usually the closing price. Similarly, a moving average of the last 20 Renko chart bricks can also be plotted by using one price from every brick. I recommend using the closing price of the brick for calculation purposes. **Remember, the closing price of a bullish brick is the high price of that brick and need not be the actual closing price on any given day. Correspondingly, the closing price of a bearish brick is the low price of that brick.**

Figure 7.1 shows a moving average plotted by connecting the closing price of each brick; that is the high prices of bullish bricks and the low prices of bearish bricks. All these prices are connected to draw the one-brick moving average line. The moving average of any length can be calculated in this manner. Thus, the plotting price of a 20-brick moving average will be calculated based on the closing prices of the previous 20 bricks. Each new brick will

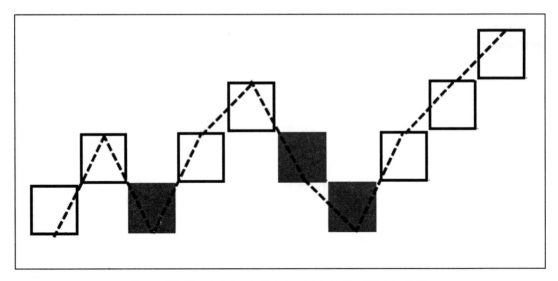

Figure 7.1: **One-brick moving average on the Renko chart**

~

come with a new closing price. The moving average will be calculated in the usual manner by taking only the latest 20 prices into account and successively dropping the first price of the series.

Now let's have a look at Figure 7.2.

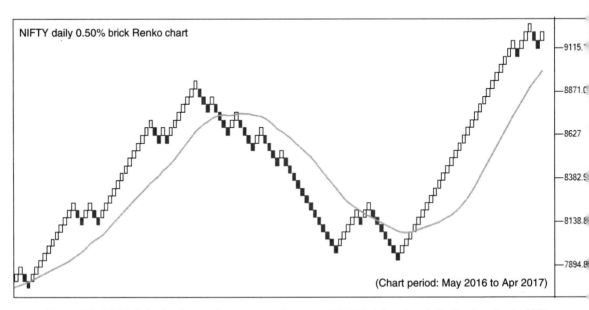

Figure 7.2: **A 20-brick simple moving average line on *a* 0.50% brick value daily Renko chart of Nifty**

~

A bullish brick going above the average line is a bullish breakout, while a bearish brick going below the moving average line is a bearish breakout.

Moving averages on Renko charts can be plotted using simple moving average (SMA), exponential moving average (EMA), weighted moving average (WMA), adaptive moving average (AMA), or any other method of calculating moving averages.

Unlike in other forms of charting, bricks in Renko charts are plotted diagonally (*see* Chapter 1). Also, there could be multiple bricks even for a single day when there is a significant price move. Hence the parameter that we normally use for the various indicators need to be increased. I recommend applying 40-brick exponential moving average on Renko charts for all instruments and all time frames. Also, I prefer exponential moving average in Renko charts because it gives more weight to the more recent bricks.

All methods of reading moving averages are equally applicable to a Renko chart. Moving averages are also useful while designing and back testing trading systems. Hence, a trend can be trailed using a moving average line, patterns can be filtered using moving averages, and pullbacks to average line can be traded with relevant patterns.

An up trend can be objectively defined as a phase when the price is trading above the moving average line and a down trend as a phase when the price is positioned below the moving average line.

Moving Average Trading System with Renko Charts

Here is a basic trading system of using moving averages with Renko charts:

- Trade long when a bullish pattern is formed above the moving average line.
- Exit long trades when a bearish pattern is formed, whether above the MA line or below it. MA filtration is required for entry.
- Trade short when a bearish pattern is formed below the moving average line.
- Cover short trades when a bullish pattern is formed, whether above or below the moving average line.

Have a look at Figure 7.3.

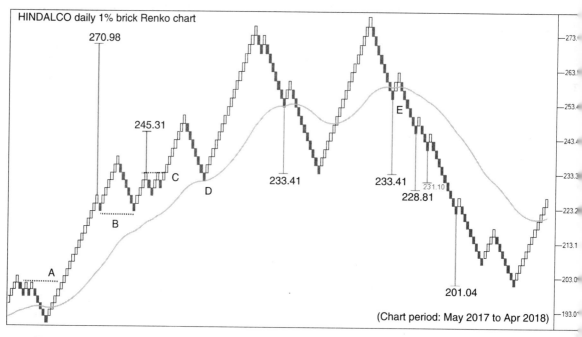

Figure 7.3: **Extensions along with 40-brick exponential moving average line on a 1% brick value daily Renko chart of Hindalco**

All extensions in Figure 7.3 are plotted from bullish one-backs or two-backs above the moving average line — and from bearish one-backs or two-backs below the moving average line. Notice the invalidation of the zigzag pattern at Point A which happens to be above the moving average line. The Renko support formation at Point B above the moving average line provides trend confirmation. Pattern C is a multi-brick breakout occurring above the moving average line. These are patterns we have discussed in the earlier chapters, but when you spot them using the moving average line as a trend filter, you get trend confirmation which adds valuable information. Point D is the culmination of a series of bearish bricks, but the price bounced back up from the moving average line. If you notice carefully, this is a bullish 123 pullback formation. The price entered into the breakout Pattern C and bounced back. Pattern E is a bearish two-back but the price flirted around the moving average and was rejected. A pullback pattern near or above the moving average line is a very effective way of trading and offers affordable initial risk. Pattern E is followed by a series of bearish continuation one-back patterns.

~

Filtering Patterns with Moving Averages

Moving averages on Renko charts are, thus, valuable in pullback formations. Pullback patterns can be filtered by using the moving average line. Here is how. The bullish pullback setups that we discussed in Chapter 3 can be utilised when these occur above the moving average line, and bearish pullback setups can be used when these price below the moving average line. Have a look at Figure 7.4.

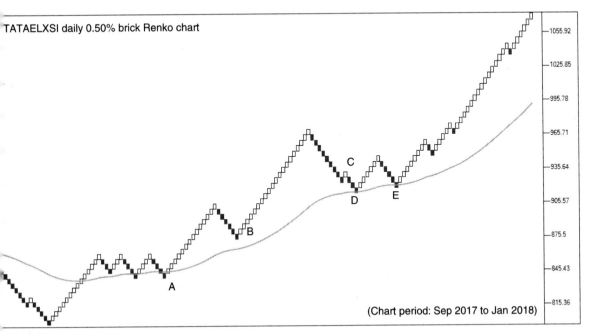

Figure 7.4: **Pullback patterns with a 40-brick exponential moving average line on the 0.50% brick value daily Renko chart of Tata Elxsi**

Pattern A is a Renko support level. The brick reversal going above the moving average line adds to the importance of this support formation. The positive brick reversal at A is followed by multi-brick breakout above the moving average line, confirming the strength of the up trend and the recent support pattern. Pattern B is a bullish retracement pattern which retraced between 25% and 66% of the earlier strong series of bullish bricks. There was a bullish brick reversal above the moving average line, suggesting that the trend was bullish. This adds a lot of context and meaning to the reversal.

Pattern C is a bullish retracement as well but turned out to be a bearish one-back formation. The price was, however, positioned above the moving average line and a bullish weak breakout at Point D at the moving average line was a bullish development. Pattern E is a bullish 123 pullback pattern testing the average line. This is additional confirmation of the pattern and offers a low risk entry opportunity. This was followed by bullish two-back and one-back continuation patterns above the moving average line.

~

Confirmation by the moving average adds to the strength of a pattern. Bullish reversal formations above the moving average line and bearish reversal formations below the moving average line are pullback patterns which are very productive from a trading perspective and are highly recommended.

Like with patterns, the moving average acts as an effective trend identification or trend filter mechanism which completes the trading setup in the case of extensions as well. We can focus on bullish extensions when the price is above the moving average line and on bearish extensions when the price is below the moving average line.

Earlier in the book we discussed the 123 swing extensions. We can use the moving average as a trend filtration tool for extensions and focus on those extensions that are in sync with the moving average. Thus:

- When the price is above the moving average level, we should consider bullish extensions.

- When the price is below the moving average line, we should focus on bearish extensions.

- Extensions plotted against the moving average line are counter-trend extensions.

Figure 7.5 is a chart of Just Dial showing extensions from swing breakouts, filtered with the help of a moving average line.

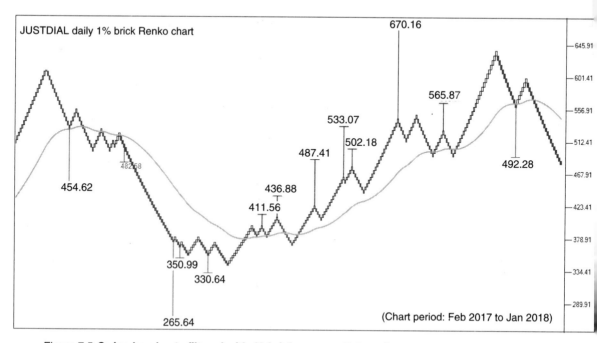

Figure 7.5: **Swing breakouts filtered with 40-brick exponential moving average on the 1% daily brick value Renko chart of Just Dial**

~

Figure 7.6 is a chart of KPIT showing extensions from swing breakouts filtered with the help of a moving average line.

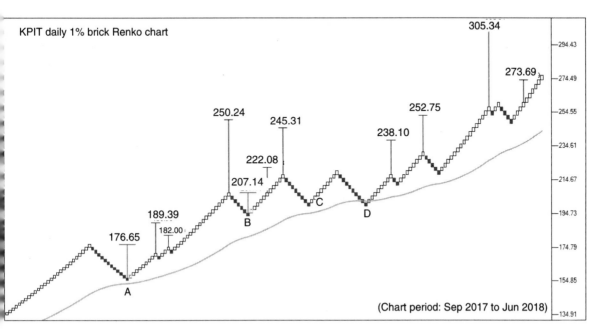

Figure 7.6: **Swing breakouts filtered with a 40-brick exponential moving average on the 1% brick value daily Renko chart of KPIT**

The price is in a clear up trend and can be traded effectively using bullish patterns occurring above the moving average line. Bullish extensions are plotted from bullish swing breakouts; notice that Pattern A and Pattern B are bullish retracement formations. They occurred above the moving average line suggesting that the price had completed the retracement. This was confirmed by a brick reversal in the direction of the established trend. Pattern C is a bullish 123 pullback above the moving average line. Pattern D is a bullish weak breakout near the moving average line, followed by a bullish strike-back follow through which is also a bullish two-back.

~

Moving averages can also be used as a stop loss for riding the trend.

Trading Moving Average and Price Crossovers

Moving average and price crossover is a trading technique which is both simple and success-ful, and one that has stood the test of time. The major problem with this technique on time based charts is the whipsaws that get generated during sideways markets. This problem is effectively dealt with in Renko charts. By default, Renko charts filter out most of the noise, resulting in fewer bricks being formed during a sideways period. The moving average will therefore remain flat during such phases. If your trading is based on patterns instead of bricks and average line crossovers, there will be far fewer trades generated and hence fewer whipsaws. The moving average line goes flat during a brick consolidation period. We have discussed trades based on Renko patterns instead of simple brick and average line crossovers. This method will generate fewer whipsaws and help in controlling the number of trades. Renko chart will produce a series of bricks during a trending phase, ensuring that a trend is not inadvertently missed when following this method.

When and which pattern must be traded can be effectively determined using a trend identification filter such as moving averages. You will notice in the chart in Figure 7.6 that a simple crossover of averages, along with pattern confirmation, could be an effective trading technique here.

In trending markets, moving averages act as an excellent tool to identify pullback trade setups. Weak breakouts, retracements and their variations that touch the moving average line indicate a rejection of the price at the moving average level and confirm the strength of the average line. They also indicate that the correction is complete and that the price is now set to resume its earlier trend.

Trading with Multiple Moving Averages

We can also plot two or three moving averages on Renko charts, in the same way as is done on other charts. Usually, crossovers of moving averages are traded when two or more moving averages are used and this logic is applicable in Renko charts, too.

With two moving averages, the trend is bullish when the short term moving average line crosses above the longer term moving average line, while it is bearish when the short term moving average line falls below the longer term moving average line.

I recommend using 20- and 40-brick exponential moving averages as the short term and the longer term average, respectively. The number of whipsaws that usually occur with the multiple moving average crossover technique during a sideways period gets significantly reduced on a Renko charts due to its inherent construction methodology, and by trading a combination of Renko patterns that we have discussed rather than trading simple crossovers.

Figure 7.7 is a 1% brick value Renko chart of Voltas plotted with 40-brick EMA and 20-brick EMA lines.

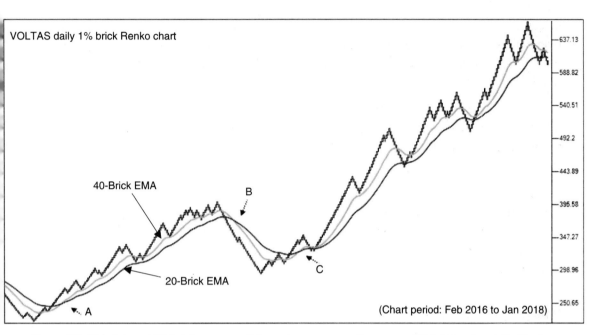

Figure 7.7: **40-brick and 20-brick exponential moving averages lines on a 1% brick value daily Renko chart of Voltas**

Point A is where the 20-brick EMA line crosses above the longer term 40-brick EMA line, which is a bullish crossover. At Point B, the 20-brick EMA line falls below the longer term 40-brick EMA line. This is a bearish crossover. Point C is again a bullish crossover.

~

The crossover method can also be applied on higher brick value charts, for riding the trend particularly for mid cap or small cap stocks. Lower brick values for investment purpose in small cap or midcap stocks might result in over-churning.

Figure 7.8 is a 3% brick value Renko chart of Tata Coffee plotted with 40-brick and 20-brick EMA lines.

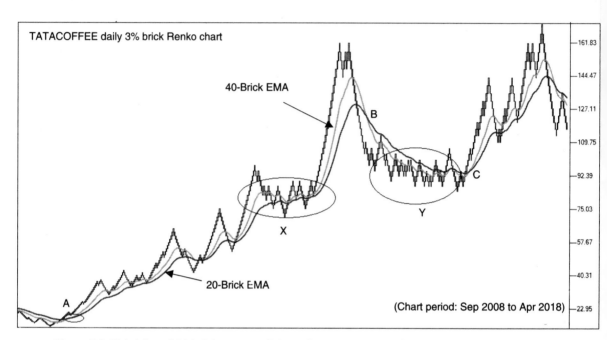

Figure 7.8: **40-brick and 20-brick exponential moving averages on the 1% brick value daily Renko chart of Tata Coffee**

This is a 10-year chart. The bullish crossover that occurred at Point A remained intact till point B. While the period X was a sideways phase but there weren't frequent crossovers of moving average lines that typically generate whipsaws. In fact, there was no whipsaw in the above case. Point C shows another bullish crossover. Notice that during Period Y, when the price was volatile, the moving averages did not produce whipsaws.

~

Figure 7.9 is a chart of Thomas Cook with two moving average lines.

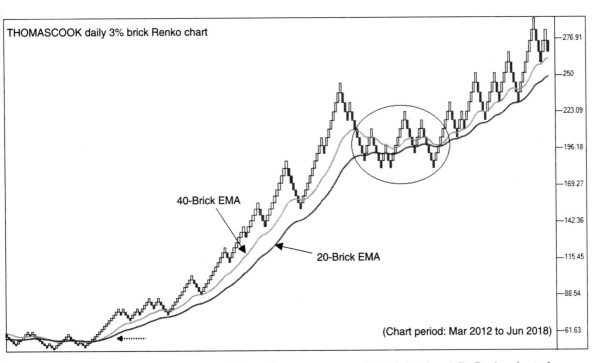

THOMASCOOK daily 3% brick Renko chart

40-Brick EMA

20-Brick EMA

(Chart period: Mar 2012 to Jun 2018)

276.91
250
223.09
196.18
169.27
142.36
115.45
88.54
61.63

Figure 7.9: **40- and 20-brick exponential moving averages on a 3% brick value daily Renko chart of Thomas Cook There is a bullish crossover at the arrow mark, and no bearish crossovers thereafter. But, more importantly, frequent crossovers are absent in the circled area where the price was volatile and stuck in a range. The reduction in whipsaws is an important trait of the Renko method, which increases the productivity of the trades.**

~

The combination of moving averages and chart patterns is an effective trading approach on Renko charts. The parameters given here are not rigid. I am not a great fan of optimising parameters. Just experience and evolve, you may find something better than what I did.

MACD

MACD is a popular indicator which was created by Gerald Appel in the late 1970s. It is a momentum indicator that calculates the difference between two moving averages. The MACD line is calculated by subtracting the longer term average from the shorter term average. An average line of MACD line is, in turn, known as the signal line.

Characteristics of MACD

- When the distance between the shorter term and longer term moving averages reduces, the slope of the MACD line moves down; and it goes up when the distance increases.

- When the MACD line is above the zero line, it means that the shorter term average line is above the longer term average line.

- When the MACD line is below the zero line, the shorter-term average line is below the longer-term average line.

- When the MACD line is above the zero line and the distance between the average lines is increasing, it is a strong bullish trend.

- When the MACD line crosses the signal line downward, it indicates that the distance has started shrinking. The price may correct, or consolidate, when the distance between the averages is reducing.

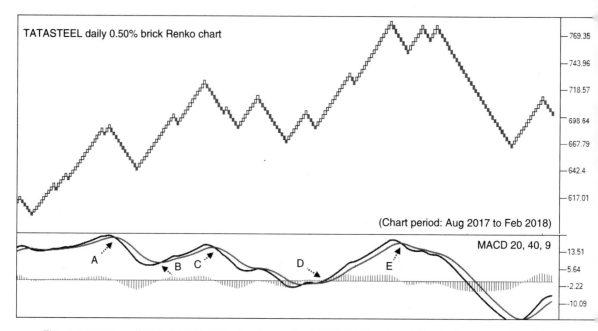

Figure 7.10: **20- and 40-brick MACD indicator on the 0.50% brick value daily Renko chart of Tata Steel**

Point A is shows that though the trend is up, the distance between the shorter term and longer term averages is reducing. Point B is a bullish crossover in an up trend, because the MACD line is above the zero line. Point C is a bearish crossover showing that distance between the two average lines is reducing. Point D is a bullish crossover above the zero line. Point E again shows that the distance between the two average lines is reducing though the trend is up. Notice the Renko resistance formation that occurs simultaneously, indicating impending bearishness.

~

- A strong downtrend is indicated when the MACD line is below the zero line and falling because the distance between the shorter term and the longer term average lines is increasing.

- With regards to the double moving average, the gap, or distance, between the averages can be a significant observation. It is for this reason that I have discussed the MACD indicator.

Figure 7.10 is a chart of Tata Steel with 20- and 40-brick EMA MACD indicator applied on a Renko chart showing crossover signals.

Once you have understood how to read the MACD indicator, you can use it to trade Renko patterns. When the distance between the shorter term and longer term average is increasing, and price is in an up trend, it means that the shorter term trend is accelerating faster than the longer term average. In other words, it means that the price is increasing rapidly. On the other hand, when the price is in a downtrend, it means that the price is falling rapidly. It indicates that while the short term trend is strong but it could be followed by a price or time correction which will be indicated by MACD and signal line crossover.

Let's consider Figure 7.11 which is a 3% brick value chart of Sobha.

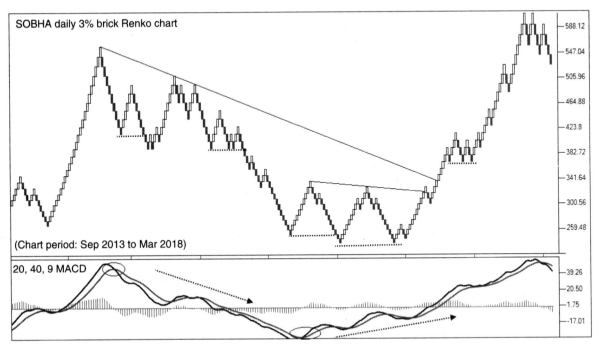

Figure 7.11: 20- and 40-brick MACD indicator on the 3% brick value daily Ronko chart of Sobha developers

~

There are times when markets are stretched and breakouts don't have enough steam. Indicators showing such kind of exhaustion can complement Renko charts.

Over the years I have observed that when the gap between price and the moving average line increases, the market reverts to the mean. It can be either through a correction or a consolidation. This is the reason why I plot the MACD line with the parameters 1 and 40. The 1-period average is just a proxy for the actual price. Calculated this way, the MACD line calculates the difference between the price and average line. The crossover of the MACD line and signal line alerts us to that there is a possibility of a change of trend, which could either be a correction or consolidation.

Figure 7.12 is a Renko chart plotted with 1, 40, 9 MACD.

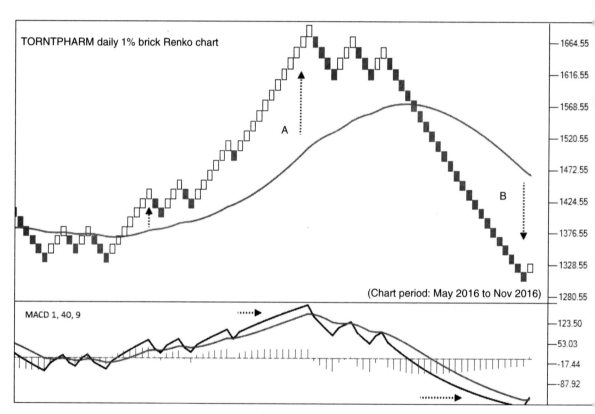

Figure 7.12: **1- and 40-brick MACD indicator on the 1% brick value daily Renko chart of Torrent Pharma**

In Zone A, the price moved far away from the moving average shown by the MACD line. Similarly, Zone B shows that the price moved away from the moving average during this downtrend.

~

A negative crossover between the MACD line and the signal line tells us that the difference between the price and the average line is reducing and the price might therefore attempt to revert to the mean. Remember, MACD line hovering around the zero line shows a consolidation phase. A negative crossover of MACD and signal line shows exhaustion which is applicable to a trending phase — while the MACD line moving away from the zero line shows a trending phase.

Figure 7.13 is a chart of SRF showing 1, 40, 9 MACD indicator.

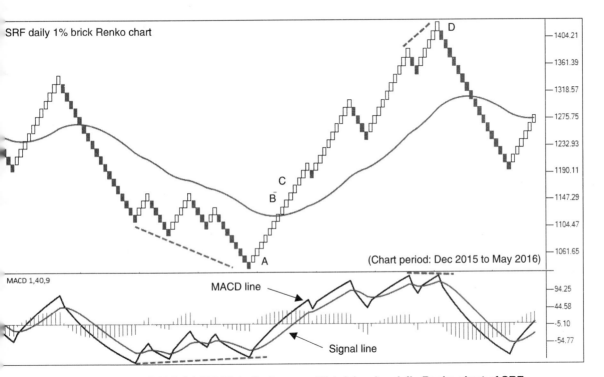

Figure 7.13: 1- and 40-brick MACD indicator on a 1% brick value daily Renko chart of SRF

In Zone A, the price is falling but the MACD indicator is not falling; rather, it made higher lows. This is a classic case of positive divergence between the price and indicator, wherein the price marks new lows while the indicator doesn't. The price then reversed, and a swing engulfing can be seen at Point B, and also invalidated a bearish two-back at Point C. This was followed by bullish continuation patterns. At Point D, the price made a new high but the indicator didn't, indicating a negative divergence. This was followed by a bearish crossover of MACD and the signal line.

～

I always stress on the logic of indicator setups.

When there is a positive divergence between the MACD and price, it means that the distance between the averages at the time of the new low has reduced compared to that at the previous low.

A negative divergence means that the distance between the price and the average has reduced compared to what it was at the previous high. This points to weakness of the new high or low. A signal line crossover after such a divergence indicates that all is not well. Renko price patterns can help in trading such observations.

This concept of price and average line distance is also known as disparity.

Disparity index is a percentage measurement for the position of the closing price relative to its moving average. This concept was introduced by Steve Nison in his book, *Beyond Candlesticks*.

Donchian Channel

Donchian channel is an indicator created by Richard Donchian that plots upper and lower bands of price based on the highest high and the lowest low of the last "n" periods. It can be plotted on Renko charts. If we plot a 40-period Donchian channel on a Renko chart, there will be three Donchian band lines plotted on the chart. The upper band shows the highest high over the last 40 bricks and the lower band will show the lowest low over the previous 40 bricks. The middle band is the average of both.

Thus, when the upper band of the 40-brick Donchian channel rises, it shows that a new high has been made over the last 40 bricks. When it falls below the 40-brick Donchian channel, it means that a new 40-brick low has been made. This makes a good trading setup with a Renko chart. There should be an important reason why an instrument is making a 40-brick high or low, right?

Observe the price breakouts shown at arrow marks in the 0.50% brick value chart of Hindustan Petroleum in Figure 7.14.

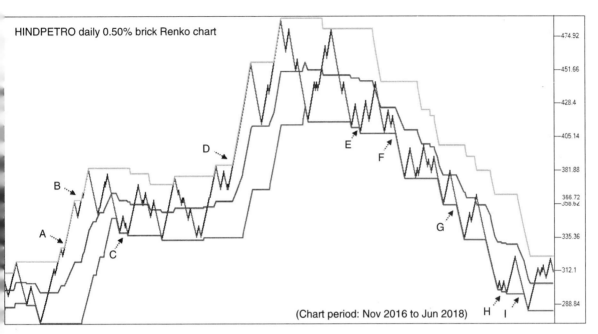

Figure 7.14: **40-brick Donchian channel on the 0.50% brick value daily Renko chart of Hindustan Petroleum**

The bullish swing breakouts happened when the Donchian channel upper band was also rising, indicating a new 40-brick high, while bearish swing breakouts were marked when Donchian channel lower band was falling, indicating the formation of a new 40-brick low.

~

We can say that the price is in a bullish zone when it is in between the middle band and the upper band. Correspondingly, it is in a bearish zone when it is in between the middle band and the lower band.

- You can trade simple bullish continuation Renko breakouts when the price is in the bullish zone.

- And trade bearish breakouts when the price is in the bearish zone.

- More importantly, you must not trade breakouts when both the bands are flat, which means when the price is in between the 40-brick high and low, i.e. when it is in a range bound mode.

- You can use mean reversion methods when the instrument is in a sideways mode.

For breakouts, find an instrument where the trend is established. Your trading performance will be better when you trade instruments with established trends.

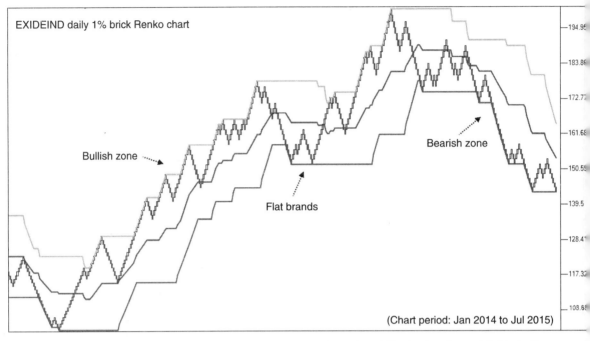

EXIDEIND daily 1% brick Renko chart

Bullish zone

Flat brands

Bearish zone

(Chart period: Jan 2014 to Jul 2015)

Figure 7.15: **40-brick Donchian channel on a 0.50% brick value daily Renko chart of Exide India**

~

Figure 7.15 is a chart of Exide India showing price patterns in both bullish and bearish zones.

Renko chart patterns are very potent when used along with Donchian channels.

At times, the price makes a new high but doesn't sustain and either gives a false breakout, or reverses, indicating the weakness of the new high, or low, that is being made.

Have a look at the 1% brick value Renko chart of Grasim Industries in Figure 7.16.

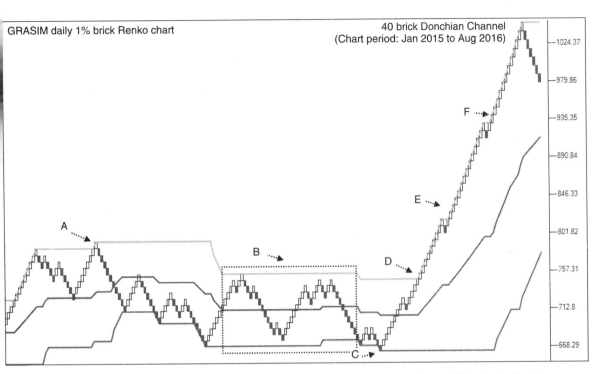

GRASIM daily 1% brick Renko chart

40 brick Donchian Channel
(Chart period: Jan 2015 to Aug 2016)

Figure 7.16: **40-brick Donchian channel on a 1% brick value daily Renko chart of Grasim Industries**

Point A is where a new 40-brick high is marked but the bearish weak breakout that formed shows that the price could not sustain the high. B is a no-breakout zone since the price bands are flat. Point C is where the price forms a bearish 40-brick low. Then there was a bearish zigzag, followed by a bullish weak breakout reversal that shows that the weak participants are out and the price has marked a significant low. It was followed by a multi-brick breakout that invalidated the bearish zigzag. Point D is where the price gained strength and marked a 40-brick high. This was followed by a series of bullish bricks. Point E and Point F are where price formed bullish one-back continuation patterns in the environment of rising bands thus showing a strong trending zone.

~

The methods described above are applicable on all brick values and instruments. I recommend higher brick values for medium term or long term investments in mid caps and small caps. For investments, ride the trend unless the price slips into a bearish zone. You should trade the bullish continuation patterns when the stock is in the bullish zone.

Figure 7.17 is a 3% brick value chart of Eros Media.

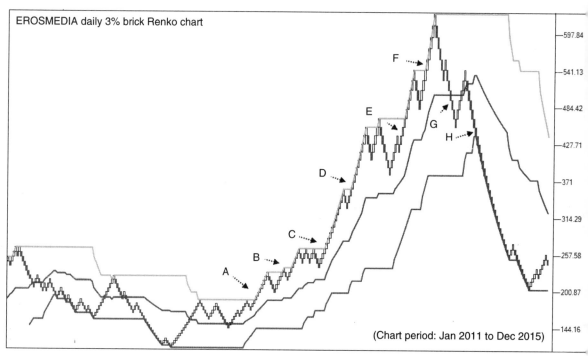

Figure 7.17: **40-brick Donchian channel on a 3% brick value daily Renko chart of Eros Media**

Notice that the upper band was falling until Point A, where the price triggered a 40-brick breakout and entered the bullish Donchian zone. It also formed a bullish two-back. Point B is also a bullish two-back. Point C is a multi-brick swing breakout. Point D is a bullish two-back. Point E is a bullish one-back with the price in a bullish zone. Point F is a bullish swing breakout. Point G is where the bearish one-back and the bearish strike-back follow through swing falls below the middle band. Point H is a new 40-brick low.

~

Bollinger Bands[*]

Bollinger bands is a wonderful innovation by John Bollinger in the field of technical analysis. Bollinger bands are standard deviation bands calculated from a moving average. Since we can plot moving averages on Renko charts, it is also possible to plot Bollinger bands alongside. If we plot 20-brick average with two standard deviation Bollinger bands on Renko charts, then three channel lines, or bands, will appear on the chart. The middle band is the moving average line, the upper and lower bands are two standard deviation lines above and below the middle band, respectively. The bands adjust with the volatility and contain the majority of the price action within them. There are many ways of using the bands. The book

---

[*] Bollinger Bands® is a registered trademark of John Bollinger.

Bollinger on Bollinger Bands, authored by John Bollinger himself is a must read to understand Bollinger bands in detail.

The major difference in using Bollinger bands on Renko charts is that the standard deviation is calculated from brick averages, not price bars. Also, Bollinger bands and Renko patterns complement each other.

All the usual methods of reading Bollinger bands are relevant in Renko charts. The 40-brick bands with two standard deviations are my preferred parameters on Renko charts.

There are two particularly important observations regarding Bollinger bands when applied to Renko charts. The strategy should be to trade the bullish swing breakout when the upper band is rising and trade the short bearish swing breakouts when the lower band is falling. Rising upper bands, and falling lower bands indicate trends. Continuation Renko patterns at band extremes are useful methods of trading such trends.

Another important observation is with regard to narrow bands, i.e. a band squeeze. This happens when the price trend is either sideways or horizontal. Figure 7.18 is a Renko chart of Hindalco with Bollinger bands plotted on it.

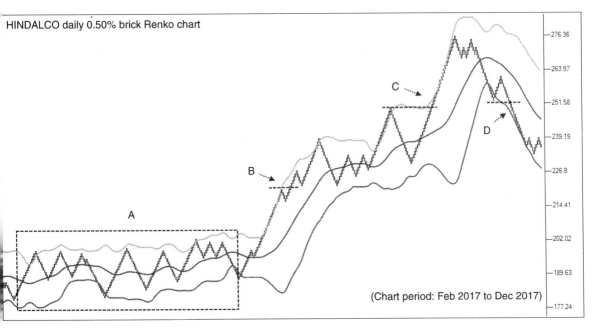

Figure 7.18: **40, 2 Bollinger bands on a 0.50% brick value daily Renko chart of Hindalco**

Zone A is when the distance between the bands was narrowing and the price was in a horizontal range. Points B and C are bullish swing breakouts at the upper band, while Point D is a bearish swing breakout at the lower band.

~

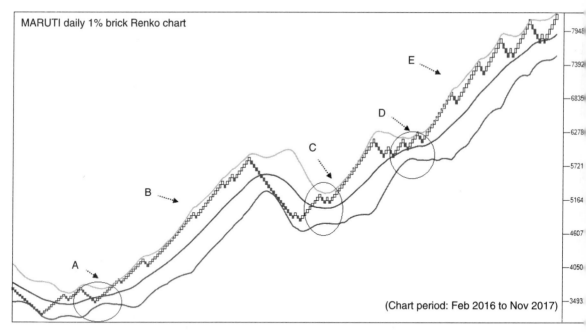

Figure 7.19: **40, 2 Bollinger bands on a 1% brick value daily Renko chart of Maruti. Points A, C and D are swing breakouts subsequent to a band squeeze. Points B and E are continuation breakouts near the rising upper band.**

~

The squeeze between the bands is a very interesting setup. On a Renko chart, a squeeze shows us that the price is consolidating, and that there is no clear trend. The pattern that emerges in a Renko chart, post the squeeze, is an interesting trading setup. This is well bought out in Figure 7.19, which is a chart of Maruti with Bollinger bands.

Bollinger Bandwidth

At times, the difference between the Bollinger bands is difficult to read visually. Bollinger bandwidth is an indicator that calculates the difference between the two bands. A rising bandwidth line means that the difference or gap between bands is widening; when the bandwidth is falling, it means that the gap between the two bands is reducing.

Figure 7.20 is a chart of JSW Steel along with Bollinger bands and also Bollinger bandwidth plotted on it.

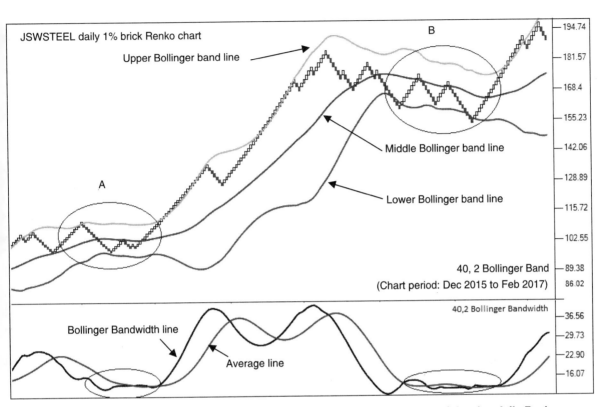

Figure 7.20: **40, 2 Bollinger bands and Bollinger bandwidth plotted on a 1% brick value daily Renko chart of JSW Steel**

Bollinger bandwidth is plotted along with the average line in the lower panel in order to read the crossover of the two lines. A crossover of the average line and the bandwidth line should be coupled with Renko pattern for trade confirmation. Points A and B in the upper panel are narrow band patterns that can be read using Bollinger bandwidth indicator. The flat Bollinger bandwidth line towards the right end of the lower panel indicates a squeeze in price.

~

The crossover of the bandwidth line and the average line doesn't necessarily mean a bullish breakout. It simply means the bands can expand but the direction of the breakout could be either up or down. For this reason, the presence of a Renko price pattern is important. A crossover of the bandwidth indicator with its a moving average line, and a Renko price breakout makes a potent trading setup.

Figure 7.21 is a 1% chart of Just Dial plotted along with Bollinger bandwidth.

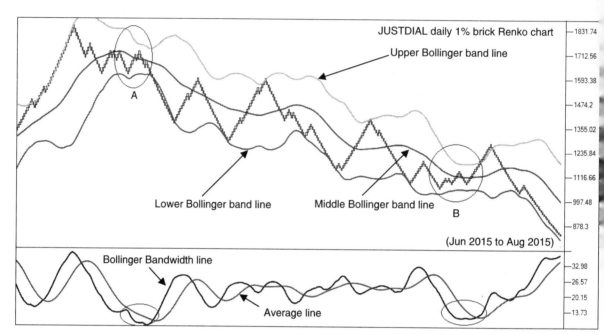

Figure 7.21: **40, 2 Bollinger bands and Bollinger bandwidth (lower panel) on a 1% brick value daily Renko chart of Just Dial**

At Point A (upper panel), the price generated a bearish swing breakout post flat bands. The crossover suggested either band expansion or an impending trending move.

At Point B, the first breakout was bullish but the price reversed immediately thereafter and triggered a bearish breakout and a sharp fall. Following price patterns along with the indicators which we have discussed proves helpful in such cases. You should look out for continuation Renko patterns at lower band extremes.

~

Relative Strength Index (RSI)

Developed by J. Welles Wilder, Relative Strength Index (RSI) is perhaps the most popular and widely used of all indicators in technical analysis. It is possible to plot RSI on Renko charts. The formula for its calculation remains the same but the underlying logic differs.

Below is the formula of calculating relative strength index:

RSI = 100 − 100 ÷ (1 + RS)
Where RS = Average gain / Average loss

A 14-day RSI is the most widely used setting for plotting RSI. This setting takes closing prices of the previous 14 sessions into account. RSI is a momentum oscillator that moves between 0 and 100. If an instrument has had more positive changes, then the RSI would be higher while if it has had more negative changes, the RSI would be lower. The level of equilibrium is 50. The corresponding RSI on Renko charts would get plotted based on 14 bricks, instead of 14 days.

Renko patterns can complement all other methods of reading RSI, such as overbought or oversold zones, mid-value crossovers, divergences, trend lines, and range rules. The trades on Renko charts are however considered based on Renko patterns. Sticking to the same parameter of 14 is fine, though it doesn't make much difference if we use some other number around that.

On Renko charts, readings of 80 and 20 could be used as overbought and oversold levels. Divergence on RSI is the most useful technique in these charts.

■ A negative divergence is said to occur when the price makes a new high but the indicator does not.

■ Correspondingly, a positive divergence occurs when the price makes a new low but the indicator does not.

The Renko technique helps determine the trend and ride it effectively. Renko chart pattern confirmation provides an opportunity to effectively trade the reversal setups suggested by divergences.

Figure 7.22 that follows is a chart of Tata Steel with 14, 9 RSI applied on it.

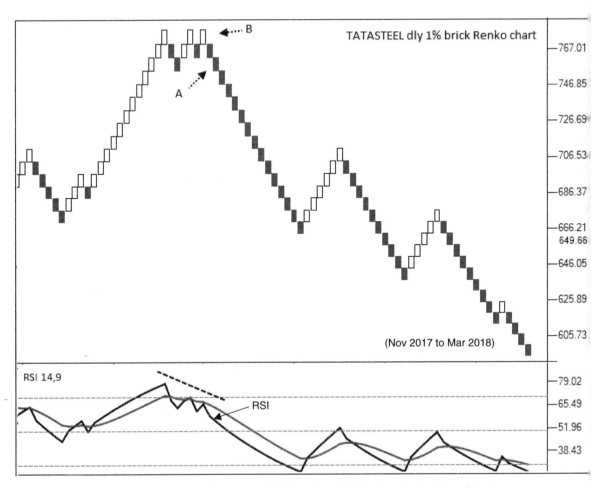

Figure 7.22: **14, 9 RSI on a 1% brick value daily Renko chart of Tata Steel**

Point A is a bearish zigzag breakout when the RSI is falling. A triple top resistance shown by the arrow at Point B indicates supply at those levels, and it's after this resistance that the price went into a decline.

~

An oversold indicator with a positive divergence and a bullish pattern, or an overbought indicator with a negative divergence and a bearish pattern, constitute setups for logical and affordable entry, with all the ingredients of an efficient reversal setup. After entry, Renko techniques should be followed to ride the trend and derive extensions.

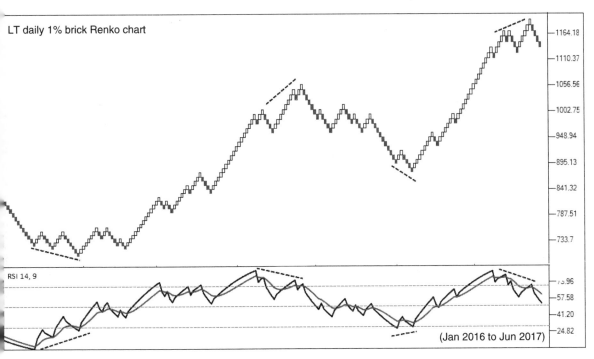

Figure 7.23: **14, 9 RSI on a 1% brick value daily Renko chart of L&T.**

~

Figure 7.23 is a chart of L&T with RSI divergences marked.

At times, divergences and other interpretations of an indicator do fail. At times, patterns too will fail. Using both in conjunction can provide greater confidence. In all cases, price patterns are always supreme.

Trade Setup

You can develop trading systems by combining the indicators we have discussed. Have a look at Figure 7.24 as an example.

The chart reading method using the RSI indicator discussed above can be applied using any other momentum indicator. The list of indicators can be lengthy and never ending. The message here is: Renko is a charting method where every indicator can be applied. You will keep coming across new indicators and the rules associated with them. Remember that you can use all of them with Renko charts as well. The only thing that you need to keep in mind is that the indicators be calculated on Renko bricks. Hence, though their formula is the same but the logic is bit different. Renko price patterns and extensions, along with indicators, can help in creating different types of trading setups which are applicable on all brick values and time frames.

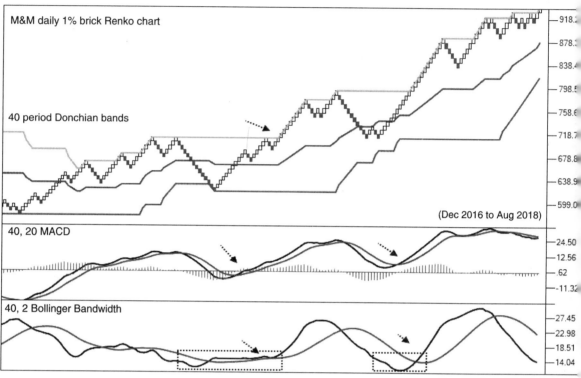

Figure 7.24: **40-brick Donchian channel, MACD and Bollinger bandwidth on a 1% brick value daily Renko chart of M&M**

Donchian channels applied on a Renko chart show 40-brick highs or lows. Rising upper band shows the 40-brick high and a falling lower band shows the 40-brick low. MACD shows the position of the shorter term moving average *vis-à-vis* the longer term one. And the Bollinger bandwidth helps in identifying any breakout from the narrow bands.

~

   While we have discussed many indicators, the basic principle is that it is the Renko patterns that should trigger a trade and not the indicators. When we have the luxury of objective price patterns, why should we trade with indicators which are derivatives of the price itself. When we trade price patterns, there are clear exit rules which makes trading profitable over time because it allows us to go wrong, keep losses small, and ride the big winners.

A word of caution: Different indicators capturing the same information on the chart should not be used that is just redundancy.

~

Chapter 8

Unique Renko Indicators

THE INDICATORS THAT WE HAVE DISCUSSED SO FAR are traditional indicators of technical analysis. We will now study some indicators that are unique to the Renko world.

Brick Count Indicator

The brick is an important property of Renko charts. Isn't it logical that if the number of bullish bricks over a look-back period is higher than the number of bearish bricks, it is then a bullish sign? Similarly, if bearish bricks over the look-back period are more in number than bullish bricks, it is a sign of weakness. This was my logic behind creating brick indicators on Renko charts.

It is possible to calculate the number of bullish and bearish bricks over a given look-back period. I call it the Brick Count Indicator. Figure 8.1 is a Renko chart showing the brick count indicator lines.

It is only logical that a bullish phase would produce more bullish bricks than bearish bricks, while a bear phase should produce more bearish bricks than bullish ones. This is thus a sensible indicator which clearly brings out where one side has gained control over the other. As we discussed earlier, this property can help us ascertain which setups can be traded. Trading patterns and pullback setups in the direction of the trend is always an effective strategy. A trend is established when the distance between the two lines tracking the numbers of bullish and bearish bricks widens while a congestion is indicated when the lines converge.

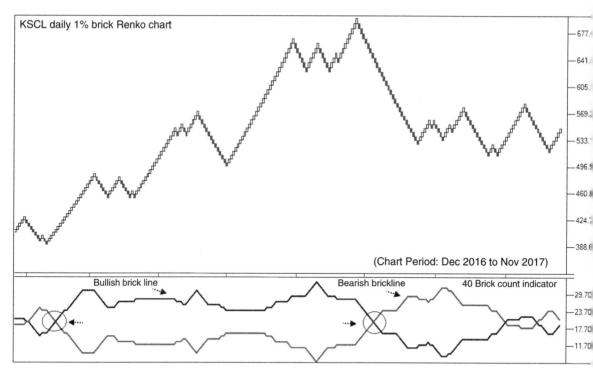

Figure 8.1: **40-brick count indicator in a 1% brick value daily Renko chart of KSCL**

The two lines in the lower panel show the number of bullish bricks and the number of bearish bricks, respectively. It is very logical to interpret that when the bullish brick line is above the bearish brick line, it means that the number of bullish bricks is greater than the number of bearish bricks. The logical interpretation in such a case is that the bulls are creating more bricks than are the bears. The circled areas in the chart show crossovers where the bullish, or the bearish, brick prints started taking over the other side.

~

Brick Zone

Bullish patterns can be traded when the brick count indicator is in a bullish zone while bearish patterns can be traded when it is in a bearish zone. For better visual appearance, the brick zone indicator is plotted by subtracting the number of bearish bricks from the number of bullish bricks. The formula for plotting the brick zone indicator, in histogram style, is given below.

Brick Zone = Number of Bullish Bricks − Number of Bearish Bricks

The brick zone indicator oscillates around the zero line and can also become negative. It will show a positive value when the number of bullish bricks is greater than the number of bearish bricks — and will turn up a negative value when the number of bullish bricks is lesser than number of bearish bricks. The indicator is called a zone because it displays positive and negative zones clearly. A positive zone is when the net brick count is either positive or above the zero line and negative zone is when it falls below the zero line.

The following are the three important readings of the brick zone indicator on a Renko chart.

Zone

There are more bullish brick prints than bearish prints when the indicator is above the zero line, thus indicating an uptrend.

When the indicator is below the zero line, the number bearish prints is more than the number of bullish prints and, hence, it is a downtrend.

Trading bullish continuation patterns in a bullish zone, and bearish continuation patterns in a bearish zone is a sensible trading approach.

Crossover

Bulls are taking over from the bears when the price crosses the zero line upward from below. Correspondingly, it should be understood that the bears have started dominating the proceedings when the price falls below the zero line. Hence, such crossovers are an important reading on this indicator.

Caution

Though price may be in a bullish zone, caution is advised when the indicator starts falling as this indicates that the number of bullish bricks has started decreasing.

Correspondingly, when the brick zone indicator starts rising from below the zero line, it means that bulls are trying to regain control. It doesn't necessarily mean reversal; Renko reversal formations can provide further confirmation.

Figure 8.2 that follows is a chart of Engineers India with a 40-period brick zone indicator.

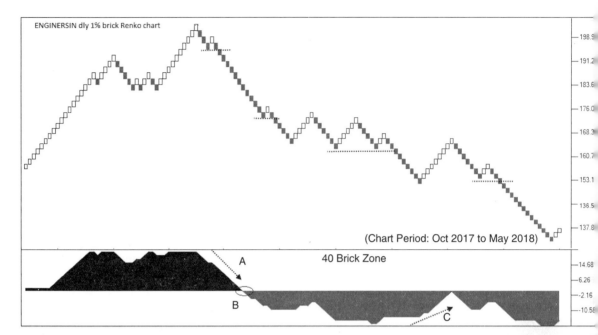

Figure 8.2: **40-brick zone indicator in a 1% brick value daily Renko chart of Engineers India**

During phase A (lower panel), the price was in a bullish zone but the indicator had started falling. The confirmation came from a Renko pattern when it triggered a bearish one-back, which is marked on the chart (upper panel).

B is a bearish crossover of the brick zone. There are continuation bearish patterns marked on the Renko chart when the price was subsequently in the bearish zone.

During C, the indicator was rising, showing that the number of bearish bricks was diminishing but the confirmation from Renko patterns was still lacking. In fact, the Renko chart gave another bearish two-back continuation pattern indicating further down side.

~

Figure 8.3 that follows is a 1% chart of L&T Finance Holdings Ltd.

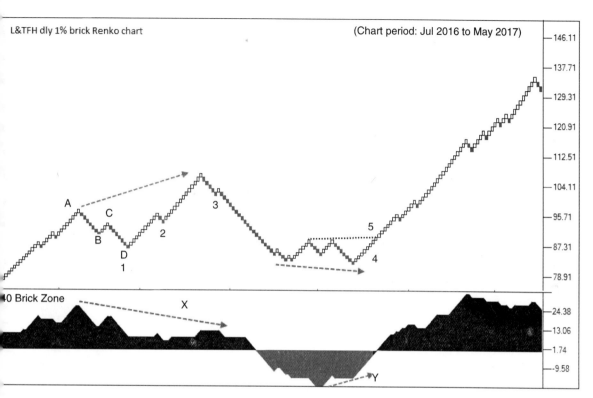

Figure 8.3: **40-brick zone indicator (lower panel) in a 1% brick value daily Renko chart of L&T Finance Holdings**

Arrows in the chart show that the brick zone indicator was falling (during period X in the lower panel) even when price was rising (during period A in the upper panel) and the Indicator started rising (during period Y in the lower panel) even when the price was making a new low. This is a divergence but Renko patterns can help from the practical trading perspective.

A bullish ABCD got formed at Point 1 (in the upper panel) when the indicator was falling though it was still in the bullish zone. The price went up and formed a bullish two-back in the uptrend at Point 2. There is a bearish one-back at Point 3, when this indicator also suggested that bears were trying to dominate. At Point 4, as the indicator began rising while in the bearish zone, there was some hint from a bullish weak breakout pattern. But a multi-brick breakout at Point 5 provided strong confirmation. Bulls regained control and then produced multiple continuations patterns in the bullish zone.

~

Can an average line be applied to the brick zone to read the crossovers? This thought led me to create the brick indicator.

Brick Indicator

Brick indicator is a brick zone indicator, plotted not in histogram style but instead with a moving average plotted along with it.

Figure 8.4 is a chart of PEL with a 40-period brick indicator line and 40-period moving average line of the brick indicator.

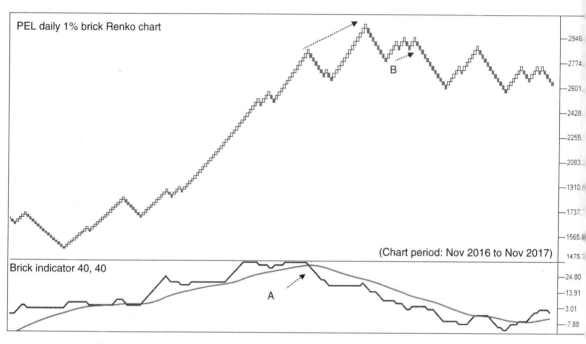

Figure 8.4: **40, 40-brick indicator on a 1% brick value daily Renko chart of PEL**

There was a bearish crossover at Point A (in the lower panel) indicating weakness, though the price (upper panel) was rising during that period. A multi-brick bearish breakout was triggered at Point B (upper panel).

~

When the price forms a new high, or a new low, after such an indicator crossover, there is the possibility of it being a weak high or weak low, at least in the short term.

Figure 8.5 that follows is a chart of Arvind Ltd.

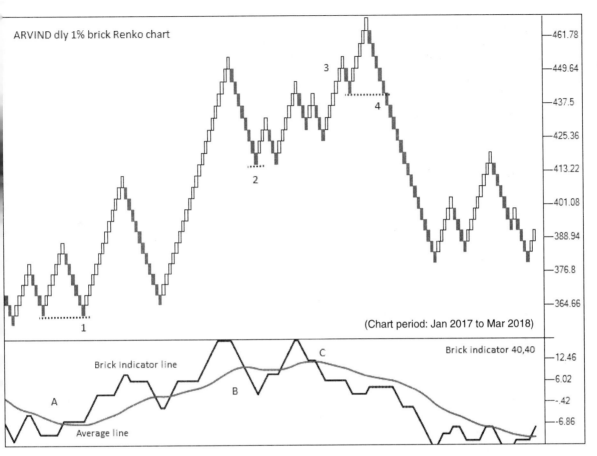

Figure 8.5: **40, 40 brick indicator in a 1% brick value daily Renko chart of Arvind Ltd**

There was a bullish crossover at Point A (in the lower panel) and a bullish Renko support pattern at Point 1 (upper panel) followed by a breakout. There was a bearish crossover at Point B but there was no confirmation from a Renko pattern. There was a bearish crossover again at Point C (lower panel), but the price continued to move up. There was a sharp reversal that produced bearish swing engulfing at Point 4 (upper, i.e. price panel).

~

The parameter of 40 is just a suggestion or an example and not a rigid rule. The brick indicator can be plotted using any other number.

Let's now move from a price indicators to a group of broader market indicators.

Breadth

Breadth is the most logical and useful indicator of market sentiment. Indicators applied on price charts help in identifying either momentum or extreme zones of a particular instrument. For example, we can apply an indicator on Nifty and measure the price exhaustion or momentum of the index. Breadth indicators are, however, not calculated on the price of an instrument. Instead, they evaluate the market sentiment by measuring the number of stocks in a sector, or a group, that satisfy some given criteria. There are several types of breadth indicators available. One dimensional charts such as P&F, Renko or line break are suitable for breadth indicators due to the objectivity that they offer. A. W. Cohen invented the first breadth indicator of markets using one-dimensional P&F chart signals during 1955 which is known as bullish percent. Jeremy Du Plessis introduced P&F X-percent breadth indicator in his book *The Definitive Guide to Point and Figure.*

One of the unique features of Renko charts is that the price will always be either bullish or bearish. It is bullish when the latest brick is bullish and bearish when latest brick is bearish.

Bullish brick percent breadth indicator is arrived at by measuring the number of stocks where the latest brick is bullish and dividing it by the total number of stocks in that particular group or sector.

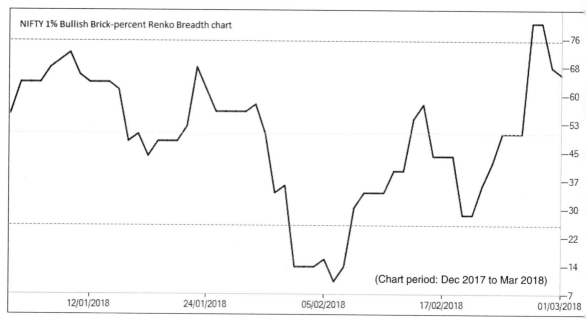

Figure 8.6: **Bullish brick percent indicator of Nifty's group of fifty stocks that calculates the percentage of Nifty stocks trading on the bullish brick in a 1% brick value Renko chart**

~

Figure 8.6 is the bullish brick percent indicator of Nifty's group of fifty stocks that calculates the percentage of Nifty stocks trading in the bullish brick on a 1% brick value Renko chart.

The breadth indicator in the chart in Figure 8.6 is plotted with a 1% brick value Renko chart. Thus, it calculates the percentage of stocks trading in the bullish brick on 1% brick individual Renko charts of Nifty's constituent stocks. This indicator oscillates between 0 and 100. A reading of 50 means that an equal number of stocks are trading with bullish and bearish bricks, thus suggesting a balanced market. The indicator scans all the stocks in the group and portrays the health of the overall market and the state of the trend. When the indicator shows a reading of 80%, it means that 40 stocks out of the Nifty's universe of 50 are in a bullish brick. Correspondingly, when the indicator drops below 20%, it suggests that 40 out of the 50 stocks forming the Nifty index are in bearish bricks.

Rising breadth is bullish because it indicates that there is participation from more stocks from the group. Falling breadth is bearish because it indicates a lack of participation.

Breadth can be calculated on different brick values but remember it is calculated on a group of stocks, and not on the index value. Hence, it reflects a true picture of the market sentiment. I can think of any number of examples when the price kept rising or falling without any indication of sentiment extreme in breadth though the price oscillators would flash overbought or oversold signal during such times.

Breadth Extreme Zones

It is often said that when you are right about the market, the maximum number of people would tend to disagree with you. Given that price shocks, or surprises, generally occur when there is consensus, I often felt the need of an indicator that gives an idea of a consensus in any one direction. When news channels, magazines or analysts are confident about the price moving in a particular direction, it's often a reason to be cautious. Even when reading fundamental reports, one may notice too many analysts sounding bullish and confident about a target level which, again, is a sign of complacency. It makes sense to get an idea of what most of the participants are doing, but it is practically impossible to read through the reports of all analysts and to know the view of all traders. Given this backdrop, would it not be handy to have a method to get an idea about such sentiment extremes? Opinions of bench sitters are not of much importance.

The trend of most stocks would be bullish when the overall market trend is strong and up. But then there comes exhaustion when there isn't much fuel left in the tank to keep the momentum progressing in the same direction. Taking long positions in such a "tiring" scenario is not advisable even though the trend may still be up and the chart still bullish. Breadth extreme zones indicate that there is a possibility of euphoria, or panic, i.e. of sentiment extremes.

There are many possible rules that can be designed using breadth. The area of extreme zone, which can be roughly defined as 75% and 25%, is very useful information.

When the breadth reading is above 75%, it means that most of the stocks of the particular group are bullish. This happens when the trend is up, and strong, but it could also indicate exhaustion, or too much bullishness. Most individual stock charts will be in a bullish mode during such phases. Overbought or oversold are extreme zones that indicate exhaustion — but not necessarily reversal. Hence, fresh longs are best avoided when the indicator is above 75% and, similarly, fresh shorts are best avoided when the indicator is below 25%. Traders should remain cautious at such extremes of the breadth indicator and reduce their position sizes during such periods.

Figure 8.7 is a 1% breadth indicator chart of Nifty.

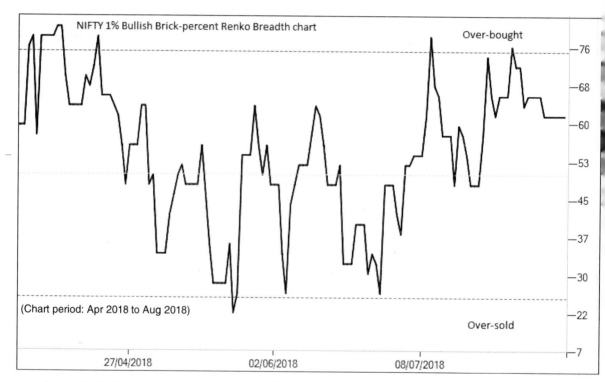

Figure 8.7: **Bullish brick percent indicator of Nifty's group of 50 stocks that calculates the percentage of stocks trading in the bullish brick on a 1% brick value Renko chart**

The chart shows overbought and oversold zones of breadth. Interestingly, Nifty went up from ₹10,400 to ₹11,400 price levels during this period. The price was going up when the breadth indicator was not in the extreme zone.

~

There are instances when the momentum is strong and pushes the breadth to the extreme zone. This is a sign that the market should be given some breathing space. When the breadth indicator is at an overbought extreme, the risk-reward parameter is not typically in favour of the bulls. Hence, position sizing should be reduced for fresh longs.

In the same way, oversold breadth suggests that the risk-reward ratio for fresh shorts is not favourable. So, breadth tells us what not to do. I call it a yellow signal. We have three traffic signal lights: green, red and yellow. **Breadth in extreme zone is analogous to the yellow traffic signal in trading.** One should take the foot off the accelerator and reduce the speed. Though markets at an extreme zone may not necessarily reverse immediately, they can get into a sideways or volatile phase. It is therefore wise to step aside until the breadth extreme condition is resolved away from the extremes.

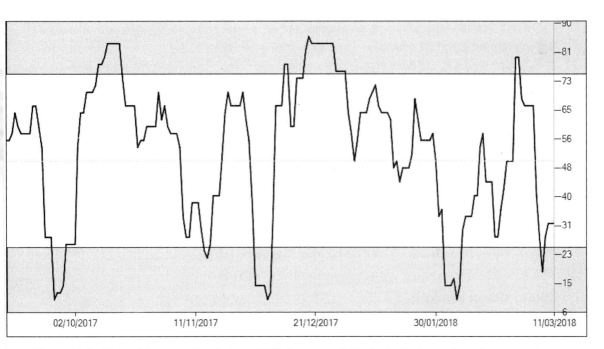

Figure 8.8: **Bullish brick percent indicator of Nifty's group of 50 stocks that calculates the percentage of stocks trading in the bullish brick on a 1% brick value Renko chart.**

~

Always remember that, overbought or oversold breadth is not a proxy for market tops and bottoms. The breadth can remain in overbought zones for a long time while the price is in a strong uptrend — and equally so at oversold zones during a strong downtrend. Rather, overbought and oversold trend represent strong trends that can produce continuation patterns. There is no reason to exit existing trades or investments when breadth reaches an extreme zone. It is just that fresh trades should be curbed until the breadth returns to the neutral zone, namely between 75 and 25. Price pattern confirmation is most important for taking a trade and one should never pre-empt or trade in its anticipation. **You can profitably trade price reversal setups when the breadth is in extreme zones.**

Price breakouts in the neutral zone tend to work well because there are no signs of exhaustion and enough room to move, whether up or down, in the direction of the breakout.

Remember, rising breadth is bullish. Extreme zone indicates scope for some exhaustion. Breadth at an extreme zone indicates exhaustion which may be followed by a time correction, something which typically happens during strong trends. A continuation breakout is often seen when breadth sustains in the extreme zone. Normally, there is the possibility of a weak high or a weak low getting formed in that zone before producing a reversal. During range bound markets, bearish formations when the breadth indicator is above 75 and bullish patterns when the indicator is below 25, are strong alerts. Always, however, wait for price patterns to form before initiating trades.

Oversold breadth when Nifty is in an uptrend, and overbought breadth when Nifty is in a downtrend, are very rare but important scenarios — and opportunities for contra trades. Relative strength, which will be discussed in the next chapter, can help us pick the right stocks to trade such scenarios.

We don't know how far the breadth indicator can go after crossing above 75, or falling below 25; nor do we know how long it may remain at those extremes. It can do so for a long time during trending markets.

Breakout patterns of Renko price chart when the breadth is in neutral zone are very interesting. Breakouts should, however, be avoided when the breadth is in the extreme zone. Breadth can help the other way round as well — by cautioning you when not to trade breakouts. In cricketing analogy, a good batsman should know when to play offence and when to defend. The various Renko patterns tell us how to hit; breadth helps us decide when to be aggressive and when it's time for defence — and which balls should be left well alone.

Sector Group Breadth

We have seen that Nifty's breadth should be followed in order to gauge the sentiment of the overall market. Breadth indicator of sectors, other indices, or groups of stocks can be built in a similar manner. Breadth indicator of Nifty 50, and midcap and small cap indices should be monitored on a regular basis. Being cautious when there is euphoria associated with mid caps and small caps can save one from getting stuck at the wrong levels.

The breadth of any sector can be plotted in a similar manner. The representation would be better if there are more than 30 stocks in a group to build the breadth indicator. If there are fewer constituents, 10% and 90% should be treated as extreme readings. Table 8.1 is an example of breadth of every sector measured on a particular day.

Table 8.1
Breadth of Every Sector on a Given Day

Group	Breadth Value	Remark
Energy Index	60%	Neutral
Auto Index-NSE	56%	Neutral
Bank Index	50%	Neutral
Media Index	93%	Upside Extreme / Momentum
Financial Services Index	55%	Neutral
FMCG Index	66%	Neutral
Service sector Index	56%	Neutral
PSU Bank Index	5%	Downside Extreme/ Momentum
IT Index	50%	Neutral
Metal Index	73%	Neutral
IT Index	50%	Neutral
Commodities Index	60%	Neutral
Consumption Index	70%	Neutral
Realty Index	30%	Neutral
MNC Index	73%	Neutral
PSE Index	55%	Neutral
Pvt Bank Index	50%	Neutral
Pharma Index	60%	Neutral

Divergences

Divergence between breadth and the Nifty index is a time to be cautious.

- Positive divergence in the breadth indicator of Nifty's group of 50 stocks occurs when the price makes a new low but breadth does not.

- Correspondingly, a negative divergence is marked when the price makes new high but the indicator is unable to do so.

If Nifty is rising but the breadth is falling, that means there isn't enough participation from most of the stocks and only a few heavyweight stocks are pulling the index. While this happens often but such type of phases are difficult to sustain. If this situation does sustain, then, typically, a major price reversal follows.

Figure 8.9 that follows is a bar price chart of Nifty Index.

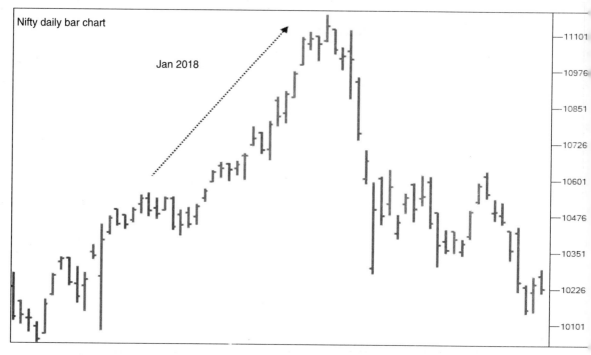

Figure 8.9: **Daily bar chart of Nifty Index**

∼

Nifty was going up during January 2018. Figure 8.10 is a breadth chart of the same period.

By now it must be clear that it is important to understand the meaning of rising breadth. The index can rise or fall due to the contribution of only a few of its constituents, but the overall market health will be positive only when most of the stocks from the group or the index are participating. The breadth indicator counts the number of stocks having bullish bricks; it is expected to have more stocks with bullish bricks or turning to bullish when the index is bullish. Therefore, the divergence between breadth and index price is an important warning sign.

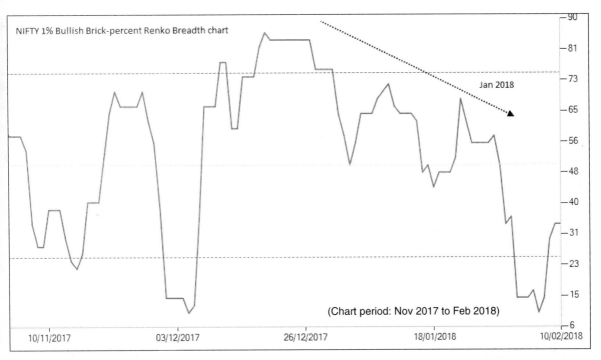

NIFTY 1% Bullish Brick-percent Renko Breadth chart

Jan 2018

(Chart period: Nov 2017 to Feb 2018)

Figure 8.10: **Bullish brick percent indicator of Nifty's group of 50 stocks that calculates the percentage of stocks trading in the bullish brick on a 1% brick value Renko chart.**

The breadth was falling indicating that the rally was fuelled by only a handful of stocks. The other logical inference is that Renko charts in most stocks were turning into bearish bricks while Nifty was going up. Thereafter, Nifty witnessed a significant fall in prices in February 2018.

~

If such divergences occur near the breadth extreme zones, i.e. positive divergence at or near an oversold zone, or a negative divergence at or near an overbought zone — they could end up being a sign of a major trend reversal.

The breadth exiting an oversold zone is when long trades have a better risk-reward while breadth exiting an overbought zone is when the risk-reward for short trades is more favourable. But the breadth indicator alone is not sufficient; price patterns of the respective chart needs to confirm whether a trade can be initiated.

Breadth is one of the most important, logical and vital tools in any trading kit. The best part is that it complements other methods of analysis.

~

~

Chapter 9

Relative Strength

THE CONCEPT OF RELATIVE STRENGTH IS VERY POPULAR and though much written about, it is under utilized by market participants. It is truly a very simple and effective method of measuring an instrument's performance. Caution: relative strength should not be confused with the RSI (Relative Strength Indicator) indicator, namely due to a similarity in names; the two represent entirely different concepts.

Strength analysis is most important to understand for all types of traders and investors as it can significantly improve their trading performance. In this chapter, we will discuss how.

Ratio Chart

If we divide the price of one instrument with that of another, what we get is a ratio of the prices of the two instruments.

For example, if Bank Nifty is trading at 20,000 and Nifty at 10,000, and if we divide the price of the former by that of the latter, we get a ratio of 2. It is the ratio of one price to another at that particular time. The ratio of two instruments can also be derived on a regular basis and plotted on a chart, which will look similar to the usual line chart plotted by connecting successive prices.

For example, Figure 9.1 that follows is the daily ratio chart of Bank Nifty and Nifty.

The ratio line shown in the chart can also be analysed in the same way as we analyse price, except that the rising or falling line is not showing the trend of the price, but of the ratio.

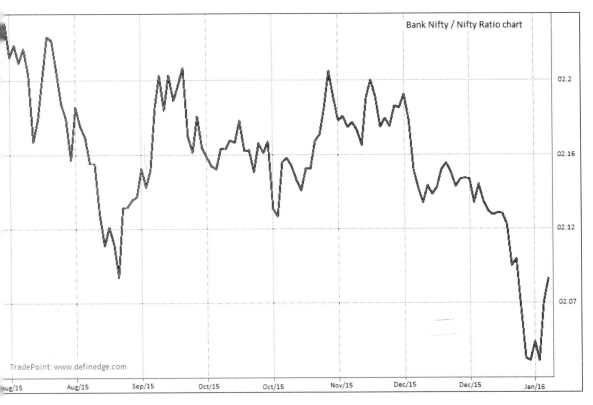

Figure 9.1: **Daily ratio chart of Bank Nifty *versus* Nifty**

~

For the ratio line to go up, the price of the instrument used in the numerator will have to go up relatively more than that of the denominator. Hence, a rising ratio line indicates that the price of the numerator security is outperforming the denominator one, while a falling ratio line indicates that the price of the numerator instrument is underperforming that of the denominator instrument. Note that outperformance doesn't necessarily mean that the numerator instrument is rising while the denominator instrument is falling. Outperformance simply means that the former is either rising more than the latter, or falling less than it.

The ratio of the two instruments may remain in a range over a period of time. Mean reversion techniques can be effectively used in such scenarios. Using this method, we can easily analyse the performance of one instrument with that of another. The concept is fascinating.

Relative strength can be a great tool for stock picking if you know what to look for. Now, let's understand how a ratio chart behaves. This is explained in Table 9.1.

Table 9.1
Ratio Chart

Denominator	Numerator	Ratio	
Up	More Up	Up	Out-performance
Down	Up	Up	Out-performance
Down	Flat	Up	Out-performance
Flat	Up	Up	Out-performance
Down	Less Down	Up	Out-performance
Up	Less Up	Down	Under-performance
Down	More Down	Down	Under-performance
Up	Down	Down	Under-performance
Up	Flat	Down	Under-performance
Flat	Down	Down	Under-performance

Renko Relative Strength

The ratio chart shown in Table 9.1 can be plotted using the Renko construction method as well. Have a look at Figure 9.2 of Bank Nifty divided by Nifty.

Now that we have a ratio chart in the Renko format, all methods of price analysis applicable to Renko charts can also be used on relative strength (RS) charts — but one must always remember that the chart captures relative strength, not price.

For me, the concept of relative strength is among the most fascinating subjects of technical analysis. I was immediately hooked to it when I realised its importance in identifying market leading stocks. If we stick to groups, sectors, or stocks that are leading the trend, we will stick to the winners. **A price breakout which occurs in combination with relative strength, presents a very interesting opportunity.** Decision making and winning probability improve significantly by picking stocks that are leading the trend.

Earlier in the book we have discussed continuation patterns, such as one-back, two-back and swing breakouts. **Continuation patterns applied to leading strong stocks offer some of the best price setups**.

If the denominator in a relative strength chart is a broader market index, such as Nifty, then the chart will show the performance of the numerator instrument against it. The numerator could comprise an individual stock, a sector, or any other instrument for that matter.

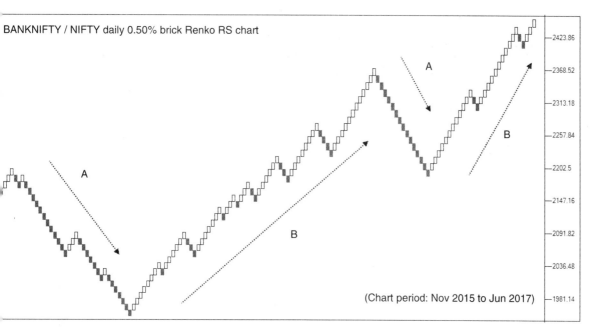

BANKNIFTY / NIFTY daily 0.50% brick Renko RS chart

(Chart period: Nov 2015 to Jun 2017)

Figure 9.2: **Bank Nifty *versus* Nifty daily 0.50% brick value Renko relative strength chart**

This is a ratio chart converted to Renko. The arrows at A show that Bank Nifty (the numerator) was underperforming the Nifty (the denominator) during these two periods, while the two arrows at B show where the Bank Nifty was outperforming Nifty.

~

Pair Trading

As the Renko relative strength chart is plotted with a ratio line of two instruments, it can be used for pair trading. Pair trading means two instruments being traded in opposite directions, that is, entered and exited simultaneously.

The relative strength chart is considered bullish when the numerator is outperforming — and is bearish when the numerator starts underperforming.

Thus, when we buy or sell a relative strength chart, we are betting on outperformance, or underperformance as the case may be, of the numerator against the denominator.

- When a Renko relative strength chart is used for pair trading, then you buy the numerator and go short in the denominator if there is a bullish pattern in the chart. This is how we buy a relative strength chart.

- When a relative strength chart produces a bearish setup, you should short the numerator instrument and trade long the denominator. This is how we short the relative strength chart.

The buying and selling should be based on the pattern in the relative strength chart; the individual price patterns should not be tracked in such cases. Also, please note that a pair should always be value neutral. For example, if the price of a particular instrument is ₹500 and its lot size is 1,000, then the contract value of that instrument is ₹5 lakh. In such a case, the contract value of the other instrument should also be ₹5 lakh for pair trading. You may need to add some quantities from spot segment to handle this, but in pair trading it is important that the value of both contracts be equal.

Take a look at Figure 9.3, which is a relative strength chart of TCS price (numerator) and Wipro price (denominator).

All techniques of trading and analysing Renko charts are equally applicable to Renko relative strength charts, the only difference being that a pair of securities is traded instead of a single instrument.

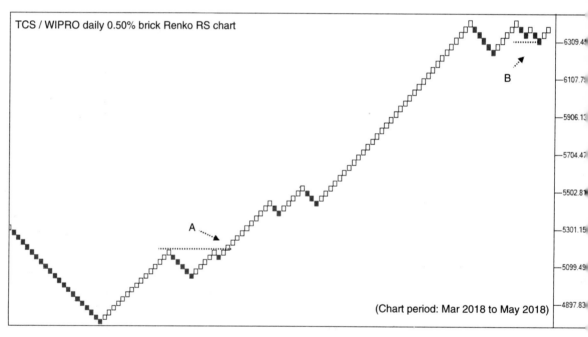

Figure 9.3: **TCS vs Wipro 0.50% brick value daily Renko relative strength chart**

The multi-brick breakout at Point A indicates the outperformance of TCS vis-à-vis Wipro. From a pair trading perspective, a long position may be considered in TCS (numerator) and a short position in Wipro (denominator) whenever there is a bullish breakout in this relative strength chart. There is a bearish swing breakout at Point B, where TCS should be sold and Wipro should be bought.

~

A set of instruments can be short listed and traded consistently as pair trades. If the selection is based on the market scenario, then I recommend picking the outperformer of a sector as the numerator and the underperformer of the same sector as the denominator. The outperformer is expected to continue its outperformance while the underperformer is likely to see further underperformance if the trend in the underlying sector reverses. Strength analysis of a sector *vis-à-vis* the broader market index plays a key role here. In the period covered in the example in Figure 9.3, the Nifty IT Index relative strength chart *vis-à-vis* Nifty for the same period generated bullish breakout during March 2018 indicating the former's outperformance over Nifty. The relative strength chart of TCS against Nifty IT was bullish, while Wipro's relative strength chart against Nifty IT was bearish. Hence, the pair of TCS and Wipro.

RS charts can also be used to create hedge positions in a derivatives portfolio. Even if one's view on the market is bullish, going short the underperformers in the portfolio can act as a safeguard in case of unfavourable overnight news, or if the market were to reverse unexpectedly.

Identifying Strength and Weakness

It is always advisable to get rid of underperformers from one's portfolio and ride strength. Strong stocks become stronger in an uptrend as the trend matures — and they also tend to resume the trend quickly after corrections. Weak counters will be beaten hard during corrective phases, making the portfolio bleed and underperform the overall market. A strength centric portfolio would deliver better returns over a period.

There will be a price breakout in many stocks when Nifty or the overall market trend is bullish. But you would also have come across instances where the stock bought on a price breakout failed to move up significantly while stocks you didn't buy might have gained handsomely. Or, what you bought might have delivered returns far lower than the ones you missed.

Focusing on a breakout in ratio charts can be very helpful in avoiding the above mentioned scenarios. Always focus on the relative outperformers, both among sectors and stocks. I can tell you with all my experience that sticking to strength will not let you get trapped on the wrong side of the market.

Price breakouts can suggest that stocks could go up. Relative strength breakouts indicate which stocks can outperform. The combination of these two factors can do wonders to your portfolio returns.

Consider this scenario: if the price of an instrument is rising but the ratio chart against the sector benchmark or the market index is not rising, what does that imply?

The simple answer is that something else is doing better, right? There should be a reason why a stock or a sector is doing better than its peers. Once we identify the strong stocks belonging to the strong sectors using relative strength chart analysis, then price breakouts in the strong stocks could be profitably traded.

Accordingly, a trader should make it a point to check the relative strength chart of a stock *vis-à-vis* Nifty before buying it. Ignoring bullish formations in a stock chart during its period of underperformance and focusing on them when it is outperforming the broader market is a logical and effective approach. In other words, you should trade the pattern formations on individual charts in the direction of the relative strength chart. Price breakouts coupled with relative strength breakouts are the key to identifying potential outperformers.

Weakness can also be analysed and traded in the same way. Shorting weak counters is more profitable when the broader market corrects. This will offer better risk reward trades than shorting the stronger counters. Pattern studies of individual stocks certainly play an important role. Remember, trades are to be placed based on a study of the individual charts. Relative strength helps in finding where to identify one's trading universe.

It should also always be remembered that what is moving will continue to move. Though the leaders of every rally change, the leaders remain leaders for a longer time than we imagine. Newton's First Law of Motion applies to relative strength, too! Thus, The stocks that outperform will continue to outperform and the underperformers will continue to underperform until there is a discontinuity (reversal). When riding a trend, it is important that you don't try to predict reversals every now and then. People are often unable to ride trends due to external noise, over analysis, or unnecessarily looking at some support or resistance. Which is why it is important to follow the price chart and not to find imaginary reversals. That is the way to continue in profitable trades.

I have seen stocks continue to remain on top in the list of relative strength performers for months. And they also continue to lead the market. Corrections in such leaders are short lived; rather, they trap the weak hands.

Trading continuation patterns in such market or sector leaders is one of the best trading approaches, and one that has stood the test of time for me.

The strength of a stock is tested when markets correct. Stocks or sectors that show relative strength when the markets are correcting in an uptrend, tend to do well when the markets recover. One should always embrace corrections and pullbacks because a buy signal in the relative strength charts when the markets are in a corrective mode indicates potential upside in those stocks when the trend resumes. Correspondingly, stocks or sectors that show weakness when markets witness a price bounce (correction) in a downtrend, tend to underperform significantly if and when the market resumes the downtrend.

Good money can also be made by trading bearish stocks in bullish markets.

People keep hoping that such weak stocks will find bottoms, but they continue to underperform, even more so when markets correct or consolidate.

In the same way, trading bullish stocks in bearish markets works well. Relative strength analysis is a very important tool for this. Keep a note of stocks that are underperforming when the market is rising, or outperforming when the market is falling. They can be great bets when the market trend reverses.

Top Down Approach

Sector performance can be compared against the broader market index to assess its relative performance. Have a look at Figure 9.4 which is a 1% brick value chart of NSE Metal index against Nifty.

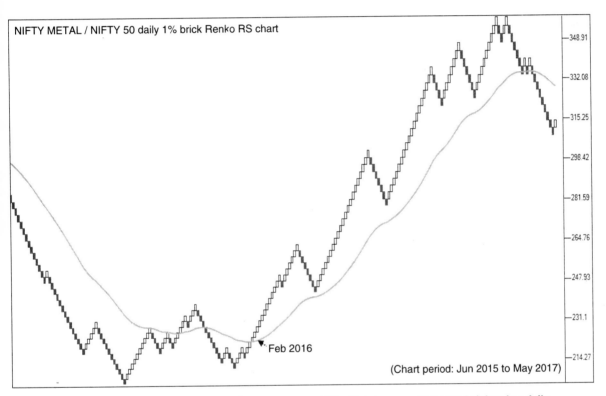

Figure 9.4: **40-brick exponential moving average on Nifty Metal *versus* Nifty 1% brick value daily Renko relative strength chart. It is apaprent that the Metal index started outperforming Nifty from February 2016.**

~

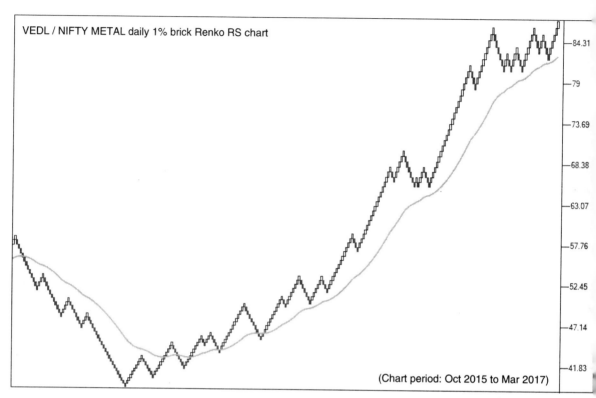

VEDL / NIFTY METAL daily 1% brick Renko RS chart

(Chart period: Oct 2015 to Mar 2017)

Figure 9.5: **40-brick exponential moving average on Vedanta *versus* Nifty Metal Index daily 1% brick value Renko relative strength chart.**

~

Now check out Figure 9.5, which is the ratio chart, of Vedanta Limited against Nifty Metal index during same period.

As the chart in Figure 9.5 shows, Vedanta was outperforming the Nifty Metal index during the same period. It was one of the leading stocks of the index which, in turn, was outperforming Nifty.

Figure 9.6 that follows is a 1% brick Renko chart of Vedanta.

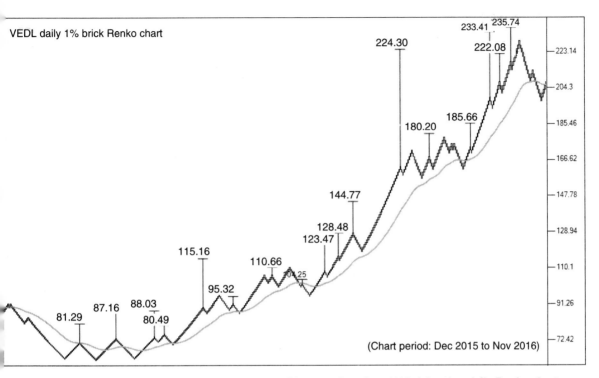

VEDL daily 1% brick Renko chart

(Chart period: Dec 2015 to Nov 2016)

Figure 9.6: **40-brick exponential moving average with extensions in a 1% brick value daily Renko chart of Vedanta. Continuation patterns in the stock could have been traded throughout this period.**

~

To summarise; bullish patterns in a ratio (relative strength) chart indicate outperformance while bearish patterns suggest weakness or underperformance. The top down approach is recommended for identifying stocks.

The top down approach begins with a study of the relative strength chart of the sectors *vis-à-vis* the broader market index. The patterns on the sector ratio charts tell us about the performance of the sector *vis-à-vis* the benchmark. This can help you identify strong sectors.

The next step is to identify strong stocks from among the outperforming sectors. This is achieved by studying the relative strength charts of the stocks from the outperforming sector(s) in relation to the sector index. Price breakout patterns in the leaders can prove more rewarding. In the same way, underperforming stocks can be identified using such a top down approach.

When a stock moves, it could be due to the individual story of the stock concerned. When an entire sector is moving, there is a bigger story at the sector level. When a micro story gets coupled with a macro, that is when a stock trends to get into an accelerated up move and the Renko chart would tell us what to do thereafter.

Sector performance analysis gives an idea of sectors that are outperforming and underperforming across various time horizons.

For short term analysis, a brick value such as 0.25% is recommended for relative strength charts. 1% to 3% brick values are recommended for intermediate and long term relative strength analysis.

The top down approach is recommended in order to identify stocks for building a portfolio[*]. Once strong stocks have been identified, then it is a question of waiting patiently for continuation patterns or buy signals to be triggered in the individual stock price charts to build a strong portfolio. Nifty 500 or Nifty Midcap indices can also be used as the denominator for this purpose.

A stock selected from a strongly performing sector is likely to perform better compared to a stock from a weak sector. Similarly, a stock from an underperforming sector is likely to fall more, and is a better bet for shorting as compared to one from a strong or stable sector. One would want to build a portfolio consisting of stocks that are outperforming the markets, and it is equally important to keep away from underperforming stocks. Relative strength is the best method for evaluating strength or weakness and to stay with the leaders.

Renko Relative Strength Matrix

Thomas Dorsey beautifully explained the DWA Relative Strength Matrix in his book *Point & Figure Charting* where he divided the price of each instrument with that of another in the group. Renko relative strength matrix is a very useful tool for reviewing the performance of all sectors or groups of stocks at a glance. If the performance of all sectors needs to be analysed, divide the price of each sector with that of every other sector. We then get to know the relative performance of every sector against every other sector. We can then check whether a brick on the relative strength chart is bullish or bearish (*see* Table 9.2).

Table 9.2
Renko Relative Strength Matrix

	Bank	Auto	Pharma	Consumption	Metal	IT
Bank		Bearish	Bearish	Bearish	Bearish	Bearish
Auto	Bullish		Bearish	Bearish	Bearish	Bearish
Pharma	Bullish	Bullish		Bullish	Bullish	Bullish
Consumption	Bullish	Bullish	Bearish		Bearish	Bearish
Metal	Bullish	Bullish	Bearish	Bullish		Bearish
IT	Bullish	Bullish	Bearish	Bullish	Bullish	

In this manner, we can analyse the performance of all the sectors. For example, the pharma sector is outperforming most sectors in Table 9.2. To make it easier to analyse, a simpler method is to score it 1 when a sector is bullish and score 0 when it is bearish. The resulting total score will help us to analyse the performance of all the sectors at a glance.

Have a look at Table 9.3.

---

[*] 0.25% brick-value chart for trading portfolio, 1% for intermediate and 3% for long-term investments.

Table 9.3

Renko Relative Strength Matrix of all NSE Sectors

Scrips	Nifty Auto	Nifty Energy	Nifty FMCG	Nifty Infra	Nifty IT	Nifty Media	Nifty Metal	Nifty MNC	Nifty Pharma	Nifty PSE	Nifty PSU Bank	Nifty Reality	Nifty Serv Sector	Nifty Fri Service	Nifty consumption	Nifty Commodi-	Nifty Bank	Nifty CPSE	Nifty Pvt Bank	Total
Nifty Realty	1	1	1	1	0	1	1	1	1	1	1	0	1	1	1	1	1	1	1	18
Nifty FMCG	1	1	0	1	1	1	1	1	1	1	1	0	1	1	1	1	1	1	0	17
Nifty Pvt Bank	1	1	1	1	0	1	1	1	1	1	1	0	1	1	1	1	1	1	0	17
Nifty IT	0	1	0	1	0	1	1	1	1	1	1	0	1	1	1	1	1	1	1	16
Nifty Atuo	0	1	0	1	1	1	1	0	1	1	1	0	0	1	0	1	1	1	1	14
Nifty Consumption	1	1	0	1	0	1	1	1	1	1	1	0	0	1	0	1	1	1	0	13
Nifty Bank	0	1	0	1	0	1	1	1	1	1	1	0	1	1	0	1	0	1	0	13
Nifty Serv Sector	1	1	0	1	0	1	1	1	1	1	1	0	0	0	1	1	0	1	0	12
Nifty Fri Service	0	1	0	1	0	1	1	1	1	1	1	0	1	0	0	1	0	1	0	12
Nifty 50	0	0	0	1	0	1	1	1	1	1	1	0	1	0	1	0	0	1	0	10
Nifty Energy	0	0	0	1	0	1	1	1	1	0	1	0	0	0	0	1	0	1	0	9
Nifty Commodities	0	0	0	1	0	1	1	1	1	1	1	0	0	0	0	0	0	1	0	9
Nifty MNC	0	0	0	1	0	1	1	0	1	1	1	0	0	0	0	0	0	1	0	7
Nifty PSE	0	1	0	1	0	1	1	0	1	0	1	0	0	0	0	0	0	1	0	7
Nifty Media	0	0	0	1	0	0	1	1	1	0	1	0	0	0	0	0	0	1	0	6
Nifty Infra	0	0	0	0	0	0	1	0	1	0	1	0	0	0	0	0	0	1	0	4
Nifty CPSE	0	0	0	0	0	0	1	0	1	0	1	0	0	0	0	0	0	0	0	3
Nifty Pharma	0	0	0	0	0	0	1	0	0	0	1	0	0	0	0	0	0	0	0	2
Nifty Metal	0	0	0	0	0	0	0	0	0	0	1	0	0	0	0	0	0	0	0	1
Nifty PSU Bank	0	0	0	0	0	0	0	0	0	0	0	0	0	0	0	0	0	0	0	0

Score is 1 if the last brick is bullish and 0 if the last brick is bearish. This way we can identify sectors that are outperforming and underperforming in relation to the other sectors. For instance, Table 9.3 shows that the Realty Index was an outperformer *vis-à-vis* most other sectors during the period covered by the table. The next step is to run the same matrix in the Realty Index.

Table 9.4 throws up the list of strong performers in the realty sector — Indiabulls Real Estate, Sobha Developers and Oberoi Realty were the leaders and were performing better than most other stocks in the sector.

Once the strong stocks among the strong sectors are identified in this manner, price analysis can identify trading opportunities in those stocks. In essence, this is like an arm-wrestling match between two indices or instruments. It gives a clearer perspective of how one instrument is performing in relation to the others. This helps to fine tune the selection after having identified the strongest sectors in relation to the benchmark.

Table 9.4

Renko Relative Strength Matrix of Realty Index

Scrip	Bri-gade	DLF	Godrej prop	HDIL	Ibrealest	Oberoirlty	Phoenixltd	Prestige	Sobha	Unitech	Total
India bulls Real Estate Ltd.	1	1	1	1	0	1	1	1	1	1	9
Sobha Ltd.	1	1	1	1	0	1	1	1	0	1	8
Oberoi Realty Limited.	1	1	1	1	0	0	1	1	0	1	7
Phoenix Mills Limited	1	1	1	1	0	0	0	1	0	1	6
Prestige Estates Projects Limited	1	1	1	1	0	0	0	0	0	1	5
Brigade Enter-prises Ltd.	0	1	1	1	0	0	0	0	0	1	4
DLF Ltd.	0	0	1	1	0	0	0	0	0	1	3
Godrej Proper-ties Ltd	0	0	0	1	0	0	0	0	0	0	1
Unitech Limited	0	0	0	1	0	0	0	0	0	0	1
Housing Development & Infrastructure	0	0	0	0	0	0	0	0	0	0	0

~

Part 2

~

Trading with Renko Charts

~

Chapter 10

Selecting Your Trading Parameters

Which Price to Use

There is a practical issue with regard to trading patterns — and breakouts occurring at the end of the day — on closing price basis. This is an issue common to all kinds of charts, not just Renko. A bar or candle gets locked at end of the day but a candle pattern seen during the day might change based on the closing price, and most of the indicators are calculated on the closing prices. Thus, any trading decision taken during the day is based either on assumption or pre-emption. End-of-the-day or positional trading systems are usually traded based on closing prices, irrespective of the charting method.

There are several ways to deal with this issue.

1. Wait for the closing price of the day and ignore intraday moves. If the closing price turns out to be so high — or low, as the case may be — that the risk becomes unaffordable, then ignore that trade and wait for the next opportunity.

2. Initiate the trade the day after the breakout gets confirmed by the previous day's closing price. If the price opens higher, and thus makes the initial risk unaffordable, then just ignore the trade. This is the safest method and one with the lowest impact cost.

3. Often times, price moves significantly intraday itself. In such cases, entry can be made when the breakout occurs in real time, and the trade exited if the closing price is below the brick value requirement. The cost of doing so should normally get offset due to the profits made over multiple such trades.

Impact Cost

Impact cost can be broadly defined as the cost of executing a transaction at the exchange. It could be governed by liquidity and spread in the instrument. It will include associated costs of doing the business of trading, such as having a backup internet and power connection, having a standby broking account, etc. The other cost that a trader will incur is associated with the cost of following the trading system. For positional traders following end of the day charts, if the signal happens on a closing basis then there will be occasions when a few trades might have to be scratched owing to false signals. And, then, there is this inevitable drawdown phase when the system is not in confluence with the underlying market condition. For instance, a trend following system will get into a drawdown phase when the price is not trending. This is another aspect of cost that a trader has to incur.

---

4. Another way to handle this issue is by taking the trades in the last hour of trading. This minimizes the impact cost to a large extent because the pattern on the daily chart may be almost locked by then and you have clear entry and exit levels in place.

5. For positional traders, this issue can be dealt with by using position sizing rules. Thus, you can commit a portion of the budgeted quantity during the day, and add more when the breakout is confirmed by the closing price. I strongly believe this is the best approach for positional traders.

6. A method most suited for an active trader would be to shift to lower time frame charts once a breakout occurs on the daily chart. One can then trade as per the formations during the day on the lower time interval chart, and get back to the daily chart at end of the day. If the breakout sustains on the daily time frame chart, you can shift back to end-of-the-day charts. The impact cost is minimum with this method because profits would also have been made on the lower time frame charts.

For example, a bullish weak breakout pattern may form during the day on the daily time frame chart but it can change at the end of the day due to the closing price. If you see some other bullish pattern during the day on lower time frame chart, you can trade that pattern as per its entry and exit rules on that time frame. Then shift trade to a positional stance if the bullish weak breakout pattern on the daily time frame chart remains valid at closing.

Things are quite simple for positional and long term traders because they use higher brick values where this issue is not much relevant.

You can select whichever method suits you best but, more importantly, you must stick to only one method and follow that method consistently.

You can exit an existing trade, if the exit price level is triggered during the day in real-time. The closed position can be reinstated if the closing price doesn't meet the exit criteria requirement. For example, if the price level for exiting the trade is ₹100, exit the trade if the price goes below that level during the day, but reinstate the position if the price closes above ₹100 at the end of the day. The impact cost debit incurred during the process would get offset over a period due to the cost saved with the same exercise. Over many trades, the impact cost debit incurred following the above process would be offset by the cost saved by using this approach.

Another method of dealing with this issue is to follow high-low charts instead of charts based on the closing price.

High-Low Renko Charts

It must be obvious by now that Renko charts can be plotted with only one price. Charts plotted with closing prices will generate patterns based on the closing price of the chosen time interval. The high-low method of plotting considers either the high, or the low, price made during the day as follows:

■ If the previous brick was bullish, and if the high price for the given time period qualifies for plotting a new brick, then a new bullish brick gets plotted and the low price is ignored.

- If the previous brick was bearish and the price falls further, a new bearish brick gets plotted and the high price is ignored.

While this method is effective but there is also a problem. We don't know whether on a given day the high occurred first or the low. The price can go high during the day and qualify for a new bullish brick, but it also can fall below the required reversal level during the same day. As per the rules of Renko, the low price will be ignored when plotting on that day even though it may have triggered the exit level. Such instances are, however, not too frequent. Within this limitation, the high-low chart is an effective method, particularly for short term traders because it is possible to take decisions in real time and there is no need to wait for the closing price.

The high-low method results in more bricks getting plotted compared to the closing price method. As the number of bricks is higher, the chart gets wider in nature, warranting the use of a higher brick value to address this.

The nature and behaviour of these high-low charts is quite different. On these charts, subjective pattern analysis, multi-swing extensions and multi-brick breakouts are more useful than simple swing breakouts. Trend lines and indicators should be applied for better analysis and simple trade execution.

Figure 10.1 is a 1% brick high-low Renko chart of Infosys.

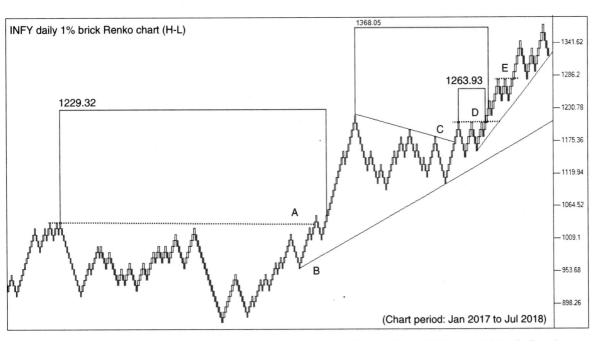

Figure 10.1: **Chart analysis of a 1% brick value daily high-low Renko chart of Infosys. Points A, D and E are multi-brick breakouts shown with multi-swing extensions. B and C are trend lines drawn from important tops and bottoms.**

~

The advantage of high-low charts is that they facilitate real time decision making for traders. One need not wait for the closing to be locked before initiating a trade. If the previous brick is bullish, and if the brick value requirement for a new bullish brick is met during the day, then the plotting of the new brick will remain in place till end of the day. In such a case, then, a decision can be taken confidently in real time. This method is more suitable for someone trading the same instrument on a consistent basis, or someone who is following a system based approach to trading. The brick will remain bullish for the day even if the price has turned down and the reversal criteria are met because the low price is not considered during such cases. But such situations are relatively uncommon and typically occur when the breakout and reversal happen on the same day. One can exit when the reversal criteria are met and then wait for the next signal to deal with the emerging situation. The impact cost in such cases is comparatively low.

One can also use both the high-low method and the closing method in conjunction charts may be traded during the day as per the levels in the high.

For momentum and derivative traders, instead of using the high-low method on daily prices, it is better to shift to intraday time interval charts.

Shadows

As discussed in Chapter 1, every Renko brick consists of two prices — and is built by connecting the two prices. This is an important feature of Renko charts. Diagonal plotting of bricks gives us an opportunity to plot shadows.

The biggest problem associated with Renko charts is that we can't see the intraday price moves when we look at daily Renko charts. The shadows in candlestick charts tell us about the high and low prices recorded during the day. Due to the diagonal method of Renko chart construction, it is possible to incorporate the high and low price as shadows to the Renko bricks as well. There are, however, a couple of issues in doing so. First, there can be too much noise if shadows are added to all the bricks because multiple bricks can get plotted for the same period when the price is in a trending phase and all bricks will show the shadows at the same levels. As a result, the chart will look cluttered. The second issue concerns the price that should be considered when the brick gets plotted after a period of inactivity in the chart. This happens when the price does not make a significant move to warrant plotting of fresh bricks.

As a solution to the first problem above, we can choose to plot shadows only when a new brick gets plotted. Then there won't be any unnecessary shadows showing on all the bricks since the shadow will only be plotted on the last brick of the period. This will also let you visually see the date when the brick's period is changed. So, for example, if five bricks get plotted for the same day in the case of a daily time frame chart, the shadows will be plotted only on the fifth brick. As for the second issue, when there are two or more periods represented in a particular brick — we'll plot the highest high and the lowest low of both the periods that comprise the brick.

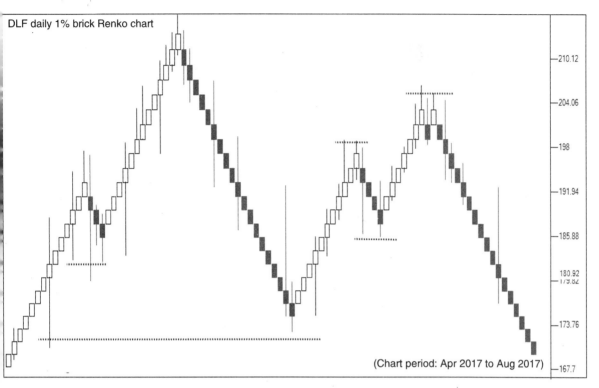

Figure 10.2: **Shadows in a 1% brick value daily Renko chart of DLF**

~

This way we can see the intraday price move on the Renko chart, as illustrated in Figure 10.2.

In Figure 10.2, it is possible to know the high or the low made during the period. Along with Renko patterns, it is possible to read high or low formed at the same levels as shown in the chart. Or, to read breakouts based on the high-low prices.

Multiple shadows appearing at the same level indicate strong demand, or supply, as the case may be. This can add value to Renko patterns.

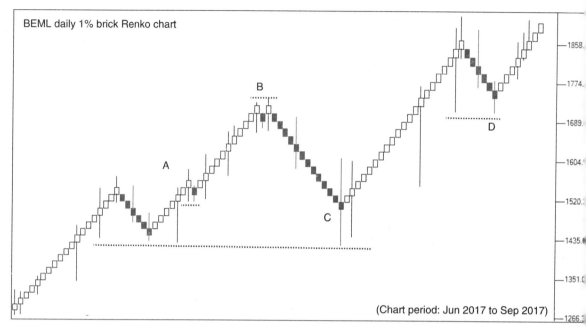

Figure 10.3: **Shadows in a 1% brick value daily Renko chart of Bharat Earth Movers Ltd.**

Pattern A is a bullish one-back. Notice the lower shadow of Pattern A. Multiple lower shadows occurred at the same level indicating demand at that particular price zone. Pattern B is a bearish zigzag with higher shadows at similar levels. Pattern C is a bullish weak breakout where the lower shadows are indicating a strong demand at the earlier zone. Lower shadows at Pattern D show that the price is taking support at the previous resistance as per the polarity principle.

~

Along with Renko patterns, you can also view on the chart in Figure 10.3 places where the price may have formed highs or lows multiple times. These can act as important reference levels, and breakouts coupled with Renko patterns can be a useful tool.

Confirmation from a shadow breakout can be used to enter upon a Renko pattern breakout. Shadows can also be utilised to locate the appropriate stop loss levels.

Shadows on 0.25%, or lower brick values, will be long because they are being plotted only on the last brick of the reversal. As discussed earlier in this chapter, at times there are multiple bricks recorded in a single day, pushing the high or the low far from the price at the last brick.

Figure 10.5 is a 0.25% brick value chart of Bharat Electronics Ltd plotted along with shadows.

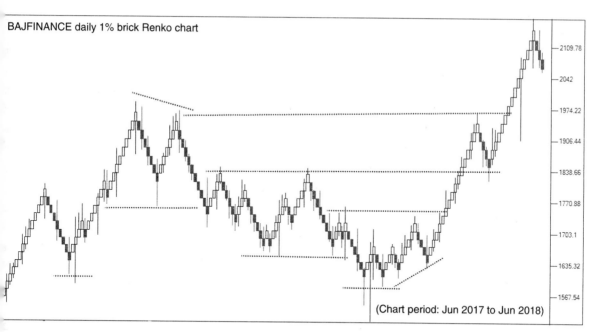

BAJFINANCE daily 1% brick Renko chart

(Chart period: Jun 2017 to Jun 2018)

Figure 10.4: **Shadows in a 1% brick value daily Renko chart of Bajaj Finance**

~

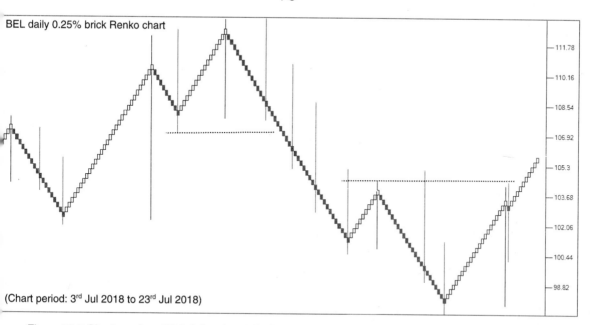

BEL daily 0.25% brick Renko chart

(Chart period: 3rd Jul 2018 to 23rd Jul 2018)

Figure 10.5: **Shadows in a 1% brick value daily Renko chart of Bharat Electronics Ltd. Shadows look relatively long when a relatively lower brick value chart is plotted. Nonetheless, they show important reference points.**

~

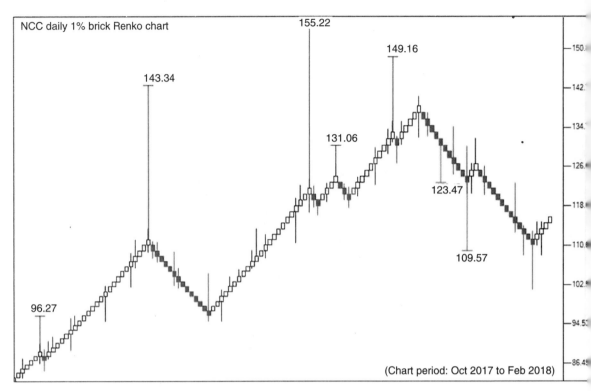

Figure 10.6: **Shadows and extensions in a 1% brick value daily Renko chart of Nagarjuna Construction Company Ltd.**

~

Figure 10.6 is a chart of Nagarjuna Construction Company Ltd. plotted along with shadows and extensions.

To sum up: shadows are important when you want to see the high or low price recorded during a day. This removes the major drawback of not being able to see intraday movements in Renko charts. Remember, shadows are just for information; only simple Renko patterns should be used for actual trading.

Volume

It is possible to plot volume too on Renko charts. There will be one volume bar for each brick date even if there are multiple bricks for that day. A new volume bar is plotted for a new date when the Renko brick date is changed.

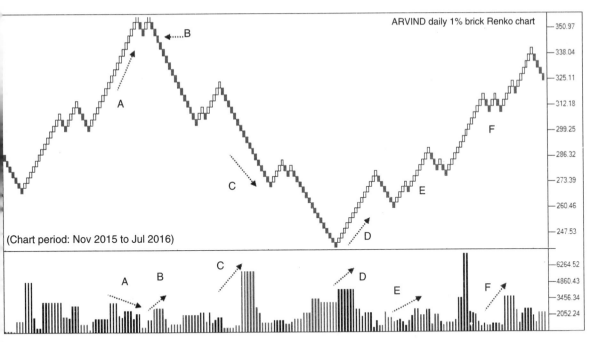

Figure 10.7: **Volume on bricks in a 1% brick value daily Renko chart of Arvind**

Every pattern is show with price and volume behaviour. Price is in the upper panel and volume in the lower one. So when we say A, one needs to observe the price and volume at A in both the panels. And so on. This chart depicts.

Volume analysis can complement price analysis. Thus, in Figure 10.7, during Pattern A (upper panel) the volume (lower panel) was reducing even though the bricks were bullish. This is followed by an M pattern shown at Point B (*see* upper panel). During Pattern C (upper panel), the price was falling with significant volume (lower panel). Pattern D is where the price bounced (*see* upper panel) with significant volume (lower panel), indicating strength. Patterns E and F (upper panel) show price rising and continuation or multi-brick breakouts were confirmed by a rise in volume (lower panel).

~

Figure 10.7 is a Renko chart of Arvind shown with volume bars.

Gaps

Many analysts and experts believe that the inability to capture gaps is a distinct disadvantage of Renko charts. I fail to understand this logic. Gaps are, in any case, irrelevant for the intra-day trader. For positional traders and investors, the issue of gaps remains even while using traditional time based charts. We can't really do much about gaps since we can't predict their occurrence beforehand. Gaps occurring in favour of one's trading position will always be most welcome. On the other hand, the trade must be exited immediately if a gap occurs against one's current trading position. Bar and candlestick charts can analyse gaps better. Renko doesn't display gaps, but which I think is fine.

~

Chapter 11

~

Selecting the Appropriate Brick Value

ALL TRADING METHODS THAT WE HAVE DISCUSSED THUS FAR are applicable on all brick values and time frames. Your trading style and trading time frame decide the brick value that you will use.

Understanding price patterns and other methods of analysis gives one a better understanding of using the appropriate brick value. Brick values vary with time frames; the same brick value cannot be used for both a daily chart and an intraday chart. Log brick values are a brilliant innovation that have not only simplified the subject but also made trading Renko charts more effective in practice. Brick values can simply be selected as per a trader or investor's time horizon. **Generally, a short term trader may use a lower brick value, while the longer term trader can settle for a higher brick value because trades and patterns appear more frequently on lower brick value charts.**

There are certain unique attributes of different brick values that should be clearly understood.

- When the brick value is higher, the number of bricks that get plotted on the chart is fewer.

- Obviously, then, some setups that are visible in lower brick value charts are not seen on a higher brick value chart.

- With practice and experience, you will understand that strike-back, swing engulfing and pullback 123 patterns are more prevalent and interesting when lower brick value charts are plotted.

- Weak breakouts and multi-brick breakouts occur more often and are better tradable when higher brick value charts are plotted.

- Understanding brick values based on the relevant setups helps understand the utility of each brick value.

One may choose to have a look at different brick values for analysis. For example, it is important for a short term trader to also know the chart pattern and trend in the medium term or the long term time frame. On the other hand, long term or medium term traders will be interested in short term patterns in order to time their entries better. The best approach is to be aware of the patterns on the higher brick value charts and trade continuation patterns or pullbacks on the lower brick value charts. This ensures that your trades are in sync with the higher order trend.

You may study different time frames, charts and brick values but I strongly recommend that you decide one time frame and one brick value for trading.

When you keep your entries, exits and time frames flexible, you can easily fall prey to excuses and play around with stops and exit rules. It also becomes difficult to enter a trade if there is a lot of subjectivity and flexibility with respect to time frames. You can always find at least one time frame and parameter that will show what you want to see!

The key job of a trader is to listen to price action, and not impose his or her opinions on the charts. As they say, the most profitable trades occur when you are least comfortable taking them. Having more objectivity in your trading rules will help you overcome emotional decision making.

I will give a range of brick values for each type of trading for you to pick one and stick to it. There is no magic in the parameters of any charting method or indicator. If there is any magic, it is in the consistency of using one method objectively.

Brick Values for Long Term Trading

Generally speaking, an investment is made keeping a longer time horizon in mind. I recommend tracking 3% to 5% brick value charts on daily time frames for long term horizons, especially for mid cap and small cap stocks. Breakouts from horizontal formations on these charts are a very useful method of investing.

There is a presumed definition about trading and investing, namely that investing is for the longer term while trading is for the short term. Sounds neat! But you need to think out of this box, though, since an investment doesn't behave as per our tax return requirements. Nor does it behave based on our definition of time horizon. You should remain in a trade, or investment, so long as the price trend is intact, and exit when the scenario is invalidated. This is the reason I get perplexed when people ask me about the right time horizon for investments. Such questions are meaningless as only the price action should dictate one's holding time period. An investor can hold on to a stock for many years if there is continuous upside potential — and if it is performing accordingly. He can book profits, or switch to better investments, when there is a change in the price scenario. Markets are dynamic and they change without serving notice. A sensible idea is to design objective setups and follow them; let the price prompt you instead of imposing your opinion on it. So, a chart can be traded for any time horizon. Thus, based on the charts you can also call an investment long term trading.

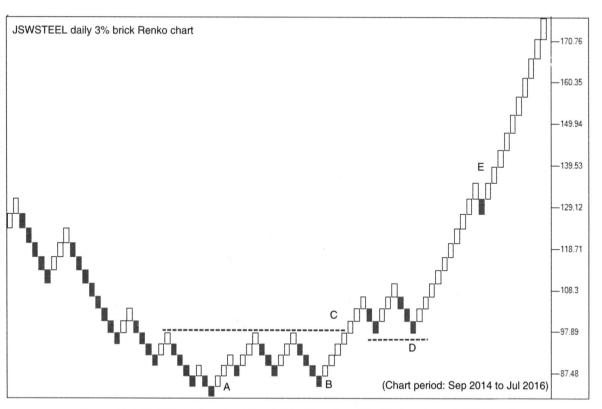

Figure 11.1: **Multi-brick breakout in a 3% brick value daily Renko chart of JSW Steel**

Point A is a bullish weak breakout giving early indication of the downtrend's weakening. Point B is a bullish weak breakout forming a higher low. Point C is a multi-brick breakout followed by polarity and Renko support pattern at Point D. Point E is a bullish one-back formation.

~

Figure 11.1 is a 3% brick value chart of JSW Steel.

You can see multi-year breakout formations on higher brick values and these tend to perform well. Typically, they will be outperforming Nifty 500 or midcaps on relative strength charts as well.

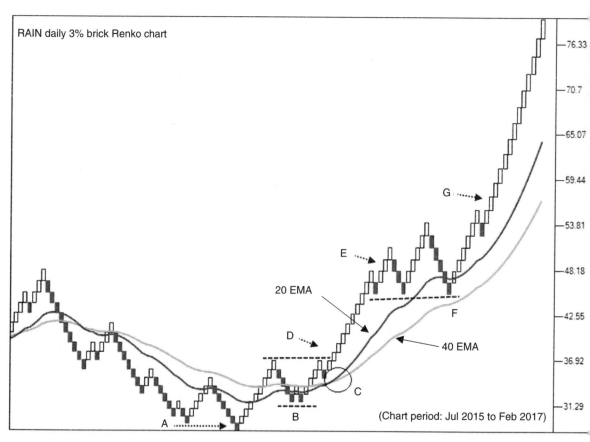

Figure 11.2: **20- and 40-brick exponential moving average lines on a 3% brick value daily Renko chart of Rain Industries. Notice the bullish moving average crossover at Point C. This occurred after the bullish weak breakout at Point A and the bullish zigzag at Point B, which makes it more important. This bullish crossover was also followed by a multi-brick breakout at Point D. Later, the bullish one-back at Point E is followed by a triple bottom support at Point F. Point G is a bullish one-back pattern. The stock went on to touch ₹450 a year later.**

~

Figure 11.2 is a 3% brick value chart of Rain Industries with 20EMA and 40EMA plotted on it.

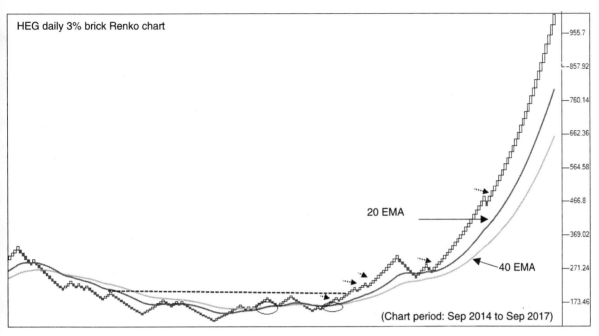

HEG daily 3% brick Renko chart

20 EMA

40 EMA

(Chart period: Sep 2014 to Sep 2017)

Figure 11.3: **20- and 40-brick exponential moving average lines on a 3% brick value daily Renko chart of HEG. The encircled areas show moving average crossovers. And the back arrows highlight one-back and two-back continuation patterns post the bullish moving average crossover. The dashed line show horizontal accumulation pattern breakout.**

~

Figure 11.3 is a 3% brick value chart of HEG with 20EMA and 40EMA lines plotted on it.

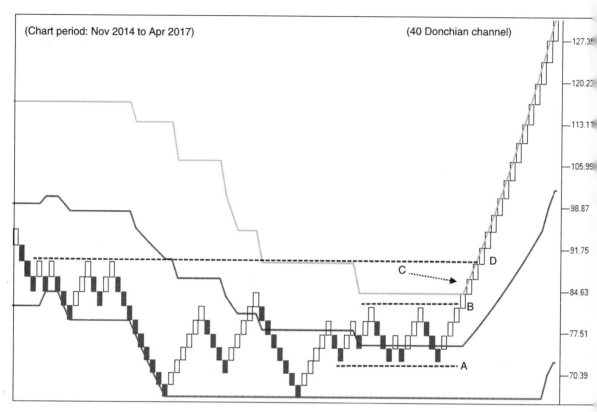

Figure 11.4: **40-brick Donchian channel plotted on a 3% brick value daily Renko chart of Graphite India**

Point A is where the price took support, something which is clearly visible on the Renko chart. Price B is a multi-brick breakout followed by a Donchian channel upper band breakout at Point C. Point D represents a significant breakout above the resistance. This happened in January 2017 around ₹90 levels. There was no 40-brick low on Donchian channel till the time of writing (August 2018) and the stock price had moved above ₹1,100.

~

Figure 11.4 is a 3% brick value chart of Graphite India with a 40-period Donchian channel plotted on it.

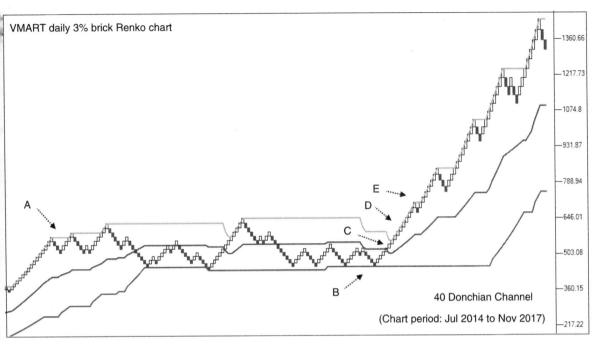

Figure 11.5: **40-brick Donchian channel on a daily 3% brick value Renko chart of VMART**

The price witnessed a sideways period, or horizontal trend, after an uptrend (Point A). Point B shows a brick taking support at the same price levels. Point C is a multi-brick breakout followed by a Donchian 40-period upper band breakout at Point D. Point E is where the bullish one-back pattern breakout confirmation occurred.

~

A combination of simple patterns with a trend identified from indictors is very useful. Figure 11.5 is a 3% brick value chart of VMart with a 40-period Donchian channel.

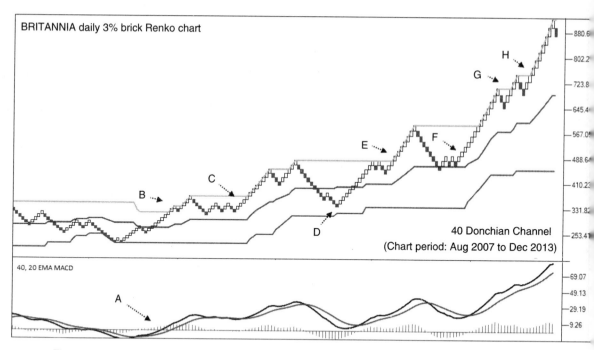

Figure 11.6: **40-brick Donchian channel and 40, 20 MACD on a 3% brick value daily Renko chart of Britannia**

Point A (in the lower MACD panel) moves above the zero line indicating bullish crossover of 20- and 40-period EMAs. Point B is a breach of the 40-period Donchian upper band. Point C is multi-brick breakout. Point D is a bullish weak breakout and polarity principle. Point E is a multi-brick breakout at the Donchian upper band. Point F is a bullish zigzag and polarity principle in the bullish Donchian zone. Points G and H are bullish two-back patterns in the bullish Donchian zone. Another highlight in this chart is that the MACD has remained above the zero line after Point A (lower panel), indicating that the moving average positioning was bullish throughout the period. The stock proved to be one of the leaders of the FMCG Index and was trading above ₹6,000 in August 2018.

~

Figure 11.6 is a 3% brick value chart of Britannia Industries with a 40-period Donchian Channel and 40, 20 EMA MACD plotted.

Now, let's have a look at Figure 11.7.

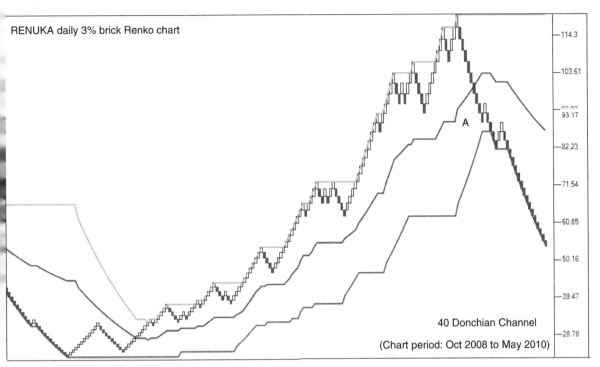

RENUKA daily 3% brick Renko chart

40 Donchian Channel

(Chart period: Oct 2008 to May 2010)

Figure 11.7: **40-brick Donchian channel on a 3% brick value daily Renko chart of Shree Renuka Sugars Ltd. Everything was bullish until Point A, when a bearish swing engulfing breakout entered in the bearish Donchian zone and triggered a follow through bearish breakout. The stock lost over 70% in value thereafter.**

~

Many such examples can be showcased to illustrate the importance of timely exits. Trading parameters can be tweaked based on personal preference but the key takeaway here is that a well defined exit method will perform well and prove beneficial over a period of time. We discussed in Chapter 8 on relative strength that not all stocks perform uniformly even when the overall market trend is bullish. The whipsaws triggered by a strategy are unavoidable and must be viewed as a premium paid for early exits to avert significant erosion in one's trading capital. But a well defined exit method will both outperform over a period of time and also safeguard one's investments when the tide turns rough. It will ensure that you exit before the situation worsens.

Stocks and sectors can remain weak even while the overall market trend is bullish; conversely, a certain set of stocks may perform well even during overall downtrend.

Fundamental Analysis

I am a firm believer in fundamental analysis. One should study valuations and invest only in companies which have a strong management and a distinctive competitive advantage. But it is very difficult for Individuals to keep track of macro- and micro-environments on a frequent basis. Price setups are often a lead indicator and help identify candidates on which further fundamental research may be conducted. But even if one is not well versed with fundamental analysis, investments and long term trading can be considered using the Renko charts methods that we have discussed.

For longer term trading, I recommend increasing the brick value while using daily charts instead of increasing the time frame of the charts from daily to weekly or monthly. This is because weekly time frame charts are not locked till the week is over and the same logic is valid for monthly charts, too. So if I see a swing breakout on a weekly chart, it cannot be considered complete until the week gets over. Trading based on a weekly chart poses practical difficulties. The price may reverse before the week is complete, or it may move farther away if you wait for the week to get over.

We can address this issue by increasing the brick value while retaining the data frequency to daily prices. The charts then get locked daily and we can decide our trade based on various price patterns. This issue of trading a pattern while the time frame is yet to complete is common to all types of charts, including candlesticks, but it is not generally highlighted. The brick value change possibility in Renko charts comes with the distinct advantage of dealing with this important and practical aspect of trading.

Brick Values for Short Term Trading

For shorter term positional trading, I would recommend brick values between 0.25% and 1% on daily time frame charts. Let us study some examples.

Figure 11.8 is a daily chart of Yes bank with a 1% brick value.

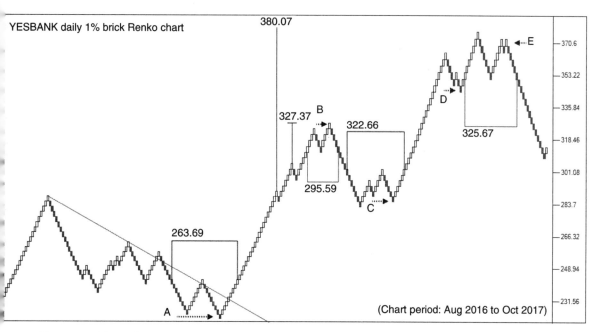

Figure 11.8: **Trend line and extension analysis on a 1% brick value daily Renko chart of Yes Bank. Trend lines and a few extensions are shown on the chart.**

Pattern A is a bullish weak breakout followed by a breakout above a significant trend line and a W formation that witnessed continuation one-back and two-back patterns. Pattern B is a bearish weak breakout followed by an M formation. Pattern C is a bullish weak breakout pattern followed by a W formation. Pattern D is a bullish weak breakout in an up trend, while pattern E is a bearish zigzag formation that marked a lower swing high following an M formation.

~

A brick value of 0.25% or 0.50% can help you time the trade once you see a significant breakout in higher brick values, such as 1%. After an important pattern breakout in a 1% brick value chart, trades may be considered on continuation patterns — such as one-backs or two-backs — on the lower brick value charts. A simple bullish swing breakout in a higher brick value chart may come across as a bullish swing engulfing or strike-back on the lower brick value charts. This will indicate that the bears are trapped and hence the breakout is important.

Let's now have look at a 1% brick value chart of Asian Paints in Figure 11.9 that follows.

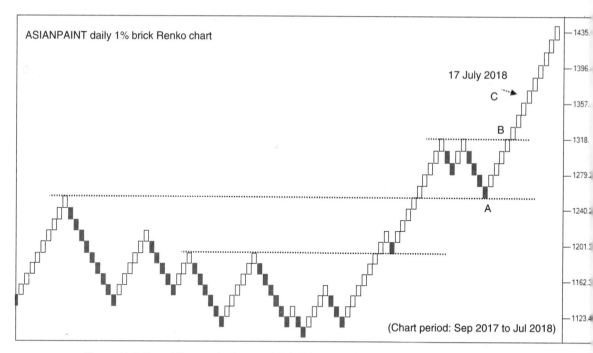

Figure 11.9: **Trend line analysis on a 1% brick value daily Renko chart of Asian Paints**

Multiple horizontal formation breakouts are seen in this chart. The stock price surpassed several previous resistances, then took support at a previous resistance at Point A, and then produced another multi-brick breakout pattern at Point B. In a nutshell, this chart analysis suggests a bullish view. But at Point C, there is a series of bullish bricks and the technical stop loss is below Point B — so the initial risk is unaffordable for short term trading.

~

Figure 11.10 that follows is a 0.25% brick value chart for the same period as when the breakout at point B in Figure 11.9 got triggered.

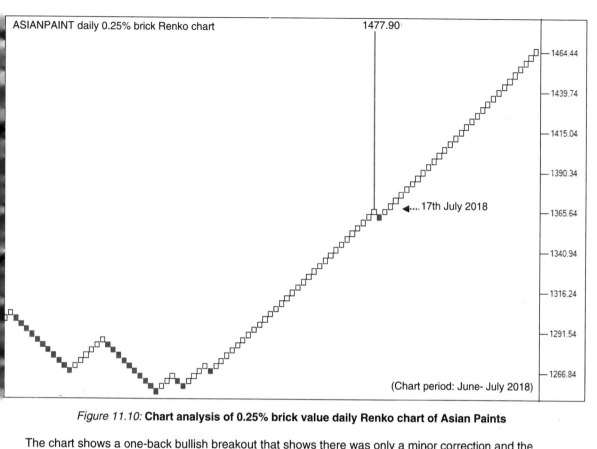

Figure 11.10: **Chart analysis of 0.25% brick value daily Renko chart of Asian Paints**

The chart shows a one-back bullish breakout that shows there was only a minor correction and the price then resumed its uptrend. This gives an opportunity to trade with affordable risk because a stop loss can be placed below the low of the bearish brick of the one-back formation, and can be trailed on this time frame. This illustrates how a view is formed by analysing on the higher brick value chart, in this case a 1% brick value chart (Figure 11.9) while price formations are traded on a lower time frame for short term trading.

~

Figure 11.10 also shows extensions from a bullish one-back. Plotting extensions on multiple brick values also helps.

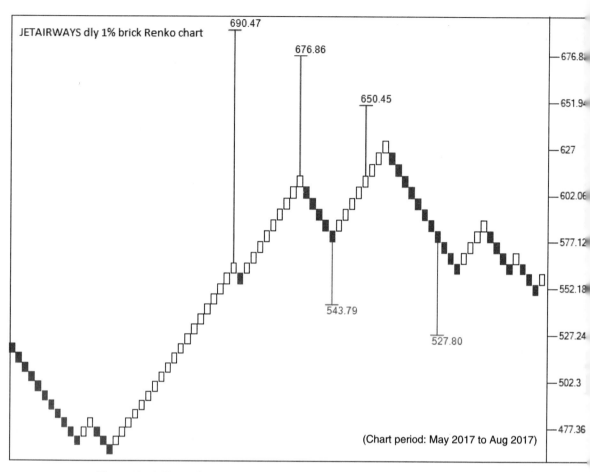

Figure 11.11: **Extensions on a 1% brick value daily Renko chart of Jet Airways**

~

Figure 11.11 is a 1% brick value chart of Jet Airways. As you can see, there are multiple bullish extensions plotted on this chart from the swing breakout patterns. From a practical trading perspective, referring to the extensions on the lower brick value chart can be of immense help.

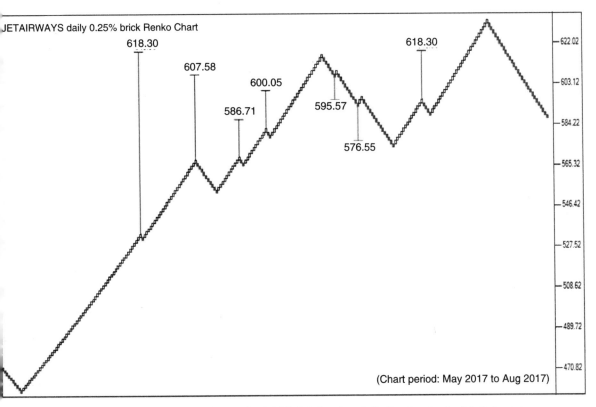

Figure 11.12: **Extension analysis on the 0.25% brick value daily Renko chart of Jet airways**

~

Figure 11.12 is a 0.25% brick value chart of Jet Airways during the same period.

Extensions on lower time frames can help a trader identify the short term reference areas. From a short term trading perspective, trading formations and extensions on the lower brick values as a confirmation to higher brick values can prove very helpful.

From a trading perspective, one can even choose to solely analyse lower brick value charts, such as 0.25% or 0.50%.

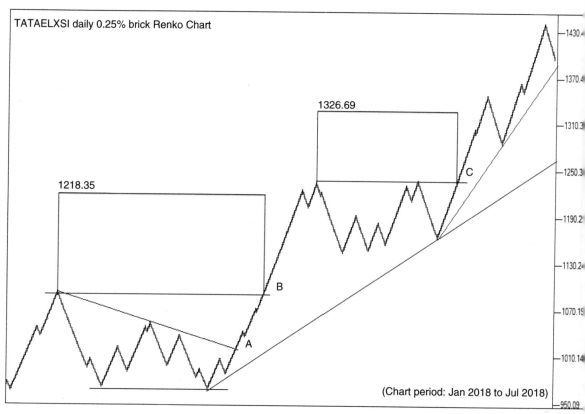

Figure 11.13: **Trend line and extension analysis on a 0.25% brick value daily Renko chart of Tata Elxsi**

Point A is a convergence formation where the price took support and registered a breakout above a significant trend line. Multi-swing extension is applied from the horizontal pattern. The price is trading above the trend line drawn from the bottom of Pattern C.

~

Figure 11.13 is an analysis of Tata Elxsi on a 0.25% brick value chart.

Figure 11.14 is a 0.50% brick value chart of Yes Bank.

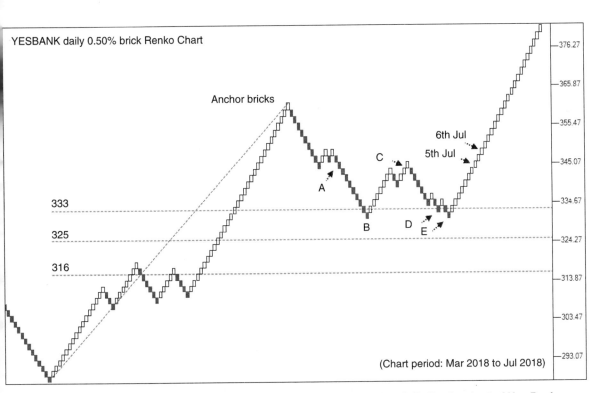

Figure 11.14: **Retracement and pattern analysis on a 0.50% brick value daily Renko chart of Yes Bank**

Point A is a bearish zigzag breakout. The price fell and took support at Point B, which is a Fibonacci retracement level of the previous bullish move. Point C is bullish two-back that morphed into a bearish weak breakout. Points D and E are consecutive bearish one-backs which turned into a bullish weak breakout that took support at the previous brick and at the Fibonacci retracement support level. This was followed by multiple bullish swing breakouts in the same swing that confirmed the strength in the trend.

~

Figure 11.15 is a 0.50% back value chart of Tata Chemicals showing Renko chart patterns without extensions.

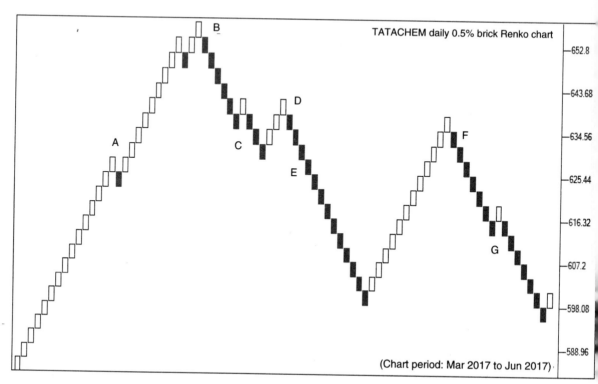

Figure 11.15: **Pattern analysis on the 0.50% brick value daily Renko chart of Tata Chemicals**

Point A is bullish one-back. Point B is also a bullish one-back but it resulted in a bearish weak breakout. Pattern C is a bearish one-back; the price bounced and faced resistance around the same levels at Point D and then produced another bearish swing breakout at Point E. A lower high and a bearish 123 pullback was marked at Point F while a bearish one-back pattern is marked at Point G.

~

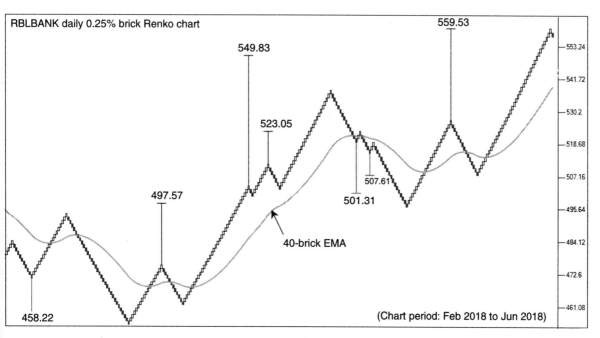

Figure 11.16: **Extensions with 40-brick exponential moving average line on the 0.25% brick value daily Renko chart of RBL Bank.**

~

In the chart in Figure 11.16, bullish swing breakout extensions are applied when the brick concerned is above the moving average, while bearish extensions are applied when the brick is below the moving average line. As earlier discussed in the Chapter 7 and Chapter 8, patterns and extensions can be filtered using indicators.

Figure 11.17 is a 0.50% brick value chart of Titan plotted with a 40-brick EMA.

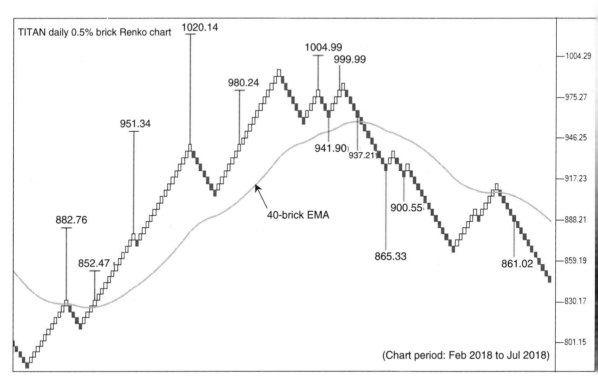

Figure 11.17: **Extensions with 40-brick exponential moving average line on a 0.50% brick value daily Renko chart of Titan.**

In Figure 11.17, you can observe the bullish patterns and extensions during the up trend when the price is above the moving average, and bearish extensions in the down trend when the price is below the moving average line. Remember, you can also use any other indicator instead of moving average.

~

Instead of looking at daily charts, for positional and short term traders, you can also increase the brick value on a one-minute time frame chart. This reduces trading impact cost and also provides information about lower time frame price patterns which is very useful for short-term or momentum trading.

The following are examples of Donchian channels applied on one-minute time interval charts for momentum trading.

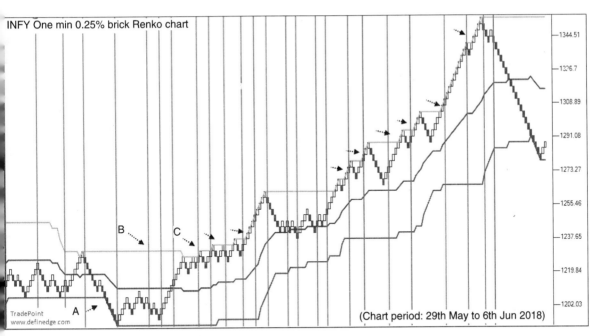

Figure 11.18: **40-brick Donchian channel on a 1-minute time interval 0.25% brick value Renko chart of Infosys. Point A shows a bearish swing breakout at the lower Donchian band. Point B shows a flat band period. And arrows at and after Point C show continuation bullish swing breakout patterns at the upper band and bullish zone of Donchian channels.**

~

You would recall we discussed the Donchian channel method on Renko charts in Chapter 7. Using Donchian channels, a trader can ride the trend for as long as the stock has momentum. Increasing the brick value on intraday time interval chart for positional trading can be a very important tool, especially for derivative traders because it makes the risk becomes more affordable and intraday volatility can be handled better (*see* Figure 11.19).

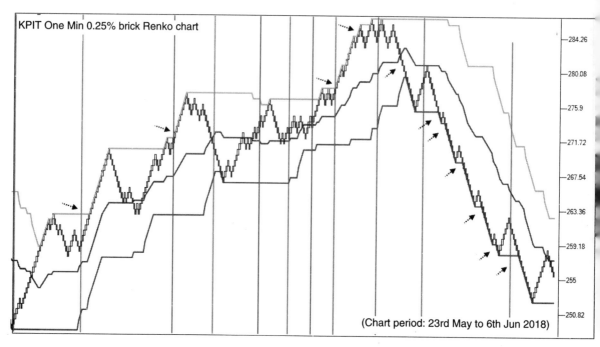

KPIT One Min 0.25% brick Renko chart

(Chart period: 23rd May to 6th Jun 2018)

Figure 11.19: **40-brick Donchian channel plotted on the 1-minute time interval 0.25% brick value Renko chart of KPIT**

~

Vertical lines are day-separating lines to help us observe intraday price moves. Information derived from higher brick values helps in identifying those instruments that are in a strong trending phase. The price action of the entire day is captured in a few Renko bricks.

Analysis of indicators, price and extensions can be carried out in lower time frames as well for momentum trading. At times, you'll get a clear ride with one-backs and two-backs, while at other times there will be zigzags and whipsaws.

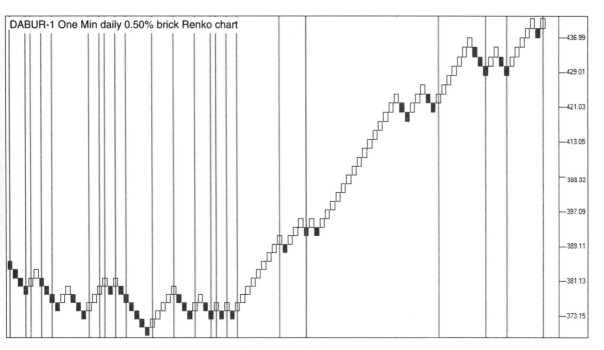

Figure 11.20: **1-minute time interval 0.50% brick value Renko chart of Dabur**

~

Vertical lines in the chart in Figure 11.20 are day separating lines and highlight the importance of Renko charts.

When there is no price action, only a limited number of brick are formed in the day. You can see that there only two or three bricks, or even a single brick, on some days because there was little price movement in the instrument concerned on that particular day. On the other hand, there are days with a series of bricks and when a clear trend is visible. This is the importance of Renko charts on lower time frames. You can read the price action clearly and trade only where there is clear action or momentum. You can easily observe multi-brick breakouts as well as one-back and two-back formations in the chart in Figure 11.20.

Gap up and gap down openings are a challenge for traders. These can result in a long series of bricks on time interval charts. If the price opens higher, and if the risk is not affordable, you should wait for a fresh entry signal. Brick reversal setups can be of help for getting an affordable entry during such times. A trading position should be exited immediately if the price gap opens against you. That is why position sizings should be different for intraday and positional trades.

Brick Values for Very Short Term Trading

Very short term trading, such as intraday trading, requires a special skill set. There is so much noise from minute to minute that it is so very easy to get led into overtrading. **The best advantage of Renko for very short term trading is that such charts reduce the number of trading signals.**

For very short term trading, such as intraday or momentum trading, intraday time interval charts are useful. There are different time frames that people use for trading intraday, such as five minutes, fifteen minutes, hourly, etc. Renko is adept at portraying or mimicking these charts using the one-minute price. Though there is the option to use hourly, or 30-minute, or any other time interval price data, I believe increasing the brick value on a one-minute time frame is a better strategy because it significantly minimizes the impact cost. On a 15-minute time frame, bricks might disappear and reappear within the 15-minute interval. Using one-minute data frequency will help in overcoming the issue. Brick value is a good tool to deal with this issue. One can simply increase the brick value to analyse the larger picture instead of viewing higher time frame charts. Remember, you essentially get to look at the bigger picture on a lower data frequency. A 15-minute candle gets locked at the end of 15 minutes; it can fluctuate wildly in between, which might increase the impact cost. The same applies to Renko as well. Nonetheless, hourly and such other time frames can also be effectively used with Renko charts.

For very short term trading, I recommend using 0.15% to 0.25% brick values for stocks on one-minute time frame Renko charts.

Of course, you can experiment and decide on higher time interval charts as well; but as noted earlier, I recommend changing the brick value instead of the time frame. Increase the brick value if you are a momentum trader; reduce it if you are a short term trader, and reduce it drastically if you are a very aggressive intraday trader. The very nature of the plotting of Renko charts will help you control the issue of overtrading on any time frame. It will also help you increase the productivity of your trades; meaning that your winners will be bigger than your losers.

One minute is a very dynamic time frame on Renko charts. Also, the one minute time frame on Renko is different from the one minute time frame on candlestick charts. As Renko charts get plotted based on bricks, so the width or the length of a chart depends on the brick value you are using. One minute is just a data frequency. One can use 0.15% brick value for very aggressive trading, though 0.25% should be enough even for those trading stocks on intraday basis.

Let's now analyse a few more charts keeping this perspective in mind.

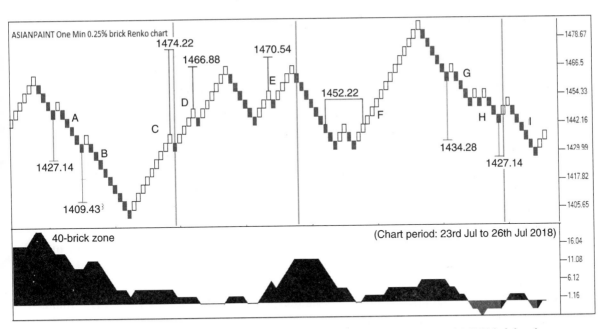

Figure 11.21: **40-brick zone indicator (lower panel) on a 1-minute time interval 0.25% brick value Renko chart of Asian Paints**

There are bearish extensions and patterns at A and B, triggered when the 40-period brick zone indicator was bullish but falling, signifying that the appearance of bearish bricks was increasing. But the price again moved up and formed bullish patterns at points C, D and E. There is a W formation from which a multi-swing extension has been plotted at Point F. A bearish one-back pattern triggered lower extensions at Point G, followed by a bearish zigzag and a bearish two-back at points H and I, respectively.

~

Let's now consider Figure 11.22, which is a chart of Ambuja Cement capturing the price action on an intraday time interval chart that can be useful for momentum traders to trade patterns. The vertical lines such time interval charts are day-separating lines.

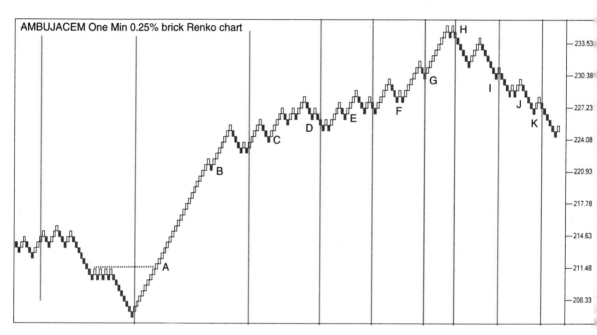

Figure 11.22: **Pattern analysis on a 1-minute time interval 0.25% brick value Renko chart of Ambuja Cement**

Point A indicates the invalidation of an extended zigzag pattern. B is a bullish one-back pattern. C is a bullish 123 pattern that was followed by a bearish multi-swing breakout at Point D. Point E is a bullish two-back continuation pattern, followed by a bullish 123 pullback at Point F. Point G is a bullish two-back pattern. Point H is a bearish zigzag pattern, which was followed by bearish one-back at Point I, a bearish multi-swing breakout with a bearish weak breakout at Point J, and a bearish two-back pattern at Point K.

~

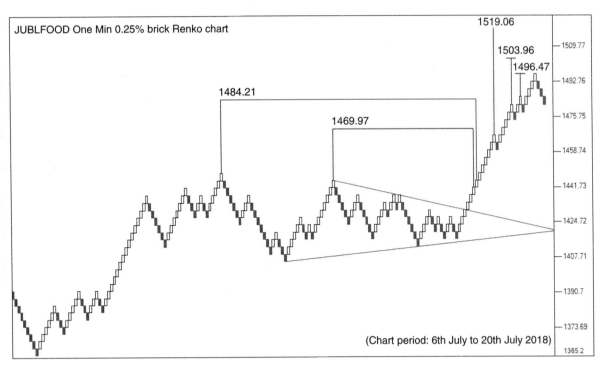

Figure 11.23: **Trend line and extension analysis on a 1-minute time interval 0.25% brick value Renko chart of Jubilant Foodworks**

~

You can use any of the indicators to read trends and divergences; they complement Renko chart pattern breakouts. One-backs, two-backs, multi-breakout and weak breakouts are the best Renko patterns for intraday traders. They are used in combination with indicators for trend filtration can be a great setup for intraday charts.

~

Chapter 12

~

Position Sizing

POSITION SIZING IS A KEY DETERMINANT OF THE RETURNS that a trader can generate on his capital. Position sizing is nothing but a logical way to determine how many shares, or how many contracts of an instrument, should a trader buy or sell in each trade; in other words, to determine the correct size of a trading position.

Determining the correct position size is very critical. This will in turn, determine if you are comfortable enough to stick to your trading system or not, and it will also determine the amount of returns you generate in your trading activity or business. There is no one-size-fits-all approach to position sizing. It differs from person to person, based on the time frame traded, capital deployed and one's risk tolerance, among others factors.

Remember: Your profit = (Exit price – Entry Price) x Number of shares.

The number of shares in the above equation is the position sizing bit. So, the ultimate determinant of your profit is the position size, or your bet size. There are many different approaches to arriving at the right position size. I recommend the book *Definitive Guide to Position Sizing* written by Van Tharp on this subject for more information.

The biggest mistake a trader makes, especially early in his or her career, is to take unusually large sized bets. Irrespective of your conviction level in any trade, as a rule of thumb, one shouldn't risk more than 1% to 2% of your capital in any single trade. For better position sizing, I recommend the strategy of testing the waters. Decide the maximum allocation per trade. I would recommend a maximum of 10% to 20% capital allocation to one trade. Divide that further into two parts. Enter the first part upon the first bullish observation and add more once you see follow through price action. In the same way, your exits could also be done in two phases. Have a look at the examples below.

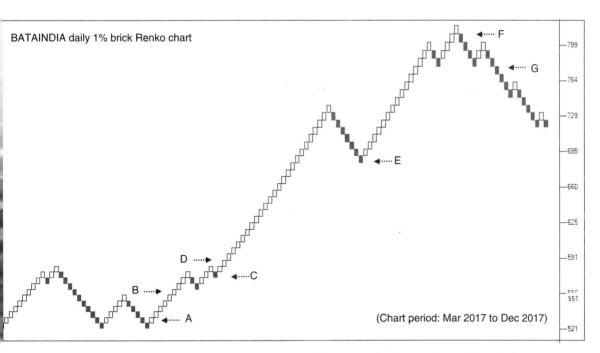

Figure 12.1: **Position sizing explained on a 1% brick value daily Renko chart of Bata India**

Point A shows a Renko support pattern which is the first entry point. Pattern B is a follow through bullish swing breakout where more quantity can be added. Pattern C is bearish weak breakout where the first portion can be sold. Pattern D is a bullish one-back pattern where the recently exited trade can be reinstated. Upon the bullish brick reversal after Point E, the stop loss for all the positions can be trailed below the bottom of Point E. Pattern F is bearish swing breakout where a part of the traded quantity should be exited. Pattern G is bearish swing breakout where the remaining quantity can be sold.

~

In this way, Renko price formations can be traded by phasing out entry and exits in a very efficient manner. Objectivity of patterns makes this job simple. You can also include indicators or other studies that we have discussed in the book to fine tune your entry and exit. You can also utilise extensions for partial exits. Have a look at the chart in Figure 12.2.

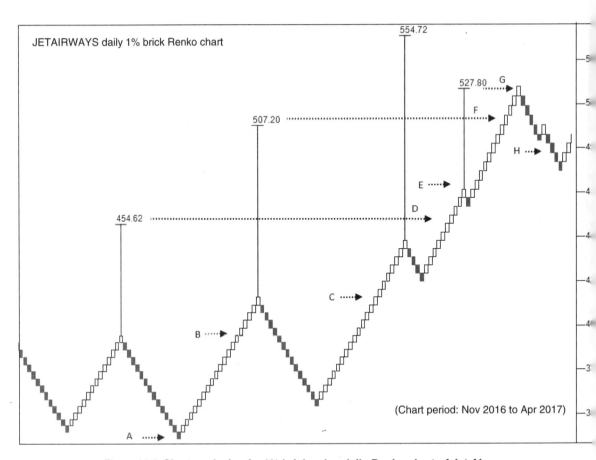

Figure 12.2: **Chart analysis of a 1% brick value daily Renko chart of Jet Airways**

Point A is bullish weak breakout pattern which is a first entry point. Pattern B is a follow through bullish swing breakout where additional quantity can be added. Pattern C is continuation bullish swing breakout. Bullish extension of ₹454.62 is achieved at Point D where partial profit can be booked. The stock can again be bought at the one-back bullish pattern at Point E. Stop loss for the entire position is trailed below the bearish brick of the one-back formation at Point E. Bullish extension of ₹507.20 is achieved at Point F where profit can again be booked. Extension of ₹527.80 is achieved at Point G where the remaining quantities can be sold. A bearish swing breakout pattern got formed at Point H.

~

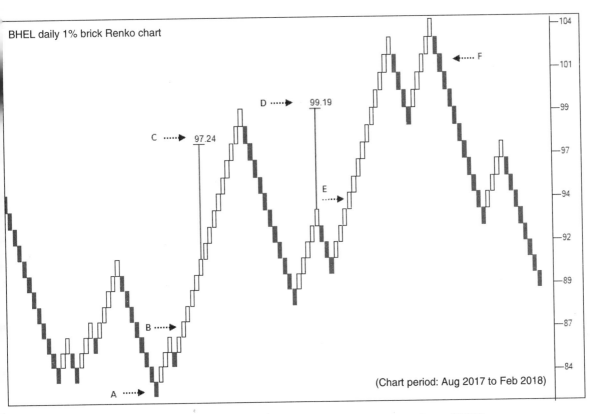

Figure 12.3 : **Chart analysis of a 1% brick value daily Renko chart of BHEL**

Point A is a bullish weak breakout pattern which is the first entry point. Pattern B is a follow through bullish one-back breakout where more quantity can be added. Bullish extension of ₹97.24 was achieved at Point C, where the first portion can be sold. The price gave another bullish swing breakout above the earlier entry level at Point E, where the quantity sold earlier can be bought again and the stop loss for the entire position can be trailed up below the bottom of the swing breakout pattern at Point E. Extension of ₹99.19 plotted from swing breakout at point E was achieved at Point D where the first portion can be sold again. Point F is a bearish weak breakout where profit can be booked in the remaining quantity.

~

The same approach is also applicable for short trades based on bearish patterns. In this way, you will be in a trade with the minimum quantity in case the price immediately reverses and the pattern fails. And you will be trading with a maximum position size when the trade goes in your favour and proves to be a winner. The follow through price action also helps in trailing the stop loss for the entire position. Once you gain confidence with this approach, you can probably divide the allocation first between three and then into four parts. The method is known as pyramiding, and it's a very nice way of trading and dealing with emotions. But it needs to be practiced and going step-wise will help you to have a hold on it and gain conviction.

The Pareto Principle, or the Rule of 80/20, applies to trading also. Over a period of time, typically, 20% of a trader's trades account for the bulk of his or her returns. With the method of riding the trend and pyramiding, those 20% trades can turn out to be huge winners. Equally, the cost of failure in losing trades can be reduced. The method of pyramiding and adding to continuation breakouts is a very effective way of trading the markets. Let's see how in the chart of Escorts in Figure 12.4.

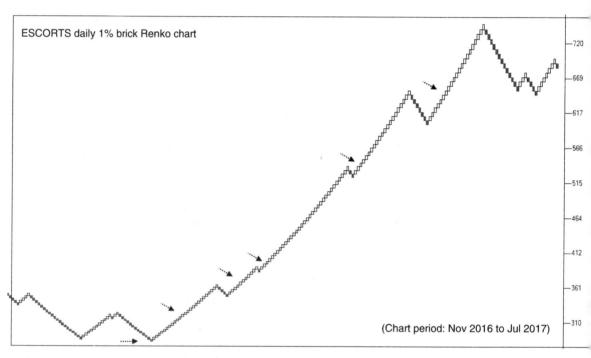

Figure 12.4: **Series of bullish breakouts in a 1% brick value daily Renko chart of Escorts**

~

Instead of exiting abruptly, adding at every continuation breakout and riding a trade would result in big winners and handsome gains in your trading portfolio.

~

Chapter 13

Short Term Trading Strategies

O N ANY GIVEN DAY, THERE WOULD BE SOME INSTRUMENTS which are trending and there would be those which you may like based on their chart formations but which are not in action.

Your trading results can be improved if you trade those patterns which have triggered a significant breakout on the higher time frame and are displaying momentum in the lower time frame.

Bull Day, Bear Day

There is objectivity and advantage in counting bricks — we can count the number of bullish and bearish bricks on a given day for any instrument and then calculate the ratio of dominating bricks.

On any given day, if the number of bullish bricks is higher than the number of bearish ones, it would mean that the price action is bullish.

Conversely, if there are more bearish bricks it would mean that the current price action is bearish.

Accordingly, if the ratio of bullish bricks to total bricks for a day is more than 50%, it is a bull day. On the other hand, if the ratio of bearish bricks is more than 50%, then it is a bear day.

A bull day, or a bear day, shows us which side is dominating and which in the direction we should focus on. At times, several instruments simultaneously witness zigzag type of days where the bullish and bearish bricks are equal or nearly equal in number. Trading on such days may not prove very rewarding simply because there is no meaningful price action. This ratio often changes as the day progresses, so I recommend tracking it every couple of hours after the market opening.

On some days there won't be many bricks, meaning there is no significant price movement. On other days, there will be many bricks showing that the stock concerned is in action. You will see this at a glance when you open a Renko chart and see the number of the current day's bricks compared to the number of bricks in the previous few days. The brick count on a day gives us an idea both about how the day is progressing and whether the bulls or bears are dominating in that instrument (*see* Figure 13.1).

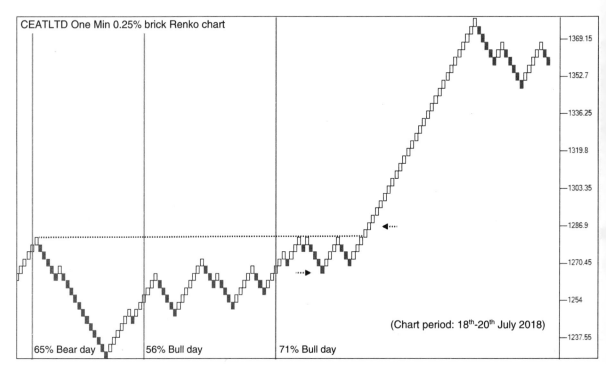

Figure 13.1: **Bull and bear days on a 1-minute time interval 0.25% brick value Renko chart of Ceat Industries Ltd. The arrow shows the bullish weak breakout followed by a higher bottom and a multi-brick breakout. The stock was witnessing resistance at a particular level and formed a multi-brick breakout from a horizontal price pattern. The price turned bullish post the breakout and remained so until the end of the day.**

~

Figure 13.2 is another example of a multi-brick breakout in intraday trading.

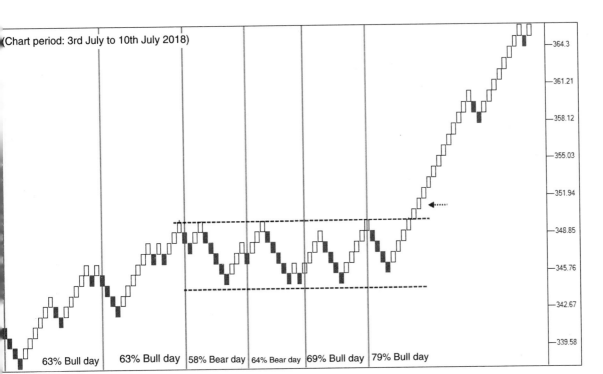

Figure 13.2: **Multi-brick breakout on a 1-minute time interval 0.25% brick value Renko chart of GAIL**

The horizontal pattern breakout that occurred in the morning session indicated that the price had broken a significant swing high in the past few sessions. More than 60% of the bricks were bullish till that time and the day remained a bull day.

~

Distinguishing bull days from bear days helps us in analysing short term sentiment and can prove useful for short term traders. Stocks logging a bull day indicate positive sentiment in the short run and can continue to do well in favourable market conditions. In the same way, a stock witnessing a bear day has more bearish prints than bullish ones, which indicates negative sentiment in the short run.

Bull days and bear days should be reckoned only on one-minute time frames.

Anchor Day

When breakouts are being traded, it is sensible to trade the instruments having a trend day. Renko bull day, bear day classification helps us to define this. Instruments having more than 60% bull day, or bear day, are anchor day instruments. You can trade continuation swing breakouts, such as one-backs or two-backs, in the anchor day instruments so long as the 60% ratio is maintained. The stop loss should be placed at the swing breakout. You can plot an indicator like the moving average for trend identification.

If it is a more than 60% bullish or bearish day, it is an anchor day for that instrument. Else, it is a neutral day. One should trade bullish patterns if it is more than 60% bull day, and bearish patterns if it turns out to be more than 60% bear day.

Anchor Bricks

A short term trader needs to identify and trade stocks displaying momentum. In fact, all that an intraday or short term trader needs to focus on is momentum. The plan should be to trade stocks that are moving, *and not try and guess which ones might move*. This way the trader can efficiently utilise his funds and generate consistent returns.

Anchor bricks is a very important tool for identifying momentum.

Whenever the price action results in the plotting of a series of more than ten bricks in either direction, any continuation pattern in that instrument should be traded. You need not know what will gap up or gap down. All you need to do is to identify the stocks that have a gap opening. You can see the series of bullish or bearish bricks in the morning in the gap opening stock. These are the stocks with momentum.

Figure 13.3 that follows is a chart of Mindtree on a day that it gapped down. Once you saw the series of bearish bricks in the morning, you knew that the sentiment for this stock was negative. One could then have traded the bearish continuation swing breakout patterns in the stock with a stop at the bullish swing breakout level. Either moving average or any other indicator can be applied for trend identification in such a case.

Trading simple Renko continuation patterns in stocks with momentum is one of the best methods I know for short term trading.

Anchor bricks set the tone of a chart. Keep a track of the recent trend of anchor bricks as that will tell you about the prevailing sentiment in the security. If you trade patterns in the direction of the recent anchor bricks, you will be saved from many whipsaws.

The 40-period brick zone indicator used in Figure 13.3 also helps in analysing the short or medium term trend of a chart. When the short term trend of a stock is aligned with its medium term trend, it should be traded because you can expect quick moves in your favour in such instruments. When the short term trend is against the medium term trend, it can be avoided for positional trading. You can treat it as dead cat bounce which you may trade intraday but I don't recommend such candidates for positional trades. One should also always wait for follow through action in such cases before considering any positional trades.

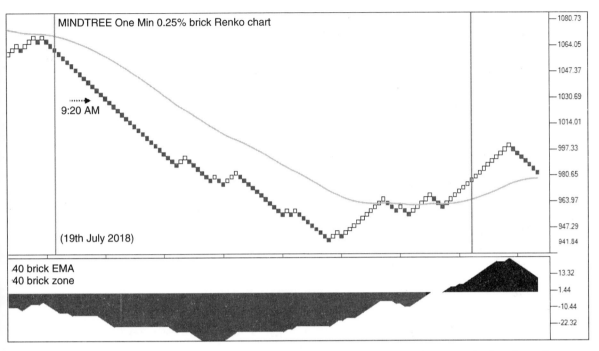

Figure 13.3: **40-brick zone indicator on a 1-minute time interval 0.25% brick value Renko chart of Mindtree**

~

A series of anchor bricks on a daily time frame chart shows that the stock has momentum, but has it already moved such that the risk reward is not favourable for positional trades any more? You need to wait for some follow through on that time frame for a trade entry. That instrument can, however, be traded intraday based on intraday chart patterns. The logic here is that if there is a breakout leading to a series of bullish bricks on the daily time frame chart, it indicates that the larger degree chart is bullish. The trend is established and the stock is in momentum. These are the best candidates for intraday trades. If you then spot some pattern in its intraday time frame chart, the stock can be traded.

Bullish-Bearish 5

A series of five consecutive bricks can be treated as an anchor brick for intraday trading with 0.25% brick value on one-minute time interval charts (*see* Figure 13.4).

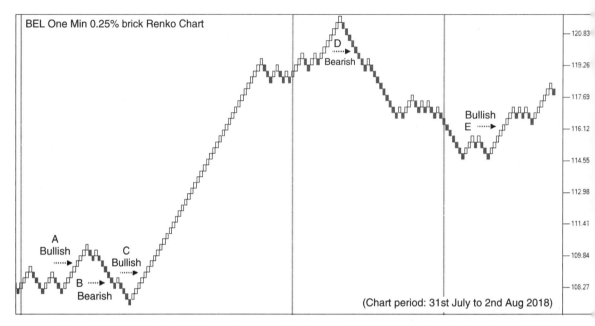

Figure 13.4: **Bullish-bearish 5 on a 1-minute time interval 0.25% brick value Renko chart of BEL futures.**

A series of five bricks at Point A sets the bullish tone, which turned to bearish at Point B. A bullish breakout and a series of five bricks triggered a bullish formation at Point C which remained bullish until Point D, when it triggered a bearish series even before the bearish swing breakout. The price remained bearish until Point E.

~

Once five consecutive bricks are printed in a direction, you should then be looking for a trade in that direction — unless five consecutive bricks in the other direction get printed. Trading continuation Renko patterns post a series of five bricks is a recommended strategy.

Multiple Time Frame Price Analysis

As we have discussed earlier, Renko is both a best representation of a line chart and an effective, noiseless method of studying price action. We can analyse a Renko chart on multiple time frames as well to get an idea of the trend and price setups across different periods. For example, if I am a short-term trader I would look at the daily time frame chart for trading, and also keep in mind the price action in the weekly or monthly chart to get an idea of the trend in those higher time frames. We can adopt a similar approach in Renko charts, too. To do so, we can adjust the brick value to perform multiple time frame analysis.

When the most recent brick is bullish, it suggests that the price is strong or bullish in that time frame. Correspondingly, if the most recent brick is bearish, the chart is construed as being bearish. Isn't it logical that the trend will be strong when an instrument is bullish, or bearish as the case may be, across multiple time frames? In other words, if the price is in a strong trending mode, it will typically have bullish bricks or bearish bricks on multiple brick values, i.e. multiple time frames.

Table 13.1
Multi-brick Value Analysis of Renko Charts of IT index stocks

Scrip	0.5%	1%	2%	3%	Total Score
INFY	1	1	1	1	4
TECHM	1	1	1	1	4
TCS	0	1	1	1	3
TATAELXSI	1	0	0	1	2
MINDTREE	1	1	0	0	2
INFIBEAM	0	0	0	1	1
HCLTECH	1	0	0	0	1
KPIT	0	0	0	1	1
OFSS	0	0	0	0	0
WIPRO	0	0	0	0	1

Given the simplicity and objectivity of Renko charts, it is very simple to build a table that will tell us about price action over multiple time frames at a glance. Here is how. If the latest brick is bullish, score it as 1 but if the latest brick is bearish, then score it as 0. Table 13.1 shows the scores as per the above rules on different brick values for IT index stocks.

There are four brick values in Table 13.1 — 0.50% representing short-term, 1% representing medium-term, 2% representing the intermediate term, and 3% representing long-term. It's scored as 1 if the brick is bullish on that particular brick value, and 0 if the brick is bearish. The last column shows the total score of all four brick values. So, if the score is 4, it means that the chart is bullish on all four brick values, i.e. on all time frames. On the other hand, if the total score is 0, that would mean the chart is bearish on all four brick values.

In Table 13.1, Infy is bullish and Wipro is bearish across all time frames. Figure 13.4 is chart of infosys from Table 13.1. As the last brick in all the four charts are bullish, hence the score is 4.

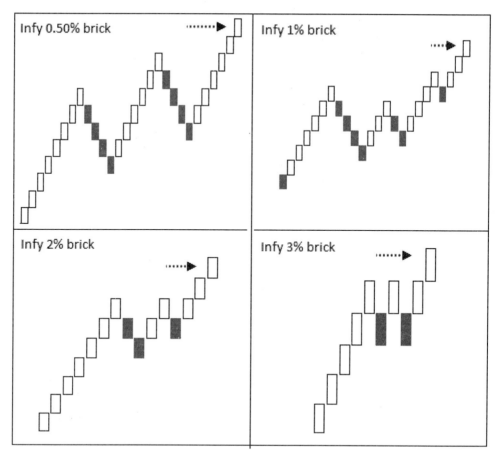

Figure 13.4: **Daily chart of Infosys corresponding of Table 13.1**

~

The Renko price matrix table gives us an idea about the performance of all the stocks in a sector or a group at a glance. So, if the IT index is performing well, and if one wishes to identify the stocks within that sector that are doing well, it is easily accomplished by just looking at the table to shortlist the candidates. Wipro, for example, has a bearish brick on multiple time frames. Accordingly, one should ignore Wipro as it is bearish even though the IT index itself is bullish.

I would give more importance to breakouts on lower time frames if the chart is bullish on the higher time frames as well. Such breakouts often produce quick and nice moves. Breakouts on a lower time frame when the larger time frame is not bullish often result in traps or whipsaws, or what is technically called a dead cat bounce.

What does it indicate If the score In Table 13.1 is positive on higher time frames but zero on the lower time frame? It shows that the trend is positive in the long and medium term, but the price is correcting in the short term. Isn't that a potential candidate that could end up being a high probability trade opportunity when the breakout happens in the lower time frame?

Let us consider TCS as an example from Table 13.1. Its score is positive on higher brick values but zero on the lower brick value. Let's now see the chart of TCS on the lower brick value of 0.50% in Figure 13.5.

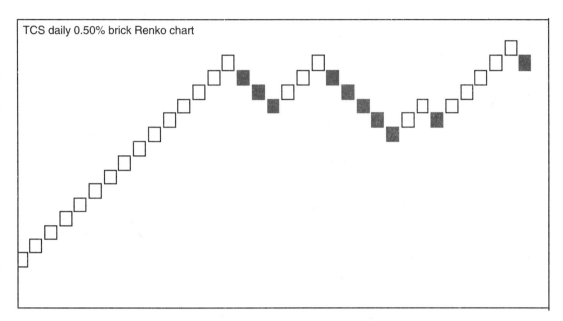

TCS daily 0.50% brick Renko chart

Figure 13.5: **Daily 0.50% brick value chart of TCS corresponding to Table 13.1**

~

Now you can analyse this chart and decipher the trade setup. It is interesting to notice that if we get two bullish bricks from here, it would trigger a bullish one-back pattern. The price has already broken a prior resistance, and a bullish continuation formation will add strength to the up trend. This is how you can trade the continuation pattern in a leading stock from an outperforming index!

This approach of trading continuation patterns in outperforming and underperforming stocks or sectors can be very rewarding.

Performance of all the sectors can be viewed at glance using a comparative table as discussed above. We can easily gather information about the sectors that are outperforming the broader market index and sectors that are either not contributing or are underperforming.

Table 13.2 shows the performance of all sectors on multiple brick values on a given day.

You can observe that the FMCG sector is the top performer in this case because the price setup is bullish across multiple time frames. PSE, CPSE, commodities and infra are underperforming sectors. There are bullish pullback opportunities in PSU banks and MNC sectors, and bearish pullback opportunities in media, pharma, auto and metals. The same matrix table can be generated for the constituent stocks of each of these sectors in order to identify trading opportunities.

Table 13.2

Multi-brick Value Analysis of Renko Charts of Sector Indices

Scrip	0.5	1	2	3	Total Score
Nifty FMCG	1	1	1	1	4
Nifty PSU Bank	0	1	1	1	3
Nifty MNC	0	1	1	1	3
Nifty Fin Service	0	0	1	1	2
Nifty 50	0	0	1	1	2
Nifty Bank	0	0	1	1	2
Nifty consumption	0	0	1	1	2
Nifty Pvt Bank	0	0	1	1	2
Nifty Serv Sector	0	0	1	1	2
Nifty IT	0	0	0	1	1
Nifty Energy	0	0	1	0	1
Nifty Realty	0	1	0	0	1
Nifty Metal	1	0	0	0	1
Nifty Auto	1	0	0	0	1
Nifty Pharma	1	0	0	0	1
Nifty Media	1	0	0	0	1
Nifty Infra	0	0	0	0	0
Nifty Commodities	0	0	0	0	0
Nifty CPSE	0	0	0	0	0
Nifty PSE	0	0	0	0	0

Identifying trade opportunities in stocks that are outperforming from a strong sector, or underperforming stocks from a weak sector, will result in more productive trades, giving increased return in a relatively short period.

You can also identify stocks that are not moving in sync with a sector's trend. Such stocks tend to be serious underperformers when the sector gets into a trend reversal.

This is a top down approach to trading and investment. I have consistently experienced that whenever a group or sector shows strength, the individual stock breakouts are very reliable in such instances.

Where the score is positive on all the brick values, those instruments are in a strong momentum phase and one can trade them on breakouts in the lower brick values or intraday time-interval charts.

~

Chapter 14

~

Index Trading

A STOCK AND AN INDEX ARE DIFFERENT IN TERMS OF THEIR UNDERLYING VOLATILITY. An index captures the price of many stocks. Typically, stocks can easily see a daily price movement of 5% to 10%, which, however, is very rare for an index. Then, too, a stock can get delisted if the company concerned goes bankrupt, but an index will seldom fall to zero unless the stock exchange itself fails.

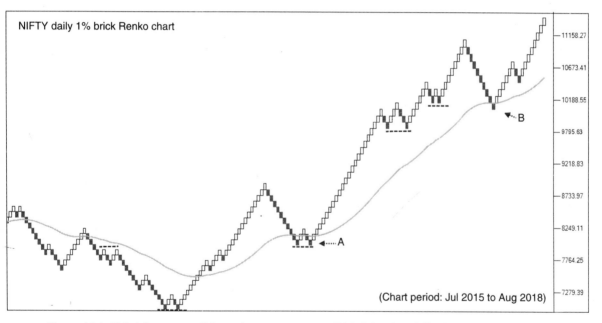

Figure 14.1: **40-brick exponential moving average on a 1% brick value daily Renko chart of Nifty**

In this chart, you can observe Renko patterns such as one-back, two-back, zigzag, etc. This chart is for a medium term analysis of Nifty. You can notice support, or resistance, at previous swing lows and swing highs shown on the chart. Point A is where the price tested the moving average line and formed a Renko support pattern. It then formed a bullish weak breakout near the moving average at Point D, followed by bullish two-back and strike-back.

~

For this reason, brick values used for trading indices are different from those used for trading stocks. For indices, I recommend a 1% brick value on the daily time frame for medium term to long term analysis, and 0.25% for short term to intermediate term analysis.

Let's consider Figure 14.1, which is a 1% brick value chart of Nifty with 40-EMA applied on it.

Figure 14.2 is a 0.25% brick value chart of Nifty with 40-EMA and extensions. Bullish extensions above the moving average, and bearish extensions below the moving average, are marked in this chart. Continuation patterns, such as one-backs, two-backs, and reversal formations such as a weak breakout in the direction of the trend (moving average) are interesting observations on this brick value.

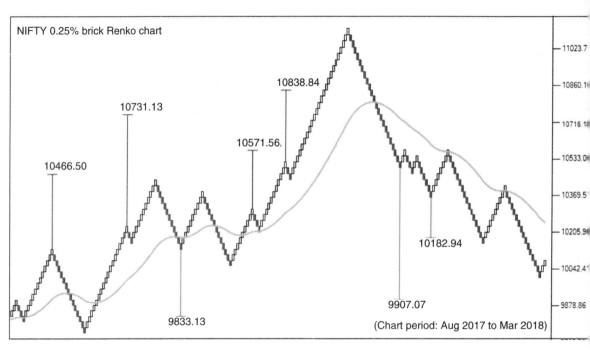

Figure 14.2: **40-brick exponential moving average and extension analysis on a 1% brick value daily Renko chart of Nifty.**

~

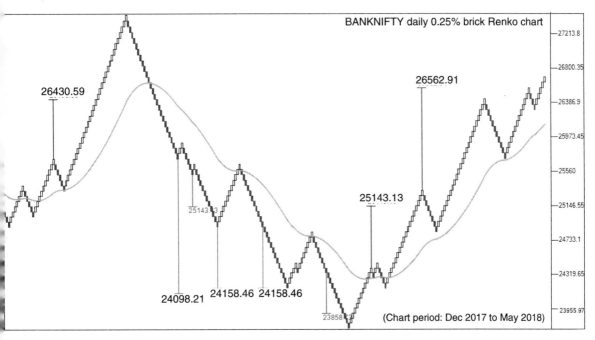

Figure 14.3: **40-brick exponential moving average and extension analysis on the 0.25% brick value daily Renko chart of Bank Nifty**

~

Figure 14.3 is a chart of Bank Nifty with 0.25% brick value plotted with 40EMA and extensions. Extensions in the direction of the moving average are plotted on the chart in Figure 14.3. 0.25% is my preferred brick value for analysing Nifty and Bank Nifty on end of the day daily charts.

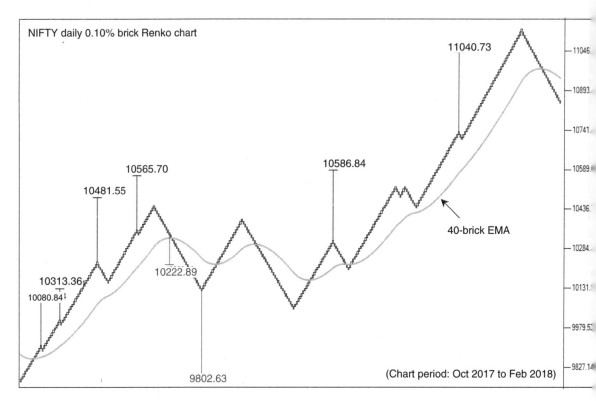

NIFTY daily 0.10% brick Renko chart

11040.73

10565.70

10481.55

10586.84

10313.36

10080.84

10222.89

40-brick EMA

9802.63

(Chart period: Oct 2017 to Feb 2018)

11046

10893

10741

10589

10436

10284

10131

9979.5

9827.14

Figure 14.4: **40-brick exponential moving average and extension analysis on the 0.10% brick value daily Renko chart of Nifty. Bullish extensions above the moving average and bearish extensions below the moving average are marked. Follow through to strike-backs and swing engulfing formations are some of the interesting observations on lower brick value charts such as this.**

~

If one wants to analyse an extreme short-term time frame, then 0.10% brick value is recommended. Figure 14.4 is a chart of Nifty with 0.10% brick value plotted with 40-brick EMA and extensions.

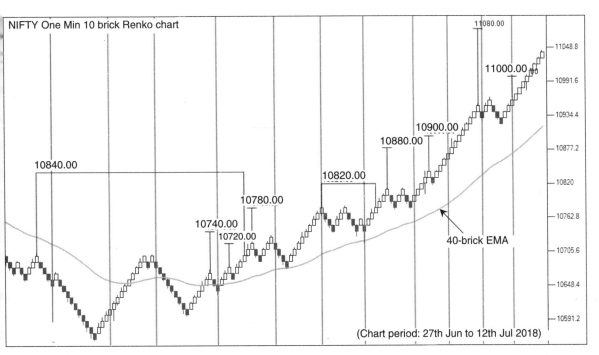

Figure 14.5: **40-brick exponential moving average and extension analysis on a 1-minute time interval 10 absolute brick value Renko chart of Nifty**

~

Figure 14.5 is a one-minute 10 absolute brick value chart of Nifty on one-minute interval shown with shadows, 40EMA and extensions applied on it.

Like in stocks, such a chart can help for momentum or positional trading in an index such as Nifty as well.

Short Term Index Trading

Brick values can be reduced further for very short term or intraday index trading.

Absolute brick values are recommended in time interval charts, particularly if an instrument is traded on a consistent basis.

This approach will be helpful both for remembering important levels and for tracking setups. As stated earlier, one-minute time interval charts are recommended for short term trading. For momentum trading, a 10-point brick value for Nifty, and a 25-points brick value for Bank Nifty may be used. A 5-point brick value in the case of Nifty, and a 10-point brick value for Bank Nifty is recommended for very short term trading, such as intraday.

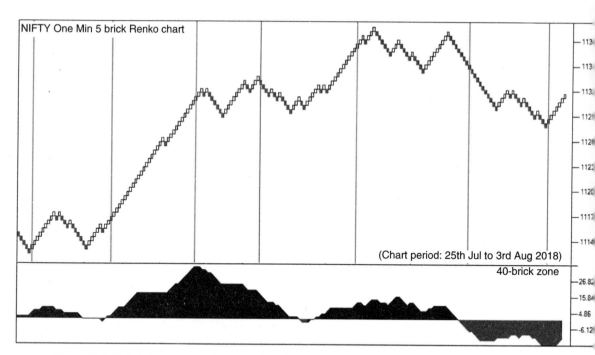

Figure 14.6: **40-brick zone on a 1-minute time interval 5 absolute brick value Renko chart of Nifty. Brick zones show bullish and bearish environments in the short term.**

~

Figure 14.6 is a 5-brick value Renko chart of Nifty shown with the brick zone indicator.

Simple Renko patterns can be very helpful for intraday trading. Have a look at the Nifty intraday one-minute Renko chart with a 5-point brick value in Figure 14.7 that follows.

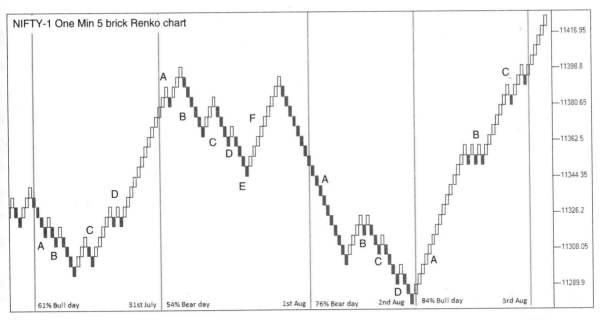

Figure 14.7: Pattern analysis on a 1-minute time interval 5 absolute brick value Renko chart of Nifty. The vertical lines are day-separating lines.

31 July: It was a 61% bull day. Patterns A and B are bearish one-backs. Pattern C is a bullish strike-back follow through, which is also a bullish two-back. Pattern D is a bullish zigzag breakout. All these are swing breakouts during the day. Patterns A and C, the only patterns that would have been traded, were swing breakouts to be traded with stop loss at swing high or swing low.

1 August: Point A is a bullish one-back that got marked upon a higher opening, but turned out to be a weak breakout. This was followed by a bearish swing breakout at Point B. Pattern C is another swing breakout. Point D is a bearish one-back followed by a bullish ABCD at Point E. A bullish swing breakout got triggered at Point F. A, B and F are signals that would have been traded in case one were actively trading swing breakout patterns. The day happened to be neutral, being a 54% bear day.

2 August: The price opened lower and triggered a bearish swing breakout at Point A. Pattern B is a bearish zigzag; Points C and D are bearish one-backs. The single bearish swing breakout triggered at Point A worked throughout the day which happened to be a 76% bear day.

3 August: The price opened higher and formed a bullish swing breakout at Point A. This was followed by an extended bullish zigzag breakout at Point B. Point C is a bullish one-back. The bullish swing breakout triggered at Point A worked throughout the day, which turned out to be an 84% bull day!

~

In Figure 14.7, you can see the price behaviour on each of the four days. You can trade such swing breakout patterns using extensions or indicators. Filtering with extensions and indicators would reduce the number of trades significantly, thus making trading more effective by using Renko charts.

The same method can be followed on Bank Nifty with an absolute brick value of 10. Roughly, round number around 0.05% of the previous day's price of an index can be opted as a brick value for plotting the next day.

For example, at the time of writing the Nifty index was trading at 10,000 level, 0.05% of that is 5 points. Accordingly, one can plot 5 brick value chart for short term trading the next day using the method discussed above. You can observe that the noise is reduced and there are a fewer numbers of trades even on such a lower time interval chart.

Anchor Day in Index Trading

We discussed anchor day instrument reading in the earlier section. It is also applicable for Nifty and Bank Nifty. It makes sense to trade continuation pattern breakouts in the indices on days when they are in momentum .

If it happens to be an anchor day in an index, meaning that it's either more than 60% bull day or more than 60% bear day, open a one-minute time frame chart as discussed above, apply moving average and trade patterns in the direction of the trend with the stop-loss of the swing high or swing low so long as the ratio of 60% is maintained. If it happens to be a trend day, you might enjoy it.

Bull day, bear day analysis will help you to judge the price setups further. Readers with market experience would agree that money earned during trending markets is often lost in sideways trends. Anchor days can be a tool to trade breakouts only in markets that show strong price action.

Figure 14.8 that follows is a 10 brick value intraday chart of Bank Nifty.

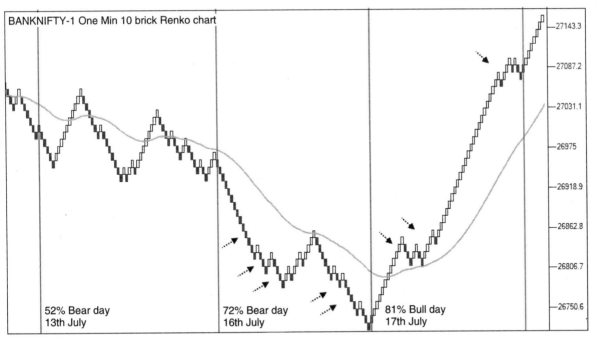

Figure 14.8: **40-brick exponential moving average on a 1-minute time interval 10 absolute brick value Renko chart of Bank Nifty**

13 July was a neutral day. As you would notice from the series of bearish bricks and bearish breakouts on the chart, 16 July was a bearish anchor day, 17 July was a strong bull day; the series of bullish bricks and bullish breakouts can be seen on the chart. Even simple continuation breakouts traded with a stop loss of swing high or swing low can prove a very effective trading strategy.

~

The brick value can be adjusted as per one's trading style. For very aggressive intraday trading, brick values can be reduced further. Aggressive traders can also use high-low Renko charts on this time frame.

Breadth Analysis in Index Trading

The breadth is a most important indicator when trading indices. We have discussed how to interpret the breadth indicator in detail in Chapter 7. We often see poor highs or lows formed during breadth exhaustion. Accordingly, one must remain cautious when the breadth is at an exhaustion zone, or when there is a divergence between the breadth and the price. **Bull days with strong breadth numbers are a bullish scenario and, by the same token, bear days with weak breadth represent a bearish scenario.**

~

Chapter 15

~

Trading Options, Commodities and Currency

OPTIONS ARE A USEFUL DERIVATIVE INSTRUMENT AND THEY CAN BE TRADED using technical analysis without having to understand the Greeks associated with them. Renko charts of options can be plotted and every Renko technique that we have discussed is applicable on them as well.

One way to trade options is to form a view on the underlying asset based on Renko chart analysis — and then build a trading strategy using option Greeks.

Another way is to plot option premium Renko charts — and then trade options as per the methods we have discussed in this book. For example, suppose the premium of 10,000 strike price of Nifty option of a particular month is trading at ₹100. We can then plot Renko chart as the premium changes.

Daily time frame has limited use in trading options. Intraday time interval Renko charts of option premiums should be plotted as other time frames are not very useful in India where the next, or far, month options contracts are still relatively illiquid. One minute is the best time frame to view option premium charts but the brick value should be higher than what is used when analysing the underlying. I recommend 3% to 5% brick value on one-minute time frame for option premium charts.

As shown in Figure 15.1, a simple brick zone indicator crossovers can also be traded.

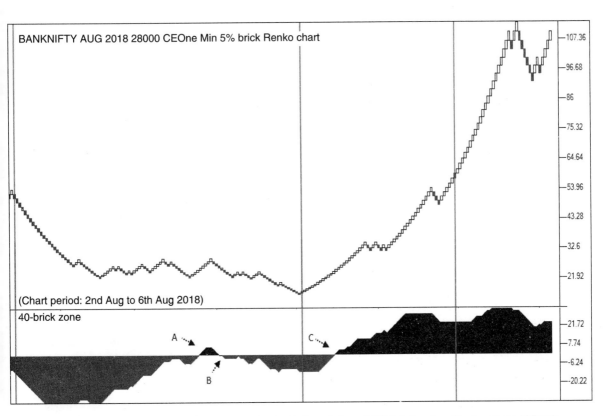

Figure 15.1: **40-brick zone indicator on a 1-minute time interval 5% brick value Renko chart of Bank Nifty 28,000 strike price call option for the month of August 2018. Notice the brick zone crossover highlighted on the chart.**

At pattern A, brick indicator turned to bullish zone at around ₹24 levels and turned to bearish zone (bearish bricks increased) around same level subsequently at pattern B. At pattern C, increment of bullish bricks resulted in bullish brick zone positive crossover at around ₹22. Brick zone indicator was still bullish when premium was trading around ₹107 on the next day.

~

You can also place a trade upon a bullish swing breakout when the brick zone is bullish; and exit at a bearish swing breakout.

When a view is formed on a chart based on the study of its underlying, the underlying's call or put option chart can be traded. Have a look at the Renko chart of Dr. Reddy's Laboratories 2,200 strike price call option shown in Figure 15.2.

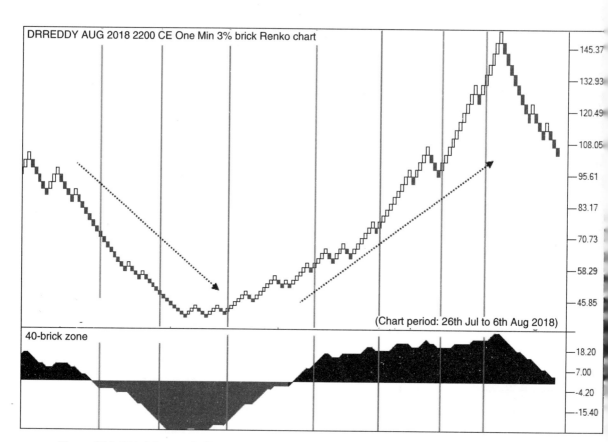

Figure 15.2: **40-brick zone indicator on a 1-minute time interval 3% brick value Renko chart of Dr. Reddy's Laboratories 2,200 strike price call option. The Y-axis is the premium.**

~

Figure 15.3 is a chart of the same period as the one in Figure 15.2, plotted along with a 40-EMA.

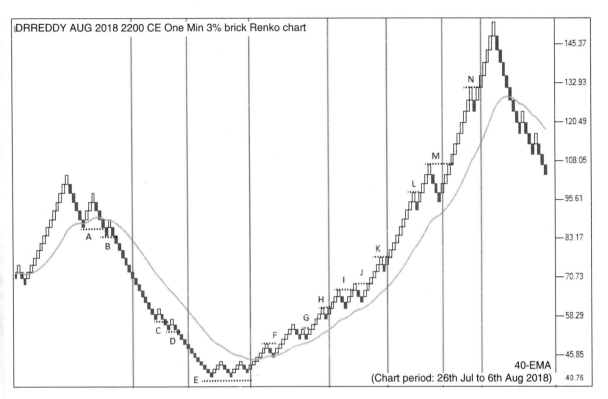

Figure 15.3: **40-brick exponential moving average on a 1-minute time interval 3% brick value Renko chart of Dr. Reddy's Laboratories 28,000 strike price call option for the same period as named in Figure 15.3.**

Patterns A to D are bearish patterns below the moving average line while patterns F to N are bullish patterns above the moving average line. Pattern A is bearish swing breakout, patterns B, C and D are bearish one-back patterns. Pattern E is a bullish Renko support pattern. Patterns F, I and J are bullish two-back patterns. Pattern G is a bullish zigzag. Patterns K, L and N are bullish one-back patterns.

~

The chart in Figure 15.3 was picked based on relative strength analysis. The pharma index was outperforming the Nifty and Dr. Reddy's was one of the top performers from the pharma sector. There were multiple trading opportunities with continuation patterns using moving average or brick zone in the call option premium chart. The strike prices would have been selected depending on the days remaining until expiry.

The bottom line is that all types of patterns and setup analysis that we discussed throughout the book are also applicable on option charts. Option premium charts can be traded as per Renko pre-defined entry and exit conditions.

Straddle (call option + put option of same strike prices) or strangle (call option + put option of different strike prices) charts can also be plotted and traded based on Renko setups.

Trading Commodities, Currencies, etc.

Renko chart analysis is possible on all types of markets and instruments.

Figure 15.4 is a 0.25% brick value chart of MCX Gold shown with extensions filtered with a moving average line.

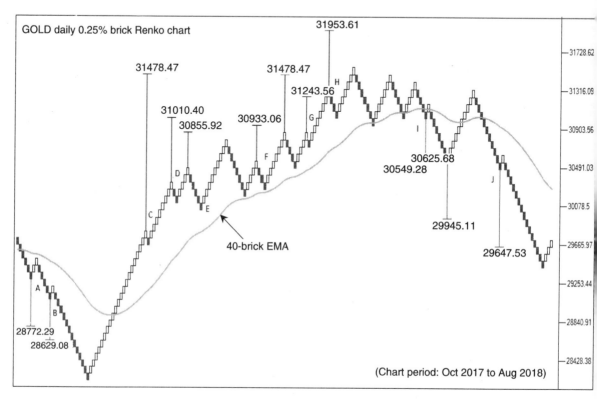

Figure 15.4: **40-brick exponential moving average and extensions on a 0.25% brick value daily Renko chart of MCX Gold.**

Patterns A and B are bearish two-back and one-back patterns respectively below the moving average. Pattern C is bullish one-back and swing engulfing follow-through above the average line. Pattern D is a bullish two-back, Pattern E is a bullish weak breakout above average line. Pattern F is a bullish strike-back follow-through. Pattern G is a multi-brick breakout and bullish one-back. Pattern H is a bullish swing breakout. All extensions on the chart till this point were achieved including extension cluster of 31,478.47. The price failed to achieve the extension from the swing breakout pattern H, and instead formed a bearish multi-brick breakout and a bearish swing engulfing follow-through pattern below the moving average at I. Pattern J is a bearish one-back pattern below the moving average line.

~

Figure 15.5 is a 0.25% brick value chart of MCX Nickel shown with extensions filtered with a moving average line.

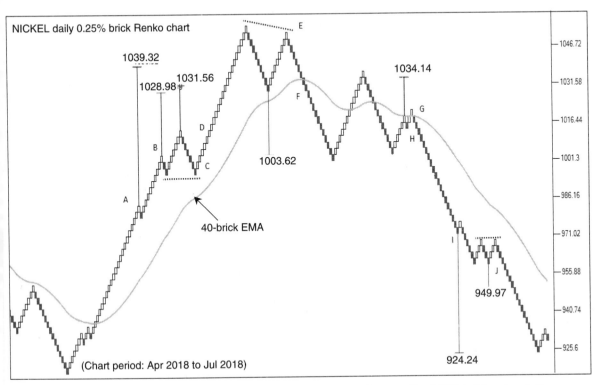

Figure 15.5: **40-brick exponential moving average and extensions on the 0.25% brick value daily Renko chart of MCX Nickel.**

Pattern A is a bullish one-back pattern above the moving average line. Pattern B is a bullish two-back pattern. Pattern C is a Renko support pattern above the average line, followed by bullish swing breakout pattern at D. Pattern E is a lower high followed by a bearish swing engulfing pattern below the average line at F which also formed a bearish M pattern. Pattern G is a bullish one-back but turned out to be a bearish weak breakout below the average line at H. Pattern I is a bearish one-back. Pattern J is a bearish multi-breakout pattern formed after a Renko resistance pattern below the average line.

~

Figure 15.6 is a 0.25% brick value chart of USDINR shown with extensions filtered with a moving average line.

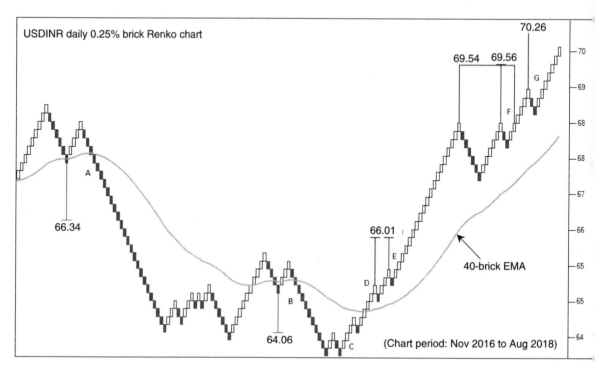

Figure 15.6: **40-brick exponential moving average and extensions on the 0.25% brick value daily Renko chart of USDINR.**

Pattern A is a bearish swing breakout below the moving average line. Pattern B is a bearish M and a swing breakout below the average line. Pattern C is a Renko support pattern followed by a series of bullish one-backs. Patterns D and E are bullish one-back patterns above the average line. Pattern F is a multi-breakout pattern and a bullish two-back. Pattern G is a bullish-two back pattern above the average line.

~

Figure 15.7 is a 0.25% brick value chart of S&P 500 shown with extensions filtered with a moving average line.

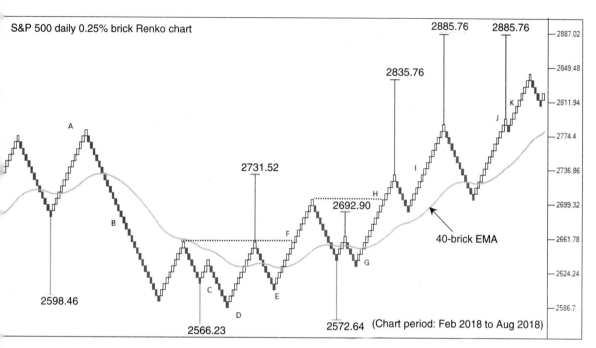

Figure 15.7: **40-brick exponential moving average and extensions on the 0.25% brick value daily Renko chart of S&P500.**

Pattern A is a bearish weak breakout. Pattern B is a bearish swing breakout below the average line with a bearish extension that got achieved subsequently. Pattern C is a bearish breakout. Pattern D is a bullish weak breakout followed by a higher low at E. Pattern F is a bullish swing breakout that invalidated the bearish extension plotted at Point C. Pattern G is a bearish swing breakout below the average line but turned out to be a bullish weak breakout above the average line. The bearish extension at Pattern G got invalidated at H. Multiple bearish extensions getting invalidated around same levels is a bullish event. It was followed by bullish swing breakout at Pattern I. Pattern J is a bullish swing breakout above the average line, followed by bullish one-back at Pattern K.

~

Chapter 16

Exit Strategies

MORE THAN THE ENTRY, IT IS THE EXIT THAT'S MORE IMPORTANT IN TRADING. Broadly, there can be three types of exit rules, namely:

1. Stop loss;
2. Trailing stop loss; and
3. Profit booking.

A swing breakout in the opposite direction is recommended as the initial and trailing stop loss technique. Moving average, trend lines, or other indicators can be used for trend filtration.

When there is a strong favourable move, such as anchor bricks, then it is advisable to follow the third consecutive brick in the opposite direction as an exit rule. I recommend the third brick rule because one-back and two-backs appear very frequently in strong trends. This third brick exit tends to avoid frequent whipsawing without missing the trend and helps achieve a nice risk-reward in trades. One can always reinstate the position upon a fresh swing breakout. Indicators such as moving averages, channel bands, etc. can be used as a trailing stop, and extensions can be used for profit booking. A reversal in the relative strength chart is another good signal for exiting an ongoing position.

Exiting at simple brick reversal may lead to overtrading. It needs to be confirmed by other observations such as support or resistance, or some other method; for example, the stock or sector has started underperforming, or breadth is showing signs of exhaustion, etc. An exit based on a reversal setup such as weak breakout or strike-back follow through is a more logical approach.

Position sizing rules improve your trading performance and also help in creating multiple entry and exit rules. Adding at follow through and continuation formations instead of risking everything at the initial signal is a logical approach, too.

You must have clear rules for dealing with the initial risk that you will take. The singular way you can better your trading performance would be a trade filter based on predefined and acceptable risk. Renko bricks can be of help here. For example, you can decide that you will not trade a swing breakout if the risk is of more than five bricks. Or, that you will ride the trend with a trailing stop loss of five bricks. Many such types of rules are possible to define the risk.

You can pick rules from the methods explained above, or you can devise your own rules but do write them down in your trading plan. I strongly recommend an objective written trading plan, at least to begin with. Everything looks good in hindsight and all analysts are great traders — on paper. Practical trade execution, however, needs a set of rules to go by. Eventually, you can enjoy the liberty of breaking rules, though with all experience I can say that breaking rules won't bring any significant advantage except the false belief of having some strong "gut feeling" which will soon be corrected by Mr. Market!

But, yes, I believe your reading of the market will improve if you practice any a technique consistently. Once you follow the same rules over a number of trades, your judgement will also improve. When some rules are traded consistently, over a period of time a judgment gets developed about suitable scenarios for that rule-set or system. It is difficult to quantify it and it comes by experience. This is why, judgment of experienced traders matter.. You will master a method and that will give you an idea about the prevailing phase. With more such experience, you will realise that there is no need for breaking the rules, and you'll then be on the path of achieving detachment.

I repeat: you can analyse a situation in as many different time frames as you like but you must stick to a single time frame when it comes to trade execution. Trade entry and exit should preferably be based on a single, pre-defined brick value and time frame. If a trading position has been taken for intraday and kept open for whatever reason, it will eventually end up being a long term investment. Many portfolios are full of stocks which were not originally bought as investments. In effect, they are a bunch of failed short term trades. It is important to realize that a lack of clear rules plus frequent style drifts will lead a trader no-where. The temptation of booking profits early will result in missing out on the big trends. The inability to take small pre-defined pattern based losses will result in holding weak stocks that turn out to be a bigger pain later. Mixing the time frames and having no clear exit rules are the trader biggest problems.

It is important to understand that there are no right or wrong exits; nor are there any perfect exits. The so-called perfect exit is a myth and doesn't exist. The sooner you realise it, the better it is. What comes across as a perfect exit for someone may not be relevant to another trader. The difference in opinions of buyers and sellers is the very nature of the market. So one needs to understand the advantages and drawbacks of all types of exit methods, accepting them and sticking to one approach — that is the key to consistent success. I have gone through that phase where I worked hard at being able to predict the exact price, and even time, for booking profits or identifying a reversal! I read lots of books and theories which claimed they could do so. The fact is that there is no such thing. An even more amazing fact is that such accuracy is actually not required to trade successfully.

What you need is to learn to embrace the market's unpredictability. It's a boon to be able to do so. Stocks will fall short of targets, or they will move after you exit. Understanding that there is no perfect exit will make you a better trader. Money in the markets can be made only by riding a trend. Period! But this is easier said than done. It takes a lot of experience to reach that stage of continuing riding the trend once you are sitting on profits.

Besides, the appropriate exit method depends a lot on the individual's style of trading and mindset. You may not need a target when you are trading one, or just a few, instruments on a regular basis. In such a scenario, you are better off riding the trend using trailing stops. But you may need different exit methods when a larger universe is being traded and the approach is to pick stocks. In such a case, you may need to keep booking profits — even if partially.

The approach is to keep rotating and betting on moving to instruments with proven momentum. Also, booking profits is important especially when markets are range bound. When markets are in a trending mode, you'll miss the ride if you exit early. To put it simply, we should not be in a hurry to exit but should continue to ride trades when markets are trending — and book profits quicker when they are in a state of consolidation. Obviously, there is no method to know these phases in advance. If this were possible, trading strategies could be tweaked according to the market's phase..

To overcome emotional trading, it is very important to make exits completely objective. It is not unusual to see stop loss getting triggered and price reversing quickly thereafter. But don't let that make you take your exit rules casually because the same rules will save you from bigger drawdowns. You must be completely faithful to your rules of exiting a trade. A good driver is not the one who can accelerate well; but one who has control over the brakes.

Patterns do fail and markets can change suddenly without prior notice. Sectors, products or commodities that looked so promising at one point are not even relevant today. Which is why you must respect your exit rules. Your focus should be more on the productivity of trades.

~

~

Chapter 17

Trading with Renko Charts in Real-Life

Renko offers an edge due to its objectivity and noiselessness.

R ENKO CHARTS ARE NOT SUPERIOR OR INFERIOR TO OTHER TYPES OF CHARTS. They are just different. There are unique features of these charts that need to be clearly understood and appreciated.

One of the biggest advantages of Renko charts is objectivity.

Renko patterns are objective in nature, they don't need great analytical or prediction skills for using them. With a little practice, one can trade them effectively. I believe money in the markets is not made through great prediction skills. From great economists and markets gurus to the average trader, everyone in the market has about equal chances of success in predicting over a longer period. When price is trading sideways, we want to know when, and in which direction, it might trend. When it's trending, we want to know how far it could go.

You have to learn to embrace unpredictability as an opportunity for profitable trading. Objectivity helps in curbing our emotions; the biggest winning trades appear when we are least comfortable in taking them.

So, it's important to focus on learning concepts and not parameters *per se*. Learning the logic and principles associated with a system or method will prove more beneficial in the long run. You need to understand the underlying logic, discuss it with experts and ask the right questions. You must aim to develop your own rules; it is very important to have an element of individuality in your trading methods. Unless there is individuality in your trading, you will not be successful. Don't focus on learning what to trade — focus on knowing how to do so.

Mastering One, or a Few, Trading Setups is Enough

"I don't fear a man who has practiced 10,000 kicks once, but I fear a man who has practiced one kick 10,000 times." — Bruce Lee

Renko is a charting method where many trading systems can be built, each having different characteristics and performance. A trader can pick a pattern that he is comfortable with and trade it consistently on his preferred instrument and time frame. For example, one-back and two-back formations can be traded across different stocks whenever they occur. This is applicable on all time frame charts.

We have discussed many techniques and patterns in this book. You can pick one or two chart patterns that you are most comfortable with from among them list and observe, backtest and practice them. Trade them whenever they occur in the stocks you follow. This is a more useful approach than drifting aimlessly from one pattern to another.

Selecting one or two patterns and trading them continuously is, however, easier said than done because it is not very easy to insulate oneself from the surrounding noise and concentrate on just a few setups. But trading can only be successful in this way, irrespective of the time frame. By using this approach, we let the market tell us what to do instead of imposing our opinions on the market. Trading, then, becomes a process that makes it a sensible business that you can scale up. The entire focus is on execution rather than endless analysis.

Being a master of one setup is better than trying to be a jack of all. You can keep learning different analytical concepts, and it is good to have more and more knowledge, but you can't trade everything. Define your core strategy or trade setups — and use your knowledge to fine tune the chosen methods.

Mastering a method by practising it consistently will give you the much needed market edge.

How to Start Trading with Renko Charts

In this book we have discussed many methods, which I hope have familiarized you with Renko charts and the different possibilities of trading them. How does one start? I followed a comprehensive approach because all types of traders should be able to pick what suits them. Some people prefer breakouts, some like reversals, while others are comfortable using indicators in their charts. And, then, there are people like me who would be happy with just relative strength and continuation price breakouts.

There is nothing right or wrong — and there is definitely more than one way to make money in the markets. So long as the underlying basics and logic are understood, all approaches are fine and should help in producing consistent and successful results.

To become an independent and successful trader, you need to understand what causes the setups that we are discussing, and listen to what the market is suggesting by following the price action and respecting exits.

Renko charts have no noise, but much noise is present between the trader's ears. Staying calm and respecting price signals help in making trading peaceful and profitable.

The view of any two analysts, be they technical or fundamental analysts, or economists for that matter, are unlikely to be the same, even though each one may be brilliant. Analysis is important, yes, but all analysis is based on assumptions. The price. however, is a reality. Rules based on price patterns can help in trading our assumptions better. Which is why it's important to relate all assumptions and analysis to price setups so that they can be traded. Otherwise, we will keep talking and discussing the markets but won't be able to trade them successfully. All "inside news" or "insider sources" that look so smart in bull markets melt down during bear markets. Trading information and news by applying certain pre-set rules is what succeeds in the long run. Let's move from *"Kya lagta hai?"* ("What do you think?") to *"Kya dikhta hai"*! ("What do you see?").

I have a trader friend who doesn't believe in charts and price action. I respect his opinion. He was telling me other day that "they" will take Nifty to 11,000 and then take it back to 10,000 from there, etc. All "weak traders will be out;" "they" will accumulate all stocks and then take the markets to new highs, and so on.

I am sure you are familiar with such comments. I am yet to understand who this "they" are? "They know everything" is another common statement heard in market circles. Are "they" operators, institutions and the big players? If so, they all don't operate in unison and they also go wrong and their shops also get shut.

No single person or entity can own the markets. It is wrong to assume that all big money is smart money or that it operates in unison in the markets.

Big funds have their own competition and challenges. "They" is a figment of our imagination. It is good for market gossip, but let's not trade based on our imagination when we have charts reflecting objective price patterns.

A Quick, Cautionary Tutorial

Let's now consider four charts of the same instrument. We'll take a pause after every chart and review the question posed.

The chart in Figure 17.1 shows a strong trend line breakout and the price is moving in a strong uptrend. But it has already moved quite a bit.

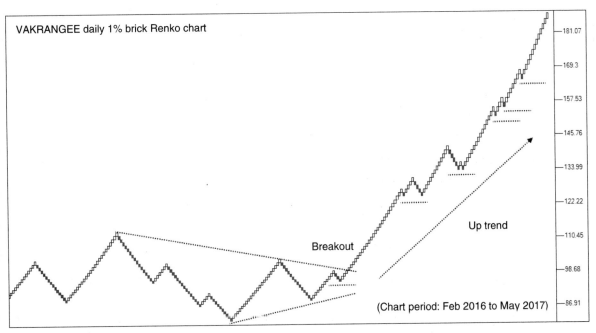

Figure 17.1: **1% brick value daily Renko chart of Vakrangee**

~

Would you feel comfortable in buying at the current price levels?
And if you did buy, where would you place your stop loss?
Now, let's see the next move.

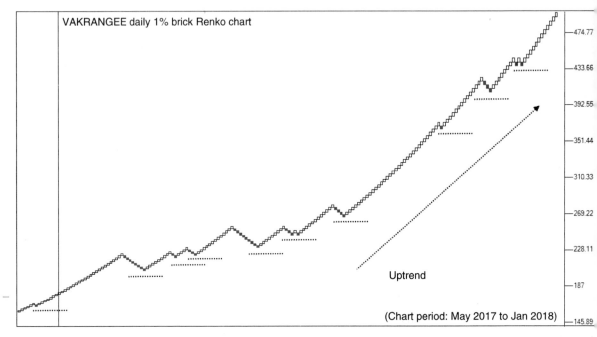

Figure 17.2: **1% brick value daily Renko chart of Vakrangee**

~

In Figure 17.2, the price has moved up further even after the phenomenal run up of the previous chart.
Are you still comfortable buying it?
Are you comfortable with the stop loss?
Now, let's see what happened next.

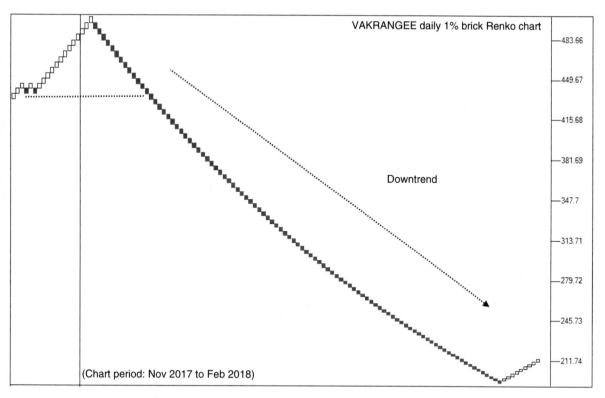

Figure 17.3: **1% brick value daily Renko chart of Vakrangee**

~

Neither the sharp rally displayed in the chart in Figure 17.2, nor the kind of fall highlighted in the chart in Figure 17.3 could have been imagined. Bullish patterns have been invalidated, and a strong downtrend has emerged instead. Now it would appear that the price has fallen considerably and might be trading at an important support or resistance.

So, should we buy now, and start accumulating?

Let's see what happened next.

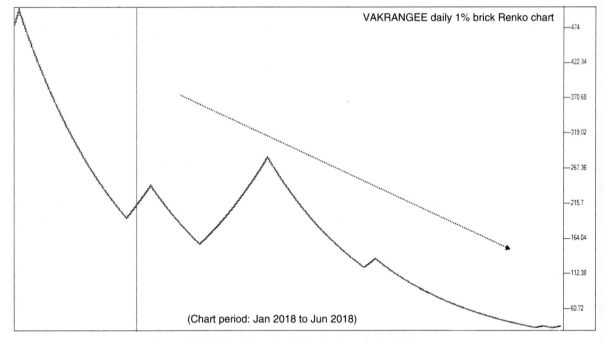

Figure 17.4: **1% brick value daily Renko chart of Vakrangee**

~

As the chart in Figure 17.4 reveals, the price fall turned out to be a serious correction. **The important learning here is that what is going up can go up way beyond your imagination. Similarly, that which is going down can keep falling beyond one's imagination and support levels.**

Don't buy simply because something has fallen "too much." Don't hold rigid opinions; everything looks perfect in hindsight. Anything can happen. And, most importantly, always have an exit plan.

The ability to handle different situations and being prepared for various outcomes is what is important. A successful trader needs to learn flexibility and adaptability along with trading techniques.

Remember:

- You make money in the markets by booking losses, not by locking profits.

- Profit is made by exiting losing positions.

- Money is not made by catching tops or bottoms; it is made by riding the trend.

- Money is not made by learning dozens of techniques; it is made by mastering one method.

Process Oriented Trading

All great and successful traders stress on the importance of process, rules and discipline. Consistent success is achieved by defining and adhering to a process. I believe Renko charts can help you to a great extent in this regard because of their simplicity, the objective price patterns they throw up, and the possibility of creating objective trading systems using Renko charts. In fact, if you wish to make trading a successful business, there is no alternative to a process oriented approach.

No business can become successful unless there is a well defined process, i.e. a set of rules, for its functioning. The same is true for trading. The biggest issue for many traders is that they have no rules. The decision to buy or sell is just a thought away. In today's world of social media, think of the amount of information you are bombarded with in a day. It certainly has an impact on your emotions and you can easily fall prey to some news or idea and enter or exit trades either unnecessarily or prematurely.

The best strategy is the one that suits your style and approach. I often say that you give me the world's best system on the 5-minute candlestick chart and I will show you how to ruin it — simply because it is not meant for me! But someone else could make millions from that system. A pattern or method has no magic in itself. The magic is in practising one method, or a few methods, consistently, and not getting distracted by the surrounding market noise.

Always remember that there are many ways to trade the markets successfully. Even if you know a method or system that someone else is successfully trading, you will not be able to replicate the other person's success because you are not him. You will eventually end up incorporating your own beliefs and knowledge into that system. More importantly, you just can't copy or replicate another trader's psychology or conviction. Conviction cannot be borrowed. And consistent success can neither be achieved with borrowed ideas nor without conviction. Trading is an individual journey; you have to learn the key concepts and develop what you are most comfortable with.

The trading system you use should suit your temperament so that you can execute it better; and knowing that by itself is a process. Which is why consistent success in trading is possible only if your trading is process oriented. The patterns we have discussed in the book are objective in nature. Hence, they need no analytical skills; only a focus on systematic execution. If your focus is on the process, you can make money in the markets, but if your focus is on money, you may even lose what you have!

Trading Plan

As great traders say, you should plan your trade and trade your plan. Below is a questionnaire you need to answer. Your answers will lead to your trading plan that you must put down in writing.

1. What time frame will I trade?
2. What brick value and reversal value will I trade?
3. What will my trading universe be?
4. What are the entry setups?

5. What is the exit setup / criteria?
6. What are the re-entry setups?
7. What will be allocation per trade?
8. What will be the risk I will take per trade?
9. What will be the maximum positions that I will keep open at a time?
10. For an intraday plan: How many trades will I take in a day?
11. For an intraday plan: What is the maximum loss that I will consider per day?
12. What is the back tested success rate and risk reward ratio of my trading system?
13. What is the review period?
14. What is the weakness of my strategy?
15. What is the strength of my strategy?
16. What is the worst scenario if this strategy is traded?
17. Am I comfortable with the rules of this strategy?

There should be no ambiguity in the answers to the above questions. Answers like, "Sometimes" or "It depends" have no place in a successful trading plan. Your trading plan is your rule book — and it should give you clear instructions for executing trades. I remember someone telling me that stocks starting with the letter "M" were unlucky for him and so he was not comfortable in trading such stocks! I don't see anything wrong even with such an unusual rule, provided it is included in the trading plan. You must review the plan periodically but not tweak it too often. We often tend to alter the trading plan too easily, and too often, typically at times when it is most needed to be followed!

A written trading plan is just the beginning of process oriented trading. Typically, it takes some time to develop a method and build conviction.

Maintaining a Trading Journal

Apart from writing a trading plan, you must maintain a trading journal to record all your trades. Whenever the trading plan is not followed, you should record the reasons that made you violate the rules. Some tweaking as per the analysis of trading records will help you to improve your plan until you are comfortable with it. Let your trading record tell you whether "M" is lucky for you or not! Beware of over-tweaking and deliberate at length before adding anything to your plan. Most of our thoughts and ideas are short-lived and fade away with the market phase.

An analysis of the rules will give you an idea about the phase the market is in. Every method has suitable and unfavourable phases. At times, buying at supports and waiting for corrections works well. At other times, breakouts are more favourable. People change their strategy when they go through a difficult period. Such mindless style drift of trading multiple methods typically results in bad phases. It's vital to understand that no method is infallible; sticking to a consistent approach is what is important. Accept a system or method with a clear understanding of its drawbacks; equally, understand the scenarios when it may not work well. A method that defines the risk clearly is most likely to outperform in the longer run.

If you have a written trading plan and also maintain written trade records, you are amongst these very few serious traders who are destined for success in the markets. Remain consistent. Success is a by product of consistency.

Real-Life Trading Stories

Let me conclude by sharing with you the stories of two real life traders who have had a great impact on me.

Story 1

In 2005, I used to work in a broking firm and my job included opening demat accounts for clients. I opened an account for a North Indian client settled in Pune. I used to place orders for him and became a fan of his trading style. He used to trade significant quantities and so he was popular in my branch and we used to look up to him. He was not a believer in charts, fundamentals, or any other type of analysis. For him, news and gut feel were all-important. He used to tell me how markets would react to a particular news and how his experience made him trade, etc. I must say he had a great understanding of the impact of news. I was witness to some of his brilliant trades and how he managed to capture some reversals right at the tops or bottoms.

When I moved to another job profile, I lost regular touch with him. But we would call each other occasionally. This person was very aggressive in nature, and also very short tempered. It was very difficult to handle his orders though I managed to build a decent rapport with him. But it was a horrible experience for others if there was a mistake or some problem with the placement of his orders. Dealers were often scared to execute his orders. I would then end up intervening and getting involved to resolve issues. In this way, I managed to keep in touch with him. I remember he was very happy when he got married to his long-time girlfriend. We decided to meet over a beer but it didn't work out then.

He moved his trading account somewhere else and I lost touch with him. He called me a couple of years ago and the pending beer finally fructified. I got to know about his two children and his well-paid job in a technology firm. He was very knowledgeable about manufacturing machine processes. I shared a few strategies with him and tried to discuss process oriented trading, etc., but he was not in a mood to listen. He had had a few bad trades but had recovered the money and was now trading options aggressively. He said he made 400-fold profit in Bank Nifty options, etc. He narrated his trading experiences and how he made amazing profits in most of his trades. I enjoyed the thrilling experiences he narrated. Once he was convinced about a view, he would build aggressive positions. It was this style of trading that helped him make big money lots of times. He also used to follow a trading guru and relied a lot on this guru's views. He explained how his guru had predicted certain moves beforehand and how he never went wrong. I could see that his trading was based on experience and he was not interested in strategies. He also had a strong opinion about politics and arguments with him in this regard would lead to long discussions. We wrapped up our meeting with some general chit chat.

A few months later I came to know that he had committed suicide. It was very shocking news. Apparently he had been in bad financial shape in the preceding few months due to over-leveraged trading. He was short in the markets based on some strong political opinion and the firm view held by his market guru whom he greatly trusted. So, he kept on adding to his losing positions. He borrowed money on interest, even sold properties to do so.

It was such a pity that the life of a very intelligent person with a well paid job, young children and a lovely family ended in this fashion.

Story 2

I used to place orders for another trader. This guy, with an average position size, enjoyed very consistent success and was always calm and to the point whenever we spoke.

I found him very interesting. I used to meet him to hand over his trading statements. Gradually, I started interacting with him and began to learn about his thought process. He would gave me a few books to read and I would go back to him with my queries. He had a very playful approach and was also very open minded. We used to discuss sports, politics, religion, etc. He would respect every opinion and believed in the adage, "Let's agree to disagree." He would always channel the discussion towards positive aspects and important things.

Arguments of this versus that kind were a waste of time and energy for him. To him, positivity was an essential aspect of achieving peace in life, and trading was no different.

One day he phoned to place an order but he couldn't do so due to some technical problem in our trading terminals. The stock ended up doing very well but he had missed the opportunity. I called him back to express my apology but he was very calm and "penalized" me with only a beer. He would say that markets offered infinite opportunities and that one should simply forget those that one may have missed. He never spent time in blaming things. This state of mind precluded any "revenge trading."

He would say that when you see your trading ledger at the end of a particular period, it is unimportant which trades contributed, or which stocks did well. It is not about which stocks or trades did well; it is the discipline of following process a rigorously that works. It can take people years to get to this level of maturity and understanding.

He held that the outcome of each trade was independent and does not influence the outcome of the next trade. He would caution against judging a method based on a few trades and would emphasize the importance of understanding the implications of long term thinking.

Once when he was going through a phase of drawdowns, I asked him if he would think of tweaking his method. He told me a very important thing then; he would never change the rules of a system during a bad phase — and neither would he fall into the temptation of booking profits and change them during good times. Most of the decisions taken during such times are short term and emotional. Instead, he would reduce his position size during a difficult phase. He would latest increase the positions once he realised that there was a favourable phase and made up the entire drawdown by following the same rules. I never saw him sound over-excited or boast of his profits to anyone. For professional and successful traders, profit and loss is routine; just like it is for other businessmen. They would not like to shout about it or advertise it.

He used to spend a lot of time with his family. I never saw him spending time worrying about overnight positions, or tracking all sorts of things to analyse their impact on his open positions. He was only concerned about order placement in the morning and the execution of his rules. He once told me that he didn't even remember the names of the stocks in which he held positions. His logic was simple; there is nothing one can do overnight by knowing all manners of news. Why then waste time on things which were not in one's control. His process was well defined and his only job was to execute it the next day. It is impossible for any analyst to factor in all possibilities. In fact, even knowing all variables will only add to confusion. He believed that time spent with friends, family, reading good books or watching interesting movies was time better spent rather than worrying about what might happen to one's trades the next day.

I asked him about a friend he had been mentoring and he said the other person could not trade the process because he had a target of making profit every month. So, most of the time his decisions were emotional, and he was constantly trying to outsmart the rules. He could not follow stops and exited early due to fear. His system had wide stop losses. This saved him from the series of small losses and overtrading as the signals were infrequent. He emphazied that accumulation of small losses does more damage than a larger stop. As I recall, he lost in about 60% of his trades in the month he made a great profit. During the same period, had he exited the positions early his success ratio would have gone up to about 70% from 40%, but he would have made lesser money overall because the success ratio and the risk reward ratio have an inverse relationship.

He was a trend rider. But he used to occasionally shift exit rules to some target based methods when a market phase did not suit his methods.

I remember he had a great run in a stock the very day he bought it. But it turned out to be a loss because the price reversed before he could trail his stop — which is what triggered the loss. What was more unfortunate was that the price again climbed to a new high after triggering his exit. I asked him at that time if he was feeling the pain. He said he used to feel it earlier, but now he was feeling good about paying the "insurance premium." He said this habit would safeguard him from many losses and early exits in the future. Very few traders can achieve such a stage of detachment.

He was an avid reader. Once when I went to his home, he was a reading a book on technical strategies. I asked him why he still read so many books when he already had a settled method. "I do so in order to keep learning new concepts," he replied. He would keep analysing trading rules and if some concept looked interesting, then he was open to experimenting with it. He stressed on the need of continuously updating one's skills. Markets have an uncanny knack of making us obsolete before we even realize what's happened, he would say.

He traded multiple strategies and his funds were allocated to different trading systems. His strategies would be divided into pilot and core. He has a three-step process for creating a system: analysis, experimentation, and implementation. Once he came across something interesting, he would analyse it, try it for some tweaks, and then backtest it. If this stage was satisfactory, then he would make it into a pilot strategy, allocate some funds to it, and try it with a limited allocation. He would keep trade records, apply necessary tweaks, and give it some time to perform. He would give a reasonable time to a strategy even if it delivered returns quickly. "Once you have observed the performance over a large enough sample size of trades, and you are comfortable with it, then allocate more funds to it and implement it as a core strategy," he would say.

I recently met this trader at the house warming function of his new bungalow. Someone was discussing with him his view of the Nifty, and explaining why he felt it would go to a certain level, and the entire logic behind his analysis. My friend listened to him patiently but did not utter a word.

Towards the end of the function, I saw group of traders animatedly discussing market trends, global economic issues and how these would impact the markets over the next few months. In another corner, my friend was rushing towards a table so as not to miss out on sharing ice cream with his children! I sensed noise on one end, and calm at the other.

Markets are the same for everyone. Some behave irresponsibly and blame the market for their losses. Others make the best use of them and build a great future.

~

There is a famous shloka in the *Bhagavad Gita*:

> "Karmanyev adhikaraste, Ma phalesh ou kadachana,
> Ma Karma Phala Hetur Bhur Matey Sangostva Akarmani"

"You have the freedom and choice about what action to take, but not over the results that ensue. Never consider yourself to be the (entire) cause of the results of your activities; neither should you be inert and, inactive." (— *Bhagavad Gita*, Chapter II, Verse 47).

~

There are brilliant traders and analysts out there and they can do wonders with Renko charts. I hope more books will get written on different trading systems and methods using these charts. I would feel highly encouraged and content even if you manage to find just one thing to take home from this book that can benefit you significantly.

You can write to me at prashant.shah@definedge.com for queries or feedback. I would welcome both.

~

Bibliography

— Aby, Carroll D. J. *Point & Figure Charting: The Complete Guide*. Grinville, SC: Traders Press Inc., 1996.

— Bollinger, John. *Bollinger on Bollinger Bands*, New York, NY: McGraw-Hill, 2002.

— Bulkowski, Thomas N. *Encyclopedia of Chart Patterns*. New York, NY: John Wiley & Sos, Inc., 2000.

— Carney, Scott M. *Harmonic Trading*, *Volume One: Profiting from the Natural Order of the Financial Markets*. FT Press; 1 edition (April 22, 2010)

— Dorsey, Thomas J. *Point & Figure charting: The Essential Applications for Forecasting and Tracking Market Prices*. Hoboken, New Jersey: John Wiley & Sons, Inc., 2007

— Douglas, Mark. *Trading in the Zone*. Prentice Hall Press, 2001.

— Du Plessis, Jeremy, *The Definitive Guide to Point and Figure: A comprehensive Guide to the Theory and Practical Use of the Point and Figure Charting Method*, Petersfield: Harriman House Publishing, 2006.

— Edwards, R., and J. Magee. *Technical Analysis of Stock Trends*, 8th ed., 2003. 1948 edition revised by W. H. C. Bassetti, St. Lucie Press, Boca Raton, FL.

— Elder, Alexander. *Trading for Living*. New York, NY: John Wiley & Sons, Inc., 1993.

— Gartley, H. M. *Profits in the Stock Market*, 3rd ed. (1981). Pomeroy, WA: Lambert-Gann Publishing Co., 1935.

— Kaufman, Perry J. *Trading Systems and Methods*, 3rd ed. New York, NY: John Wiley & Sons, Inc., 1998.

— Kirkpatrick, Charles D., and Dahlquist, Julie R. *The Complete Resource for Financial Market Technicians*. New Jersey: Pearson Education, Inc., 2007

— Murphy, John J., *Intermarket Analysis*, New Jersey: John Wiley & Sons, Inc., 2004.

— Nison, Steve, Japanese *Candlestick Charting Techniques*, New York, NY: New York Institute of Finance, 2001.

— Pring, Martin J., *Technical Analysis Explained: The Successful Investor's Guide to Spotting Investment Trends and Turning Points* , McGraw-Hill, 2002.

— Schwager, Jack D. *Market Wizards*. New York, NY: New York Institute of Finance, 1989.

— Taleb, Nassim. *Fooled by Randomness*. Penguin, 2007.

— Tharp, Van K. *Trade Your Way to Financial Freedom* . McGraw-Hill Education; 2nd edition.,2006.

— Tharp, Van K. *Definitive Guide to Position Sizing Strategies*. The Van Tharp Institute, 2nd edition, 2013.

— Wheelan, Alexander, *Study Helps in Point and Figure Technique* , Morgan Rogers and Roberts, New York, 1954 and Traders Press, Greenville, 1990.

— Wilder, J. Welles Jr. *New Concepts in Technical Trading Systems*. Greensboro, SC: Trend Research, 1978.

— Zieg, Kermit C., *Point & Figure Commodity & Stock Trading Techniques* , Traders Press, Greenville, 1997.

~

Acknowledgements

AS THEY SAY, WE ARE SUM A TOTAL OF OUR EXPERIENCES. There are many people who have been instrumental in helping and guiding me to be where I am today, and turning the dream of this book into a reality.

Thanks to my father, Pravin Shah, and mother, Rekha Shah, for all their support and guidance, and for moulding me into the person I am today.

To my grandmother (Baa), the late Savita Shah, who single-handedly raised my father ever since he was a few months old. I know the sacrifices she made to give us a life. Her late night stories of bravery and victory of good over evil have left an indelible mark on my persona. I try to continue her legacy and teach the same values to the apple of my eye, Ahaan, who makes me smile every day.

Many thanks to my precious wife and best friend Isha, for all the encouragement and support she has given me in writing this book — be it my perparation for international exams while working, or my leaving a job in order to write a research paper and eventually a book. After marriage, all this is only possible when there is a companion like her, an unending inspiration. She is my best support system.

My sister Payal and my brother in-law Deepak Gupta are my best friends and critics. I am also fortunate to have a very understanding extended family; my in-laws have supported me in every decision I took and have always stood by me during my good and bad times. I am blessed to receive their unwavering emotional support and encouragement.

The hero of my life, Ravi mama (maternal uncle), is the one I have always looked up to. The childhood memories, and his love and support at every stage are the strong pillars of my life. I thank him for existing.

I am truly thankful to my colleagues at Definedge, Vinay Shah, Nitin Gajbhiye, Abhijit Phatak, Raju Ranjan, B. Krishnakumar, Nagin Kothari and all others. We would spend hours discussing and brainstorming on market trends, sentiment, trading psychology and trading techniques. All these discussions have greatly contributed to my thought process while writing this book. I thank the technology team who coded limitless things for the research I was conducting on Renko charts. My special thanks to B. Krishnakumar for proof reading and initial editing of the book, and for keeping me in line.

Thanks to Biren Patel, who first taught me OHLC and sent me to my first ever training seminar on technical analysis during 2005. I have benefited from many helpful suggestions and comments from Nitin Mude, Rajesh Badiye, Prashant Gupta, Sumeet Jain, Brijesh Bhatia, and K. Anant Rao.

The origins of Renko charts are in Japan. I can't thank Steve Nison enough for his idea and effort of brining Renko charts to the notice of the rest of the world. I would like to express my sincere gratitude to Jeremy Du Plessis and Tomas Dorsey; I have learnt a lot about one-dimensional charts from their work. Martin Pring, John Murphy, John Bollinger, Kermit Zieg and many other authors are teachers from whom I have learnt chart analysis. The works of Alexander Elder, Mark Douglas, Van Tharp, Nassim Taleb have played an immense role in my understanding of the markets. The list is endless. These people have had a very deep and significant impact on my work and personality. I feel a debt of gratitude to so many professionals, traders and authors who have generously shared their valuable knowledge on trading and investing.

Thanks to the CMT Association and International Federation of Technical Analysis, through which I have got introduced to the best of the works in the field of technical analysis. They have greatly contributed to my knowledge of trading and analysis.

Thanks to all my students, event participants and product subscribers for keeping me on my toes with their wonderful observations and queries.

My special thanks to the editor and publisher of this book, Kapil Malhotra, and the entire team at Vision Books. His eye for detail and the discussion on different topics while editing has added great value to the book. This book is much better for his contribution.

All the charts in this book are from TradePoint software by Definedge Solutions. Though I am a founder member of the company, the software and the company are a result of the unwavering hard work by many. It is because of them that this book has become a reality today.

This book is my attempt to contribute to the growth of one-dimensional charts and technical analysis. I have presented the concepts the way I understood them with consistent practice of so many years. I have attempted to keep the discussion relevant from a trading perspective. Everything that I have written is borrowed in one or the other way from these predecessors and brilliant minds in the field of trading and technical analysis. The credit for anything that you might learn from this book goes to them. What you don't like is my weakness.

— PRASHANT SHAH

~